The Library and the Workshop

The Library and the Workshop

Social Democracy and Capitalism in the Knowledge Age

Jenny Andersson

Stanford University Press
Stanford, California

Stanford University Press
Stanford, California

Printed in the United States of America on acid-free, archival-quality paper

Library of Congress Cataloging-in-Publication Data
Andersson, Jenny
  The library and the workshop : social democracy and capitalism in the knowledge age /
Jenny Andersson.
    p. cm.
  Includes bibliographical references and index.
  ISBN 978-0-8047-6263-2 (cloth : alk. paper)
  1. Mixed economy—Europe. 2. Human capital—Europe. 3. Knowledge, Sociology of. 4.
Europe—Economic conditions—1945– I. Title.
  HC240.A799 2010
  330.12'6094—dc22
                              2009014490

Typeset by Thompson Type in 10/14 Minion Pro

Contents

Acknowledgments

I have been working on this book for a rather long time, and I'm grateful to many people for their generous help. Thanks go in particular to Ed Miliband, Patrick Legalès, Olivier Borraz, Chris Howell, Alan Finlayson, Magnus Ryner, Geoff Eley, Peter Hall, Andrew Martin, Jonas Pontusson, Andrew Scott, Mary Hilson, Victor Perez Diaz, Bo Rothstein, and Joakim Palme. I would also like to thank the Swedish Institute for Futures Studies and my colleagues for their interest in this book. As I write the last words, my thoughts go to two wonderful people in a beautiful house in Somerville, Massachusetts, who gave me a home during my stay at Harvard: Ann Gallagher and Frank Roselli.

Introduction

In recent years, much attention has been devoted to the repositioning of social democracy known as the Third Way, particularly in its Anglo-Saxon form, but far less to its place in the history of social democracy. The first wave of studies of the Third Way saw it as neoliberal, as a continuation of significant elements of Thatcherism as regards the economy, industrial relations, and social justice.[1] Rather, I suggest, the Third Way draws on fundamental continuities in the social democratic project, continuities that are, however, not unproblematic. In particular, this book explores the Third Way's relationship to the knowledge economy and the way in which the Third Way's understanding of the knowledge economy leads to a reinterpretation of fundamental postulates of social democracy around capitalism.

The knowledge economy has been a central element of the Third Way, almost to the point of being its raison d'être. Just as earlier processes of social democratic revisionism took place around processes of industrial transformation, so the Third Way can be understood as the rearticulation of a set of ideological postulates in relationship to its conception of a new economic and social order. Similar to the way in which Social Democrats in the 1950s and 1960s tried to provide ideological coherence to the industrial economy and the social and cultural changes it brought with it, the Third Way is an ideological project that attempts to establish coherent articulations of the knowledge economy. Some of its articulations are indeed strikingly similar to social democracy's discourses on the need for adaptation to the industrial economy during the Wilson era in the United Kingdom and the Erlander years in Sweden. Since the mid-1990s, the notion of the knowledge economy has occupied a similar function in social democratic discourse, as the cornerstone of a modernization narrative around information technology, education and lifelong learning, innovation, and entrepreneurship. Where Social Democrats in the postwar period saw the industrial economy as the promise of an affluence that would lead away from class conflict and poverty, the Third Way saw the knowledge economy as a new stage of capitalism that promised "prosperity for all."[2] Moreover, the knowledge economy provided a new progressive narrative around questions of social justice—because social exclusion and the unequal distribution of opportunity are understood as problems for the development of the human capital that is at a premium in the new economy. The knowledge economy seemed to give a new role to the social democratic state for the creation of value, by investing in learning, education, and information technology—the drivers of prosperity in the new economy. Thus it was seen, by a nascent new center Left, as offering a way out of the neoliberal "there is no such thing as society" while also providing a reason for breaking with the legacies of Fordism and the mechanistic notions of change of the old Left.

The knowledge economy concerns core issues in social democracy's understanding of contemporary capitalism—the creation of value and its distribution, the role of markets and the balance between public and private, the balance between labor and capital, the nature of need and want, the role of social justice, the dream of equality. Indeed, the knowledge economy has new implications for age-old social democratic questions of class, exploitation, and emancipation. To the British, then Chancellor of the Exchequer Gordon Brown, in texts from the mid-1990s when New Labour was taking shape, the knowledge economy was an "opportunity economics," a new economic egalitarianism that was truly dependent on "exploiting the potential of all." People's potential was the driving force of the modern economy, and it was the capacity to enhance the value of labor through education and learning that made a modern economy succeed or fail. The challenge to social democratic politics, then, was to "ensure labour can use capital to the benefit of all," rather than "let capital exploit labor for the benefit of the few."[3] To Brown, this was the point of departure for a new relationship between capital and labour. The knowledge economy signified the final reversal of Marx's power relationship between labor and capital as the skills revolution made capital a mere commodity and put labor in control of the production of value. Hence, the knowledge economy was the promise of socialism.

The important conclusion that we reach is that the Left's century-old case—that we must enhance the value of labor as the key to economic prosperity—is now realizable in the modern economy. If this analysis is right, socialist analysis fits the economic facts of the 1990s more closely than those of the 1890s.[4]

This analysis of a new balance of power between labor and capital stemmed from the idea, inspired by endogenous growth theory, that because knowledge is a kind of capital located within the worker, it also makes workers the owners of their capital and no longer subject to other logics of capital. This is a mindboggling suggestion to socialist thinking. If capital is within us, then how can it exploit us? And if, as Brown suggested, capital is no longer an exploiting force but a force that, in the hands of a Labour government, works for the emancipation of labor, then what is capitalism?

This book explores the way that social democracy makes sense of a new economic and social order based on knowledge. In particular, it points to the different interpretations of the knowledge economy and the knowledge society that exist within Third Way discourse, through an analysis of the different interpretations of a knowledge age of New Labour and the Swedish Social Democratic Party, SAP (*socialdemokraterna*). These differences, the book argues, can be brought back to different definitions of what kind of good knowledge is, how knowledge acts as an economic and social resource, and what that means in terms of economy and society, individuals and politics. To the SAP, knowledge is a democratic, public good that should be created and redistributed on the basis of universalism. Its discourse on the knowledge economy is highly egalitarian, drawing on ideological legacies from the universal welfare state and the party's historic project, the People's Home. To quote the Swedish slogan, "knowledge grows the more we share it."[5] Key metaphors used in party rhetoric to describe the knowledge economy have been the library or the study circle, both of which draw on the idea of knowledge as produced and distributed on the basis of solidarity and also allude to central elements in party history—the public libraries and study circles that laid the foundation for worker education in the nineteenth century. New Labour, in contrast, spoke in the 1990s of the knowledge economy as the chance for Britain to rise again, as the electronic workshop of the world. To New Labour, knowledge is a competitive commodity and an individual good, to be bartered and sold on the markets of the knowledge economy.

At the same time that these differences evoke central questions concerning the social democratic project, past, present, and future, they also reflect tensions at the heart of the knowledge economy. These are tensions that go back even to those embodied in the idea of knowledge that informs European modernity, between notions of knowledge as economic capital, defined by applicability and use, and knowledge as democratic or public capital, defined by democracy and the virtues of citizenship.[6] Thus, through its focus on contemporary narratives of the knowledge economy, this book sheds light on a wider issue, namely, social democracy and its ambiguous place in the history of modernity and capitalism.

Coined in the late 1990s to describe a new and youthful social democratic project, the *Third Way* is now an awkward term, indeed one that is often regarded with some embarrassment by Third Way proponents themselves. For lack of a better term, however, it still functions as an analytical description of the ideological content of contemporary social democracy. At the very least, it is hard to discern any viable alternative to it. However, and contrary to what one might think due to the dominance of Anglo-Saxon literature, the Third Way is not and was never a one-way political space but a deeply heterogeneous project across time and space, with complex origins in ideologies in social democracy's past and complex relationships to national legacies and cultures.[7] As I finish this book, social democracy is struggling to find a new sense of identity in a time when its infatuation with the market has suddenly become its largest liability. From the Third Way a contested field of discourses and counterdiscourses, ideologies and counterideologies, some with their origins in the 1990s, some with origins in historical discourses of social democracy, some new, all struggling to define the future of social democracy, has emerged. This book also aspires to shed light on these points of change.

Structure of This Book

This book's point of departure is that the idea of the knowledge economy and the modernization narrative to which it gives rise in both countries are dependent on a highly specific idea of knowledge, indeed, a form of capital, an intangible but marketable commodity located within those individuals whose brainpower constitutes the skills revolution. This has particular implications in the knowledge economy, where ideas of self-realization through learning and education are also at a premium. This book suggests that this represents a process of capitalization—a process whereby forms of good, previously not primarily thought of as economic goods, become defined as forms of economic capital. The growth discourses of the Third Way focus on "tapping potential," on ways to turn curiosity, talent, originality, and creativity into value. In this process, the socialist notion of exploring potential, of helping everyone "bridge the gap between what they are and what they have it in themselves to become" acquires a new meaning, and the distinction between emancipation and exploitation becomes fundamentally blurred.

The first chapter of this book, "Dilemmas of Social Democracy," establishes a framework for understanding the Third Way in the context of the history of social democracy and capitalism. Chapter 2, "The Political Economy of Knowledge," discusses the main features of what might be called a political economy of knowledge, the Third Way's macro-micro strategy, and its understanding of a global order where "capital moves at the strike of a key," and growth strategies increasingly built around the value of human capital. It argues that this political economy of knowledge is distinct from neoliberalism and that it brings with it a plethora of new means of governance that change the nature of social democracy's intervention into the economic and the social. Chapter 3, "Defining Old and New Times," traces the genealogy of the Third Way and its narrative of a new economy through its various trajectories, beginning in the 1970s. It maps the strategic ideological choices made by social democracy in this period and highlights the role of struggle around futures chosen and futures closed.

The three chapters that make up the second part of the book deal with the question of how social democracy understands knowledge capital, that is, the role and nature of capital in an era of knowledge. Chapter 4, "Capitalism?," lays out the differences in the parties' interpretation of knowledge capitalism, including notions of class and conflict, ownership, and equality. It puts this in the context of social democracy's historic interpretations of capitalism and asks how it is different. Chapter 5, "Politics of Growth," deals with the ambiguous notion of growth in the knowledge economy. As it is most clearly expressed in the concept of learning, growth in the knowledge economy takes on a double meaning of economic and individual improvement, hence, of accumulation and profit as well as of self-realization and self-fulfilment. The chapter probes this double bind and argues that the Third Way, through its articulations of potential, talent, and skill as forms of economic capital, rearticulates radical utopian notions in education or culture in terms of technocratic notions of efficiency, thus silencing other ideological heritages in the history of social democracy.

Chapter 6, "Knowledge Societies," treats the social democratic vision of the knowledge *society* and its interpretation of the social organization of knowledge as equality or meritocracy. It explores the differences between New Labour's meritocratic notion of community and the SAP's more egalitarian notion of society as *samhälle*, a notion that still occupies a central place in Swedish politics but that is today, after decades of ideological change, full of tensions and ambiguities that are demonstrated in the chapter with the example of voucher schools. Chapter 7, "Investing in People," is concerned with the different strategies for welfare state modernization of New Labour and the SAP and the different role that the parties give to social citizenship in the process of change. In the 1990s and 2000s, both parties emphasized and continue to emphasize the positive relationship between social justice and economic efficiency; they do so, however, in very different ways, reflecting different understandings in the liberal and social democratic tradition of the defining virtues of citizenship and the role of social citizenship for the efficient functioning of capitalism.

Chapter 8, "Creating the Knowledge Individual," explores the idea of the knowledge citizen, the constantly learning and relearning individual who supposedly inhabits the knowledge society. It argues that social democracy, preoccupied in the 1950s with the creation of industrial man, is equally preoccupied today with the idea of knowledge man and that many of the Third Way's means of governance are designed to actively create this utopic citizen. The Third Way's notion of improvement is inherently individualized, seeing, in actual fact, the process of modernization as one that essentially takes place within each individual. The chapter argues that the political construction of this knowledgeable individual has an other, discernable in discourses of social exclusion, in the form of those individuals and groups who are seen as lacking knowledge, talent, and potential. Chapter 9, "The Future of Social Democracy," opens a window to the future of social democracy by positing the conclusions of this book in the light of current debates in social democratic discourse at the end of the Third Way.

1 Dilemmas of Social Democracy

The History of Social Democracy

Any history of social democracy is inevitably the history of its context. Social democracy is a political movement umbilically linked to capitalism and modernity, dependent on these forces for its very existence. Just as it once grappled with questions of industrial modernity, it continues to grapple with the issues and dilemmas posed by (post)industrial modernity.

The relationship between social democracy and its surrounding context—the field on which it operates, the parameters that it takes as given or changeable—is, however, far from simple. Historically, social democracy has built its platform around the idea of progress, around interpreting modernity, defining it, indeed, representing modern times and carrying the future. From its birth somewhere between the French and the Industrial Revolutions, it recognized capitalism as a force capable of bringing about that modernity. It saw its own role as that of the catalyst. The fundamental paradox of social democracy is that the recognition of capitalism as the fundamental means to social progress brings about the recognition of capitalism itself. There is an important but rather fine line between socialism and capitalism in the history of social democracy.[1]

Social democracy, then, is not a social movement that is simply adapting to new orders of production. It is intimately involved in bringing them about. It is not possible to separate the economy as an objective sphere from our understanding and interpretation of it and from the way that historical agents intervene into it, thus creating in the process the boundaries between the economic and the social or the cultural. The making sense of new times is also creating them, through discourse and ideology and through policy and institutions. Here, the notion of the knowledge society fulfils a similar function for the Third Way that the notion of the industrial society did for nascent social democracy in the 1880s or that the idea of the affluent society did for social democratic revisionists in the 1950s. As Bob Jessop suggests, the idea of a knowledge-based economy has emerged in the post-Fordist world as a pervasive metanarrative, the function of which is not just interpretative but constitutive of the new economy because it motivates modes and means of governance designed to bring it about.[2] Just as social democracy was a central historical agent behind the bringing about of industrial modernity, the Third Way with its notion of the new economy is a key agent in creating knowledge capitalism.[3]

The relationship between interpretation and construction is one of the fundamental dilemmas of social democracy, following its ambiguous relationship with capitalism. Social democracy has not, in history, been primarily concerned with the overthrow of capitalism and hence with the radical alternative. Rather, it is a social movement firmly caught between its radical critique of capitalism and its emphasis on the gradual improvement of capitalism. These two seemingly irreconcilable political strategies are not irreconcilable in the history of social democracy. Rather its history is the history of trying to marry utopian critique and pragmatic stances in its various bouts of revisionism. In the history of social democracy, modernization discourse is about such attempts at reconciliation. In the late nineteenth century, social democracy broke away from utopian socialism by presenting itself as the practical alternative.[4] With the rise of reformism in the interwar period, it replaced notions of revolution with an appeal to nation and prosperity. In the 1950s, it took a further step down the revisionist road when it focused on the efficient management of affluence.[5] Nevertheless, utopian critique and discourses of improvement are distinct political and discursive strategies, leading in different directions, with the former calling for radical alternatives and another future and the latter leading to political compromise and the wish to bring about efficiency and prosperity within the framework of the market economy. The tension between utopian critique and discourses of pragmatic improvement is a fundamental dilemma of social democracy.

This has important implications for the substantial discussion in the literature on how to define the "new" social democracy in relation to what "old" social democracy was. There are two problems here. The first one is the construction of radical newness, break, and discontinuity, which has characterized much of the political and academic writing on contemporary social democracy. In particular, the literature about New Labour saw this newness in its abdication of socialism in favor of market capitalism or even neoliberalism.[6] This has set in place a dichotomy between old and new, which is not very helpful for understanding the complex origins and trajectories of social democracy either historically or in the present. It is clearly not possible, from any reading of social democracy's history, to argue that the Third Way's embracing of the market signifies a decisive break with old social democracy because social democracy has always grappled with questions of markets and capitalist efficiency. On the other hand, suggestions that the Third Way stands in continuity with "old" social democracy have often been simplistic. Studies of ideological change have often led to accounts of the evolutionary nature of social democratic ideology, where revisionism becomes a kind of learning process, an unproblematic adaptation to altered socioeconomic circumstances. From this perspective, the Third Way tends to become equated with previous periods of revisionism as if social democratic ideology evolved in a historical continuity of revisionism and ideological change was an unproblematic question of adaptation to altered socioeconomic circumstances. From this perspective, the meaning of modernization in each period in the history of social democracy is not problematized, and the Third Way becomes "a further step towards the reassessment of issues which leftwing parties have long been confronted with and addressed."[7]

In a recent study, Sheri Berman suggests that the historic project of social democracy was its marrying of capitalism and democracy and that the twentieth century can be seen as the historic victory of social democracy over fascism and market fundamentalism.[8] This is an important point, and it reminds us of the importance of social democracy's past achievements. But one might argue that the relevance of the Third Way is exactly the manner in which it has undone this "victory" by abdicating central principles of democracy and equality—all in the name of the market. Somehow I do not think that this would have been possible were it not for the fact that the market has always occupied a central place in social democratic ideology. In another study of British Labour and Swedish social democracy, Jonas Hinnfors argues that social democracy was always "market friendly," and so there is nothing fundamentally new in the market orientation of the Third Way.[9] While this is clearly true on some level, it does not seem to provide us with the bigger picture. Clearly, social democracy did things before that it does not do today, and it does some things today that it did not do before, and moreover it does them differently. Indeed, its notion of the market is not the same, nor is its notion of intervention. Social democracy has "always" been concerned with prosperity, which is why the concept of growth is a key element in social democratic ideology. However, its understanding of what drives the process of value creation, the relationship of growth as means or end to other ideological objectives, and the role of the market economy to create it, are key elements of ideological change. What distinguishes the Third Way from "old" social democracy, then, is not a sudden acceptance of market forces or a new procapitalist stance; rather it is the way that it gives new meaning to its historic articulations around capitalism in relationship to new ideas of what drives prosperity in the new economy. This is by no means an innocuous process. On the contrary, it is a process that changes the very meaning of social democracy.

Sassoon writes that "revisionism involves rejecting old policies, not old ethical principles, old ways of achieving desirable ends, not the ends."[10] The problem with this argument, often repeated by social democracy's modernizers, is that what is a means to an end is not a constant in social democratic history; rather, the hierarchy between means and ends is historically specific. The concept of equality, for instance, has become equality of opportunity in British discourse, which is, moreover, not the same concept in Gordon Brown's use as it was in Anthony Crosland's.[11] Is equality a means for opportunity, or is opportunity the means for equality? In Swedish social democratic discourse, strong links exist between the notions of growth and security. But is security the means for growth or growth the means for security?[12] The meaning of concepts such as equality or security change in periods of revisionism, even if the words remain the same, and they must therefore be considered historic objectives, defined again at each specific period in time. This is not an innocuous process of evolution: It involves strategic ideological choices and, arguably, these choices are what define the soul of social democracy. The discussions of means and ends, eternal values and new realities, are necessarily about ideological change.

This does not mean that each period of revisionism makes a radical break with the social democratic past, as was suggested by many Third Way proponents in the mid-1990s. Part of revisionist projects is the relocation of undesired ideological luggage to the past and the claim to break with previous ideologies. However, there is an important element of intertextuality and interdependency between periods of revisionism, as modernizers lean on and reread the modernizers who preceded them. Social democracy is not a movement that likes to break with its past; rather, it goes to great lengths to establish continuities backwards. History is one of its main sources of legitimacy. Swedish Social Democrats are at pains to stay within a carefully choreographed story of continuity that begins with Hjalmar Branting, Per Albin Hansson, and Ernst Wigforss; and New Labour, despite its need to claim new territory, has kept returning to Anthony Crosland, R. H. Tawney, and William Beveridge.[13] Even archmodernizers are, in this sense, anchored in rereadings of past ideologies, and even New Labour's Third Way, in its self-proclaimed newness, drew on the Third Ways that came before it. There is revisionism, then, also in the historiographical meaning of the term, in the sense of rereading, reinterpreting, and redefining the social democratic past itself, thereby laying down the ideological heritage for new times. Revisionism does not take place as a break with the past but as the reinterpretation and rearticulation of the past. This is a selective and quintessentially ideological process. The SAP's reading of the Keynesian economist Wigforss, in defence of its 1980s austerity policies, and New Labour's reading of Crosland in 1994, in defence of its reinvented concept of equality of opportunity, are examples of this historiographical nature of revisionism.[14]

But what kind of ideology, then, guides social democracy today? Indisputably, the Third Way represents a form of social democracy reformatted, as it were, for a new era. The Third Way was and is social democracy's attempt to put a social face on capitalism with the means that it sees at its disposition. From a historical perspective, however, until now the Third Way has been strangely myopic. It contains a number of assumptions and postulates that seem distinct from old social democracy, not only in means but in the fundamental values that define what social democracy is. In an excellent study, Gerassimos Moschonas argues that the Third Way signifies a "decisive ideological leap," through which social democracy has been transformed "from a political force for the moderate promotion of equality within an economic system that is by definition inegalitarian, to a force for the moderate promotion of inequality in the face of forces that are even more inegalitarian."[15] In this way, Moschonas suggests, the transformation of social democracy has meant the dissolution of an historical node of social reformism: the idea that the role of the state is to protect the wage earners, the disadvantaged, and society's weakest against the forces of deregulation and the market, a node that has not been questioned during previous periods of revisionism. This is a tough verdict on the Third Way. The decisiveness of the leap, for instance, is debatable because social democracy is a contradictory, multifaceted project across time and space. It is also questionable whether social democracy is really no longer interested in society's weakest (or, alternatively, if it really ever was, in its historical form, organized around a historic subject of the male industrial worker). Indisputably, the Third Way contains a strong interest in questions of inequality and social cohesion, but the meaning of these terms in the contemporary is crucial.[16] Further, the Third Way clearly links issues of inequalities and social exclusion to the efficient functioning of capitalism, as social democracy has traditionally done. New Labour has argued passionately that what is fair is also efficient and that neoliberalism was not efficient, with the social costs that it brought in terms of unemployment and poverty.[17] But this leaves us with the question of what social democracy today considers to be an efficient society.

In this book, my perspective on the Third Way is that it does add up to a fundamental ideological change in social democracy's outlook on capitalism. Social democratic ideology today, I argue, is distinct from ideologies in the history of social democracy because it turns arguments that historically were arguments *in critique of* capitalist structures into arguments *for* these structures. In this process, discourses of utopian alternative become discourses of improvement and efficiency—discourses of the management of knowledge capitalism. It is clear that since 1989 there has not been, in the established Left, any serious debate on alternatives to capitalism.[18] What we know as the Third Way is an expression of social democracy in the new political space that this absence of radical alternative creates. What is left, in the absence of utopia and radical critique, is the sphere of improvement and regulation, of managing progress and of steering change. On the one hand, this seems like a sea change. On the other, one has to ask the question, How different is such managerialism from social democracy's historical discourses of rationalization, improvement, and efficiency?

Answering this question calls for a very careful approach to what is old and new in social democratic thinking. It requires, I maintain, a historical reading of the Third Way, a reading that places it within the history of the social democratic project but also distinguishes what sets it apart from previous social democratic thinking. Rather than juxtaposing "old" and "new," I propose that the Third Way and its narrative of the knowledge economy can be thought of in terms of key dilemmas at the heart of the social democratic project. One of these dilemmas is, as discussed, the relationship between social democracy's critique of capitalism and its desire to improve it. Another is the tension between what I call *socializing capital* and *capitalizing the social*, between social democracy's desire to intervene into capitalist structures in reaction to their social effects and its equally important strand, through history, of using social intervention to create economic efficiency and thus, of embedding capitalism in society and social relations. Social democracy and the welfare state are intimately involved in both commodifying and decommodifying practices.[19] Social democracy is a historical agent that, throughout the history of welfare capitalism, has intervened into the relationship between the economic and the social, mediating it and arbitrating it, indeed constructing economy and society as fields of action, existence, and intervention. Throughout history, its various modernization and rationalization discourses have been concerned with the rational organization and restructuring of this relationship, usually in response to notions of crisis and breakdown. The notion of the Third Way is, in the multitude of different forms that it takes in history, closely connoted to such notions of crisis, concerned with finding a new way out of them, of recreating harmony and efficiency.[20] In the 1930s, the Depression and its social effects led to discourses of rationalization and social engineering, which went hand in hand with the economic doctrines of Keynesianism.[21] In the 1990s, the social effects of neoliberalism led to new concerns of social crisis in the wake of market integration, and the Third Way can be seen as a reaction to these in its search for the social institutions in which to embed knowledge capitalism. In so doing, it has displayed an at times thoroughgoing social interventionism that is closer to rationalization discourses in the history of social democracy than it is to neoliberalism.

These tensions between utopian critique and improvement, and between regulating capitalism or rationalizing the social (along with others, such as the relationship between collective advancement and individual emancipation, or between economic dynamism and equality) are part of a social democratic *grammaire*. They have defined it historically and continue to define it today, at the possible end of the Third road. They are questions at the heart of processes of revisionism and modernization. The Third Way gave them new form in relationship to what it perceived as a new world. While there are elements to the Third Way that seem highly specific to the present, such as the relationship between information communication technology (ICT) and individual freedom, for example, nevertheless, these are reminiscent of old socialist debates, such as the one on technology and alienation in the late nineteenth century or the discussion of increasing expectations in the affluent society in the

1950s. Similarly, the alleged individualism of the globalized knowledge era brings back a deeply individualistic strand in the history of social democracy. Indeed, one of the utopias of social democracy, besides that of the efficient capitalist society, is the idea of the fulfilled individual, the educated, aware citizen capable of both seeing through the structures of bourgeois society and of finding happiness. In the knowledge era, this utopic individual preoccupies social democracy more than ever. Hence, when social democracy speaks of a knowledge society, it taps into, advertently or inadvertently, a long historical legacy of notions of self-improvement and the cultivation of the self.[22]

Focusing on the tensions embedded in such dilemmas is a way of opening up the Third Way to point to the contradictions, tensions, and incoherences that it seemed to envelop and that are perhaps becoming clearer today. Indeed, an important aspect of social democratic ideology is the fact that contradictory or seemingly incoherent standpoints coexist within it, within parties in ongoing disputes between traditionalists and modernizers or possibly even within the same person. These tensions are crucial. They provide for ideological incoherence, for tension or glitches between discourse and policies, or even for contradictory measures and ideas, and as such they need to be elucidated and criticized. But these tensions are also the possible embryos of other political futures because ideological change originates in the disputes and struggles over exactly such incoherences and tensions.[23] As Geoff Eley has suggested, history can be a way of opening up such tensions, of bringing back the past futures of social democracy, thus permitting us to critique its contemporary orthodoxies. The use of the comparative method also holds such emancipatory potential because it shows that social democracy is involved in thinking otherwise.[24]

This book is based on a comparative approach to social democracy across time and space, designed to bring out questions of continuity and change in social democracy's relationship to capitalism. The cases that form the point of departure of the book offer a singular opportunity for this approach because over time they seem both strikingly similar and deeply contradictory, both soul mates and opposites. While New Labour has been the primary focus of observers of the Third Way, the transformation of Swedish SAP in recent decades has attracted far less attention. Swedish social democracy has an almost iconic status among international observers of social democracy and welfare policy, as a paradigmatic case of social democracy.[25] To these observers, the SAP is seemingly resilient to neoliberalism, holding on to the traditional values of the "Model."[26] This is partly wishful thinking because Swedish social democracy has gone through substantial ideological transformations in the period following the 1980s.[27] It is also hard to think of a more managerialist, pragmatic, and modernist example of social democracy than the Swedish SAP. Its historical pragmatism and relative market friendliness are exactly what make it stand out among social democratic parties.[28] Whereas SAP discourse of the 1990s comes off as more radical than New Labour discourse—in the sense of being more critical of capitalism—throughout its history the SAP has been quintessentially reformist, its utopian stances reduced to brief interludes and generally subdued in relation to its predominant productivism. This stands in contrast to a much more radical tradition of British Labourism and to the lasting influence on the British Left of utopian thinkers, such as William Morris or Raymond Williams. This permits us to illustrate the tensions in social democracy's relationship to capitalism over time. As one British interviewee suggests, Swedish social democracy never wanted to abolish capitalism in the first place, which makes it much easier for the SAP to critique it, while "our problem is that for a long time we looked like we wanted to abolish it."[29] It also permits us to consider the suggestion that today, New Labour does, or attempts to do, what Swedish social democracy historically did, only adapted to a new era of globalization, flexible production patterns, and individualization.[30] This is an argument that requires analysis, I argue, not only on the level of policies and institutional change but also on the normative level of the values and objectives of contemporary social democracy, its discourses, and worldviews, essentially, on the level of ideology.

Modernization and Utopia

The Third Way, as the notion emerged in the mid-1990s following the advent of social democratic governments in Europe, Bill Clinton's election as president of the United States, Anthony Giddens' book with the same name, and the Blair-Schröder article laying out the territory for a new center Left, corresponded to a set of wider changes in European politics, which seemed to mark the end of neoliberalism and the rise of something more social.[31] The European creation of the Lisbon strategy and the debate on Social Europe that followed were also important markers in this process. The notion of the Third Way became a term for a big project involved in rethinking the welfare state, of finding new means of social intervention after the deregulation and market liberalization of the 1980s and 1990s, and of finding new economic and social policies for the knowledge economy, which was almost unanimously hailed as the way forward.[32] The metaphor of the Third Way was also quickly adopted by the social sciences to describe an institutional approach to social policy in search of a systemic fit or "optimal policy mixes" in adaptation to the new economy.[33] The outcome of this was the creation of a modernization discourse, which on both the national and the European level was intimately linked to notions such as employability, social investment, knowledge economy, and welfare-to-work, all of which seemed to add up to a global imperative for change.

The influence of the liberal center-left thesis, as it was put forward not only by Giddens but with variations by observers from John Gray in the United Kingdom to Francis Fukuyama in the United States, was substantial.[34] It seemed, as David Marquand once put it, to mark a social democratic moment and provide a new rationale for social democracy in the modern era.[35] It linked this rationale to forces of globalization, individualization, and information technology. Particularly in the United Kingdom, the idea of a new economy came together with a call for the forging of new politics, the defining characteristic of which was the rejection of ideology and notions of class, conflict, and interest.[36] The Third Way was a new, modern political space, beyond old and outdated Left and Right, defined by the pragmatism that suits modern times.[37] Modernization was represented as a process undogmatically centered on the means of reform, a logic of adaptation to a new stage of capitalism.

Giddens's call for adaptation to the irrevocable changes brought on by a runaway world has been met with considerable critique in the ten years since its publication, particularly for the determinism underlying its portrayal of globalization and information technology.[38] Modernization is a keyword that figures less prominently in political discourse today, particularly as financial crisis seems to rapidly undo much of what it was about; liberalization of markets, marketizations of welfare. The problem with the notion of modernization as a pragmatic process of reform that underpinned much of political discourse in the late 1990s and early 2000s was of course that it downplayed normative aspects of policy change and the elements of choice, will, and power—that is, the sphere of ideology. Modernization became portrayed as an evolutionary necessity rather than what it was arguably really about, namely the normative construction of economy and society. *Modernization* is an inherently teleological term, which carries with it a heavy heritage of Enlightenment values and normative assumptions of the nature of progress.[39] Indeed, there were elements of Third Way discourse, particularly New Labour's determinism around information technology, that were reminiscent of tenets of scientific socialism, with all the problems associated with it. In 1968, Raymond Williams wrote of the concept of modernization that it is the "theology of capitalism": a technocratic vision of society, where social conflicts are silenced in the praise of the scientific revolution.[40]

Modernization is a powered discourse, with central disciplining and governing functions. In the words of the political philosopher Nicholas Rose, modernization discourse is a language, which "gives authority authority" and connects the "molars with the molecular," thereby defining the governing and the governed and the role and technologies of government.[41] Modernization discourse speaks of certain parts of change while it silences others, and in the process it also speaks of some experiences and silences others. The claim of a new era is also the claim that the old is no longer relevant.

An important consequence of the modernization discourse of the Third Way was the way that it rejected the notion of utopia. Politics is however necessarily a futures-oriented business. A key function of modernization discourse is that of establishing a sense of direction and of creating coherence around this particular way forward rather than another. In doing so, modernization discourse is dependent on ideas, silent or articulated, of a desired future, a future that defines the trajectory of change and lends meaning to the process of modernization—where to go and why. In consequence, pragmatism is not a value-free zone of politics. Rather it is a specific discursive strategy drawing on the representation of particular politics as something more modern, rational, progressive, and futures oriented than its alternatives. Pragmatism appeals to normative postulates as if they were commonsense values, usually the values of the "people." This is an essentially hegemonic strategy, an attempt to create consensus around certain values and experiences and exclude others.[42] The hegemony of Swedish social democracy from the 1930s onwards drew exactly on such an appeal to mainstream values and consensus, the values of the Swedish *folk*, and in this respect it was similar to other *volk*-ideologies that were prominent in Europe at that time.[43] The success of this strategy, arguably, is the reason for New Labour's own interest in it, in its search for a progressive consensus or for a way of entrenching its values in the British electorate. Indeed, New Labour, in the 1990s, also appealed to the "people" and the "nation," an appeal it has continued to promote in its recurrent theme of Britishness.

In this appeal to national harmony, the Third Way has included elements of historic nationalist discourses, something that is increasingly evident in the need to make speeches on Britishness in the United Kingdom or in the constant reassertion, in Sweden, of a self-image as the most modern country in the world. However, the politics of the Third Way are also close to the

1950s managerialism, focused on the administering of affluence. There was something in the Third Way's hope that "prosperity for all" would lead to the withering away of social problems that was highly reminiscent of social democracy's 1950s idea that industrial affluence would make redistribution without class conflict possible. By the 1990s something was different, though. The postwar end-of-ideology thesis was deeply optimistic and presumed the near end of all social evils. The managerialism of the Third Way was infinitely more pessimistic. It was more closely related to the risk society thesis of Giddens and Beck, of societies that no longer dream of utopias but are content with the rational administering of the status quo.[44] And while postwar social democratic modernizers, such as Harold Wilson in the United Kingdom or Tage Erlander in Sweden, might have been technocrats in their fundamental beliefs in the power of technology and growth, they were concerned with building the good society, in Sweden conceptualized as the Strong Society of collective solidarity and public responsibility.[45] The Third Way shied away from such utopian articulations. Indeed, the notion of the knowledge society, despite its centrality as a future metaphor for social democratic politics in the 1990s and 2000s, never seemed to contain a specific vision of the good society. Rather, it depicted change as a perpetual process of improvement. The notion of learning, as in the notion of the learning society or indeed, in the term life-long-learning, denotes this process of never-ending change. To that extent, the notion of modernization that informed the Third Way's managerialism brings to mind what the sociologist Zygmunt Bauman has called modernization without *telos*, a notion of modernization without endpoint, a politics without utopia.[46] The focal point of politics is change itself. Alongside this shift in notions of progress from end to motion, says Bauman, is an individualization of the future, a process in which utopian aspiration is relocated to the individual sphere. To Bauman, this is the search for individual fulfilment and happiness, the self-expression of which, indeed, much is made in contemporary societies. However, the other side of this individualization are political discourses of improvement that no longer focus on social and economic structures but on aspects of individual motivations and behavior, adding up to a notion of modernization that centers in on the individual as the key locus of change.

Utopia, post-1968 and 1989, became a pejorative term, one that denoted the authoritarian elements of visions of the good society gone astray.[47] This refusal to speak of the good society was the Third Way's motivation, but it has also rapidly become its limit, in a time when all are fighting over the political center. Again, the dilemma of reformism is that radical critique questions the basis of reform—while on the other hand, discourses of improvement are ultimately dependent on a notion of utopia to maintain their creed. Contrary to social democracy's current beliefs, the utopian alternative does not demand the overthrow of the status quo. A critique of capitalism does not demand the abolition of capitalism. Utopia, in the words of the liberal philosopher Charles Taylor, is not the prescription for exactly what society demands full realization in the here and now but a notion of possibility, "a way of things that may be realised in some eventually possible conditions, but that meanwhile serve as a standard to steer by."[48] Taylor points to the crucial field of political imaginary and aspiration, the kind of aspiration that gives voice to critique of the present. The contemporary torment of social democracy, in the United Kingdom and in Sweden, is that it has lost sight of this crucial vision of the better society that can stem from such utopian critique. This does not mean that social democracy's Third Way project is not utopian. Ultimately, the chapters of this book suggest that the Third Way, in all its self-proclaimed pragmatism, is a highly normative worldview, construed around pervasive assumptions of the organization of economy and society, of the relationship between individual and collective, and, indeed, of what kind of individuals are desirable in a knowledge society. It is dangerous when such utopian assumptions are disguised as value-free pragmatics. Therefore, the Third Way needs to be discussed in terms of politics and ideology and in terms of the economy, society, and individual that it projects.

Ideology and History: Discourse and Institutional Change

The impetus behind this book is the desire to take ideology seriously, that is, to grapple not with the logics of institutional change that have been the focus of contemporary social science for the last decade but with the worldviews of contemporary politics. From this it follows that the ideas dealt with herein are not dealt with merely as a set of discourses or rhetoric but as elements in the shaping of a social democratic worldview, an ontology of economy and society. Taking ideology seriously requires grappling with history because ideology is not a set of new postulates; rather, every process of ideological change draws on ideologies past. Moreover, as we will see in upcoming chapters, modernization is, to a striking extent, a national discourse, one that reflects and asserts self-images.[49] In both countries, the narrative of the new economy is embedded in representations of the national past. Change is reacted to and interpreted against the backdrop of understandings of national cultural specificity and even national character. In this process, Esping-Andersen's famous models have taken on a role of trope and identity construction. In both countries, there is a preoccupation with finding strategies of reform that fit the historical institutions of the social or the liberal model and their underlying values of "Swedishness" and "Britishness."[50]

My argument here goes beyond questions of path dependency or institutional stickiness. Rather, it points to the way that political change is dependent on the values and symbols that make up the political consciousness. Consider the way that the SAP, in the 1990s and 2000s, has been concerned with creating a sense of belonging, while New Labour has been equally concerned with the idea of creating a culture of obligation. Consider, too, the way that Tony Blair, in a speech to the Progressive Governance summit in Budapest in 2004, announced a crackdown on welfare claimants, while the former Swedish Prime Minister Göran Persson stated that welfare is productive.[51] These differences fall back, I argue, on the different norms and values that surround welfare capitalism and what we might call the social contract in both countries.[52]

This calls for a different concept of history than the one that dominated social science in previous decades. In recent years, the literature on welfare state change has pointed to the role of history for prevailing continuities in the form of specific varieties of capitalism and the divergence of national policy models, despite the pressure of globalization or European integration.[53] However, institutional path dependence is a narrow conception of history, one that draws on past legacies to account for institutional continuities but gives a lesser role to political culture, language, and the norms and values that make up the political consciousness and create what might be called varieties of reformism. Notions of what constitutes a fair and efficient society differ among political cultures. Political change is not just a question of institutional divergence or convergence but of the renegotiation of cultural and ideological legacies around welfare and of key values that distinguish one society from another and uphold national self-images in times of change. Modernity is ultimately a kind of self-understanding, inseparable from a set of images and symbols for how we fit together, how we got to where we are, and how we relate to other versions of modernity.[54] The values surrounding political economy, the organization of capitalism, and the virtues of citizenship are central parts of our social imaginaries. Moreover, history has acquired a new role in the knowledge economy because, in the post-Fordist era, shared identity is considered constitutive of the trust relations that foster growth and prosperity. The question of how we grow as a nation has become intimately linked to the question of *who we are* and to the presumed values of the nation and its people. Identity politics are an integral feature of the Third Way in its appeal to identities beyond class, influenced by the idea of a new economy, where identity is also a brand name.

From Model to Model

The faces of Swedish and British politics have changed substantially in the decades since Gösta Esping Andersen wrote his *Three Worlds of Welfare Capitalism*. Indeed, the meaning of the social and the liberal model in a new era is unclear, after decades of retrenchment and reform.[55] This book points to important continuities in discursive legacies around the welfare state and in the framings around policy change, even when the policies are sometimes similar. This calls for a complicated argument, namely, that in the process of renegotiating national welfare heritages the historic values of the social contract seem to have a crucial role. This is not unimportant, because the values reproduced in political discourse are constitutive of the relationship between politics and citizen and between citizens in a society, and they determine how it is politically possible to speak of change. In this way, the values of discourse thus define the content and direction of the process of modernization.[56] In her late-1990s article, Vivienne Schmidt argued that Sweden was the country where "neoliberal values have penetrated the least" because of a resilience of historical Swedish values of equality and universalism.[57] Schmidt pointed to a hesitation in Swedish modernization discourse between an emphasis on continuity with the postwar model and notions of change. As will be developed in the coming pages, this vacillation between continuity and change is at the core of the Swedish interpretation of modernization as "safeguarding" the historical edifice of the People's Home. This discursive emphasis on safeguarding does not mean, however, that nothing has changed in Sweden. The literature on welfare state retrenchment has argued that Sweden has successfully dealt with the 1990s crisis and upheld labor market and social policies that stand in continuity with the institutions of the postwar model. This is also what Swedish Social Democrats will say.[58] However, it is an indisputable fact that the Swedish welfare state has seen some substantial changes in recent decades. Some Swedish policies of the 1990s, such as the all-party pension reform in 1994, have gone very far. The pension reform made future compensation levels dependent on macroeconomic and demographic trends and, moreover, included a small but symbolic individual saving to be placed on the stock market.[59] Swedish macroeconomic policies in the 1990s saw the effective replacement of the goal of full employment with norm policies, even if full employment also quickly reappeared on the agenda once the objective of stability was achieved.[60] While Swedish labor market policies in the 1990s can appear to stand in continuity with the supply-side orientation and active labor market policies of the postwar Rehn Meidner model, Swedish labor market policies have also seen a clear shift to the employability and flexibility discourses that have structured the process of welfare state modernization in the last two decades.[61] The restructuring of the public sector in the 1990s opened the way for far-reaching marketizations. Sweden has introduced a voucher system in schools that seems directly at odds with the principle of universalism and that has contributed to economic and social segregation.[62] Most of this has taken place under the slogan of "safeguarding."

During the decade that New Labour has been in power, the United Kingdom has seen an ambitious reform agenda on poverty, unemployment, and literacy; major institutional changes in social and labor market policies; and massive investment in education and child care.[63] The Institute for Public Policy Research's follow-up to the Commission on Social Justice argued that New Labour has developed a new model of anglo-social welfare, drawing on the historical elements of liberalism, as well as on elements borrowed from Scandinavian-style welfare arrangements, particularly the day-care strategy and the creation of the New Deal for the unemployed.[64] There are many contradictions in this. Just as there is tension, in the Swedish case, between a discourse that holds on to traditional values and important change on the policy level, British discourse is often more cautious than the policies implemented, for reasons having to do with New Labour's break with old Labourism and with its perception of the British electorate as deeply conservative. Thus some of its policies, such as the Sure Start program or the radically redistributive emphasis in asset-based welfare policies such as the baby bonds, seem much more radical in content than are the framings around them. Another contradiction is the relationship between elements from the liberal model and its means-testing and workfare strategies, and elements of universalism imported from the Scandinavian model. In an interview, Ed Balls, the main architect of New Labour's macro-micro strategy, says that the New Deal drew on Swedish active labor market policies and quotes Allan Larsson, the Swedish Minister of Finance who designed the European Employment Strategy.[65] But in the early years of New Labour the influence behind new employment policies was not Sweden but the supply-side policies developed in the Clinton administration.[66] These involved not only investment in education but also activation program and the pledge to "cut welfare as we know it."[67] In the 1990s, New Labour's interest in Sweden was in the voucher schools that were introduced in Sweden in 1992 by the conservative Bildt government. This reform was modelled on Thatcher's attempt to create a market in education in the United Kingdom.

By the end of the Blair era, British ideas of the Swedish model changed, and Sweden emerged as a kind of Brownite utopia, a northern light of modern socioeconomic rationality and bold modernizing spirit.[68] In the summer of 2005, Gordon Brown was invited to speak at the SAP's annual economic seminar in Almedalen on the island of Gotland in the Baltic Sea. There he launched a joint research program on security and change in European labor markets with then Minister of Finance Pär Nuder. In 2005, the Labour Party conference included a fringe meeting organised by the left-flank Compass Group on the subject "Can We Do a Sweden?," inspired by a pamphlet written by the former *Financial Times* journalist Robert Taylor with the telling title *Sweden, Proof That a Better World Is Possible.* Taylor's pamphlet fell neatly into a tradition in the British (and American) Left of looking to Sweden for the utopian alternative.[69] In *The Future of Socialism*, Crosland used Sweden as proof that equality and social progress could be achieved without suffocating the liberty of the middle classes, and in the Compass pamphlet Robert Taylor argued that Sweden, renewed after the 1990s crisis, provided proof that social justice and economic dynamism could be combined.[70]

Swedish outlooks on Britain have also changed in the last decade. In the mid-1990s, when no one wanted to be Swedish, not even the Swedes, the youthfulness of New Labour was also alluring to the SAP. Göran Persson told the party conference in 1997 that Tony Blair's communitarian socialism was also his socialism.[71] Geoff Mulgan and Tom Bentley came to Stockholm in 1998 to present the work of the think tank Demos to an enthusiastic audience at party headquarters. As Swedish social democracy has regained confidence in the Swedish model in recent years, party discourse has moved away from the Third Way project as too market liberal—thereby also silencing the heritage from its own Third Way experiment in the 1980s. In the 2006 election, it was the Swedish Right who turned to New Labour for inspiration for its project of renewal.

2 The Political Economy of Knowledge

In the following pages, I sketch out the defining characteristics of what might be called a political economy of knowledge. Third Way ideology is informed, I argue, by a discursive logic of capitalization, a logic whereby social democracy identifies human potential—human knowledge, talent, creativity—as economic goods and ultimately new forms of capital, indeed as the raw material of the new economy. This capitalization is not a new phenomenon to social democracy. Processes of social democratic revisionism have, to a large extent, been about new definitions of what capital is and of how capitalist value is created. Social democratic growth discourses have always been concerned with the rationalization and utilization of labor. In the Keynesian era, social democracy was concerned with manpower and labor resources. In the knowledge era, it is concerned with the rationalization of the human capital of the skills revolution and with exploiting the intellectual resources that drive a knowledge-based economy.

Perhaps we should not overstate the role of the knowledge economy to contemporary social democracy. Social democracy is involved in traditional policies, such as apprenticeships, that had relevance long before the idea of the information revolution. However, the idea of the knowledge economy has provided a neat narrative to bring together policies of the industrial society with new ones, such as distance learning and ICT. The understanding of knowledge as a form of commodity also leads to a rethinking of the postulates of political economy. Unlike the coal and steel of the Industrial Revolution, knowledge is defined by its location within us, in the human capital of knowledge workers. Knowledge is "brainpower," not steam power. As other production factors lose importance, growth stems from the improvement of the factor of labor through knowledge and learning.[1]

This understanding of knowledge as a kind of capital within people leads to the creation of new means of economic governance to bring it out. Social policies, education policies, and cultural policies have, thus, become part of modern growth strategies. In this process, somewhat paradoxically, the parameters of state intervention in the age of globalization become, if anything, larger, as virtually everything becomes the object of economic policies. As Alan Finlayson has pointed out, the economy, in New Labour thinking, is almost omnipresent. Almost all New Labour policies, whether they be aimed at social inclusion, the preschooling of young children, or the preservation of the historical heritage, have been primarily *economic*, in the sense of being given a role for the strategic creation of the human and social capital of the knowledge economy. In the same way, virtually all social and cultural values from trust to curiosity and aesthetics are, in New Labour thinking, also economic values and therefore legitimate objects of economic intervention.[2] We might say the same for Sweden, where everything from initiatives for children's culture to the environment is framed in a pragmatic growth discourse, even if there are also differences, to which we will return.

This expansion of the sphere of economic governance is directly related to the capitalization of knowledge in the Third Way's economic theory:

> When knowledge is understood as the central commodity flowing in the economy, it is a short step to such a cultural mode of governance. After all a culture can, at one level, be understood as a set of shared knowledges. As such the analysis of economic production and the analysis of culture begin to fuse.[3]

The literature around the knowledge economy includes many references to this expansion of the economic, but it has a particular relevance in the history of social democracy because notions of human potential, culture, and education are notions that historically have referred to values in conflict with the idea of profit. Now they become drawn into the process of capitalist improvement. We can take this back to the argument set out in the Introduction; while the Third Way cannot be set apart from "old" social democracy by means of its fundamental market acceptance, what the Third Way does is to turn arguments that in the history of social democracy were arguments against capitalism into arguments *for* capitalism.

Neoliberal Social Democracy?

For the sake of this argument, let us revisit the theory that the Third Way is neo-liberal, which was the suggestion of the first wave of studies on the Third Way.

The point of departure of the Third Way project was, as we know, the end of Keynesian demand management and national economic policies in a world dominated by globalization. In contrast to the way that "old" social democra-cy's Keynesian policies were focused on controlling capital within the bound-aries of the nation-state through macroeconomic policies and demand man-agement, a central tenet of the Third Way, from the mid-1990s, was the idea of globalization and of an open economy, where capital cannot be controlled by the boundaries of the nation-state and where the scope of macroeconomic policies is circumscribed by the constant flux of capital.[4] Hence, the Third Way can be described as a political project based on a rethinking of the nature of contemporary capitalism and the logic of capital, as well as of the role of state intervention and the scope of economic policies in this new world. This rearticulation of politics around the imperative of globalization is what has often been described as the neoliberalization of social democracy.

In the British context, New Labour's economic policies have been seen as the continuation of Thatcherism because of their fundamental acceptance of the monetarist framework, their rejection of collective action, and the refusal to undo the changes in labor law introduced by Thatcher.[5] Colin Hay put it most critically when he described New Labour's political economy as "studi-ously courting capital," a "reconception of the parameters of political possi-bility in terms of the imperatives imposed by economic integration, financial liberalisation and heightened capital mobility—in short globalisation."[6] Based on the political presumption that capital is in a fundamentally uncontrollable liquid state, what is left in terms of macroeconomic strategy is, in Hay's terms, an accommodation to the perceived interest of capital for political, economic, and social survival. Similar arguments have been made for Sweden by Magnus Ryner.[7] According to this interpretation, social democracy accepts the ideo-logical parameters set by Thatcherism, including its use of a strong state in the interest of the market.[8] This is clearly so. But the Third Way also contains a strong rejection of both the social philosophy of neoliberalism and the eco-nomic doctrine of monetarism, as if not entirely ideologically misconstrued at least economically inefficient in an era driven by skill, knowledge, and in-formation. These are all drivers of change that are understood to require a rethinking of the very scope of politics, similar to the redefinition of politics carried out by neoliberalism. As Hay and others have shown, the Third Way is a political economy based on the assumption of the reality of globalization, and, accordingly, it redefines the role of social democratic politics to act for the creation of wealth within the parameters set by globalization. Because capital is uncontrollable, what government must do is provide a stable framework and infrastructure so as to attract capital and inward investment. The other leg of this strategy, however, is to increase the value of the capital within its borders, that is, the human capital of the nation. Attracting foreign investment has a parallel here in those labor market policies, education policies, and asylum policies that attempt to attract the "best brains." If the macro strategy can be described, then, in Hay's terms, as a courting of the liquid financial capital of the information age, the micro strategy could be described as a capitalization of those human, social, and cultural resources that are defined as productive capital. We can bring this macro–micro strategy back to Gordon Brown's statement—that, in an economy where capital moves "at the press of a key," the fundamental resource of the nation state is the potential and talent of its people, the "brainpower" that makes up the skills revolution.[9] In a manner of speaking, labor's earlier attempts to control capital have been replaced, in the economic policies of contemporary social democracy, by the attempts to control the capital embedded in labor. New cultural modes of governance aim at creating this capital and at changing the values and dispositions within knowledge workers—in other words, "build human capital."[10]

Neoliberalism is not an adequate concept to describe this. The Third Way is, I suggest, better understood as a political economy based on an understanding of knowledge as a specific form of capital that requires new forms of intervention and a new balance between macro and micro, state and individual, economy and society.

Social Democracy from Austerity to Prosperity: The Macro-Micro Strategy of the Third Way

The allure of the knowledge economy in social democratic politics from the mid-1990s was its promise of a new industrial revolution that seemed to recreate conditions of prosperity. As we will see in the following chapter, this idea of a revolutionary economic transformation was much more prominent in the United Kingdom, where it fit into a general narrative of renewal, than in Sweden. The Downing Street advisor Charles Leadbeater wrote of an age where you could virtually live on thin air and where growth could be conjured up from the intangible resources of human ingenuity and creativity.[11] However, in Sweden too the idea of electronic railways and the promises of new Swedish new economy multinationals, such as Framfab and Spray, seduced a Social Democratic Party coming out of the worst recession since the 1930s.[12]

Leadbeater's wildly optimistic account of the knowledge economy was, in fact, not too different from descriptions of the knowledge economy of actors such as the Organisation of Economic Co-operation and Development.[13] These 1990s accounts drew on very specific assumptions as to how knowledge behaves as good and capital. Knowledge, because of its fundamental intangibility and the difficulty of measuring it and reining it in, is often presumed to be a virtually infinite resource and a nonrival good.[14] Its consumption is also its production. There was a silent assumption, or perhaps dream, that the human capital of the third industrial revolution would prove to be the source of an unprecedented productivity expansion, leading the way out of the austerity of the 1970s and 1980s.[15] This dream of the productivity potential embedded in the knowledge-driven economy mirrors social democracy's postwar growth utopia. This optimistic prospect for a new golden era is what explains the hype around the new economy in the 1990s.

Although much of the new economy hyperbole ended with the dot.com bubble, the knowledge economy has also been the object of a more traditional social democratic growth discourse, focused on the conditions for business and the skills of the labor force.[16] Central to this growth discourse as it took shape in the 1990s was the drawing up of a macro–micro strategy designed to promote stability and prosperity. In both countries, the experiences of the devastating social effects of capital flight, in Britain after the European Exchange Rate Mechanism (ERM) debacle and in Sweden after the 1992 collapse of the krona, led to the conclusion that the survival of social democracy and the capacity for social reform hinged on the creation of a stable macroeconomic framework and the restoration of sound finances.[17] This led to the emergence of a social democratic economic language construed around the watchword of prudence and the setting in place of a macroeconomic framework designed to foster long-term stability. In the United Kingdom, macroeconomic stability was seen as the key to building international and domestic credibility and facilitating long-term investment decisions, thus breaking with the "boom and bust" of the British economy.[18] In Sweden, the main motivation for macroeconomic policy change was to restore sound finances and recreate legitimacy for the Swedish welfare state, which was blamed both domestically and internationally for the economic crisis and galloping budget deficits.[19] In both countries, this macro strategy included new framings around public spending, based on New Public Management policies and the principle of "value for money," created through innovation in management techniques and the strategic use of audits and standards.[20] The golden rule in the United Kingdom, which states that borrowing should be undertaken only with the purpose to invest over the current economic cycle, had a cousin in Sweden in the *utgiftstak,* the cap that was placed on public expenditure after 1992. In both countries, a central strategy of reform was the restructuring of the budget process to increase control over public spending. In the United Kingdom, the Comprehensive Spending Review was designed to monitor the substantial investment in public services that has taken place, while in Sweden the overhaul of the budget process was put in place to tighten public spending, without any significant shifts in its use as a means of governance.[21]

On the one hand, this approach to public spending and the public sector clearly reflected the neoliberal critique of public expenditure since the 1970s. On the other, particularly in the United Kingdom, it also broke with the blunt privatizations and the internal markets introduced by Thatcher in the public sector, notably in the National Health Service (NHS). Thus crude competition was replaced by such means as spreading best practice through collaboration and learning, a process that nevertheless was based on competition as the best way to create "best value regimes."[22] This remained an approach to the public sector and to key welfare services explicitly based on a market template, an approach that appealed to consumerism; indeed, one that spoke of the public as consumers, used NPM policies to create markets of demand and supply in key services, and also served as a critique of the very notion of public as a special sphere in society. An important aspect of this, to which we will return shortly, was replacing the idea of public good with the notion of public value, defined as value for money and ensured though the strategic use of audits. This was a very different idea of the public than that which shaped postwar public sectors, and in both countries it came with a more or less explicit mistrust of both public sector activities and public sector workers. Arguably, this went further in the United Kingdom, but the critique of the public sector and the introduction of NPM policies was a central part of the Swedish Third Way beginning in the 1980s.[23]

In both countries, the macro politics of purpose were coupled with a new micro orientation centered on the fostering of knowledge, skill, and innovation.[24] The 1990s saw the articulation of new growth policies around small- and medium-sized enterprises (SMEs) and entrepreneurship and new regional policies around the promotion of clusters of innovation, influenced by endogenous growth theory.

Endogenous growth theory sees growth as stemming from investment in knowledge and skills, a postulate that gives a clear role to the state for investment in ICT and education.[25] In the mid-1990s, endogenous growth theory was coupled with the new supply-side economics, aimed at increasing the quantity and quality of labor, which were developed by leading architects of economic and labor market policy in the Clinton administration.[26] The rise of supply-side economics was, in many ways, a logical consequence of the abdication of the demand side and the self-binding that followed the breakdown of Keynesian arrangements from the early 1970s; however, the supply side was also given a specific role in new growth theory because of its emphasis on endogenous investment in education and training. The new emphasis on the supply side came with a shift in employment discourses, from Keynesian discourses on full employment to discourses of employability, which focus on individual skill.[27] The notion of employability is indicative of a substantial shift in notions of need, risk, and responsibility in modern labor markets . Public responsibility is no longer job protection or job creation but investment in human capital to help workers deal with the risks of a globalized era. The individual is responsible for obtaining and maintaining skills. The shift from employment to employability discourses arguably constitutes a bigger difference for Sweden because the public responsibility for work in the United Kingdom was always more conditional and has in some ways been strengthened under New Labour, while in Sweden it was at the heart of the Social Democratic state. [28]

The emphasis on the supply side has also brought about a new coupling of economic and social policies, where welfare reform has become an integral part of growth policies. In the United Kingdom, the first reforms of the New Labour government in 1997 were the spectacular decision of giving independence to the Bank of England, immediately followed by the creation of the New Deal for the unemployed. The Treasury's productivity strategy for the modernization of the British economy has been tightly coupled with a modernization strategy for the welfare state, including an overhaul of the tax and benefits system and the introduction of tax credits with the specific purpose of moving people off benefits and into work. In the New Deals and the welfare-to-work programs, this involved a careful recalibration of the relationship between rights and responsibilities and incentives and benefits to "make work pay."[29] In that way, the creation of a macroeconomic framework for efficiency and parameters for spending on the macro level was combined with means of governance explicitly aimed at modernizing the welfare subject, through supply-side policies and welfare state intervention.[30] In Sweden, welfare reform in the 1990s might seem to stand in continuity with the postwar model because supply-side policies and the coordination of economic and social policy were central elements of the Swedish welfare state as it developed from the interwar period onward. However, mass unemployment, fiscal crisis, and new ideological currents in the 1990s have also given these policies new content, closer to the activation and workfare strategies of the liberal model.[31]

The relative laissez-faire on the macro level has been matched, then, by macro strategies, that, if anything, contain a strengthened emphasis on the role of social democracy for the creation of prosperity. This is more of a break for the United Kingdom. As David Coates has pointed out, from the beginning New Labour profiled itself as the party of wealth creation, more concerned with the creation of wealth than it was with its redistribution. This celebration of prosperity through key elements of the market and the entrepreneur was a central part of its break with old Labour and its "tax and spend" mentality.[32] In contrast, Swedish social democracy has always been a party of wealth creation. The party's 1994 economic report, which introduced the theme of endogenous growth theory, placed itself firmly in the tradition of the labor movement's economic committees of the postwar period, even though its themes of entrepreneurs and SMEs were new in social democratic ideology.[33] The economic strategy drawn up for the 1990s drew on the party's rejection of Keynesianism in the 1980s, to which were added elements from the conservative growth policies of the early 1990s. These focused on competition, competence, and knowledge. The policies of the conservative Bildt government, in turn, were influenced by the critique of the Swedish model put forward by the Lindbeck Commission in its program for the decorporization of the Swedish economy and the improvement of incentives structures for entrepreneurship.[34] On social democracy's return in 1994, these themes were merged into a new social democratic concept of growth.

Knowledge and the Common Good: Politics of Partnership

In their policies from the mid-1990s, both New Labour and the SAP argue, following the postulates of new growth theory, that knowledge is a particular kind of capital that is essentially owned and controlled by the worker and that has fundamental externalities in terms of its social returns (a higher level of knowledge in society promoting further learning and resulting in a skilled, adaptable labor force; better climate for innovation; and the like). Hence the state has to take a larger responsibility for its creation because, if left to the market, the lack of incentives and property rights and the problems of control for the individual firm will result in fundamental market failures, causing fatal underinvestment in knowledge. In consequence, both parties see a new balance between state and market, where the role of the state is to put in place an infrastructure for knowledge, learning, and information technology while the role of economic actors is that of innovation, and creativity—processes that are seen as beyond the capacity of the state.[35] As the slogan goes, it is not for the state to pick the winners (or subsidize the losers) but to remove barriers to entry and obstacles for learning, to put in place a stable framework for business and individuals, to foster entrepreneurs and creativity, and to encourage so-called competitive collaboration in clusters and networks. In Sweden, this seems to point to continuities with the corporatist legacies of the Swedish model, despite the novelty of some of the regional policies such as the *tillväxtavtal* (the partnerships for growth), which are based on local agreements between regional governments and regional industries. In the United Kingdom, the idea of a new economy somehow driven by the common good was the basis of New Labour's New Deal with business, a new "partnership for prosperity" based on mutual trust and collaboration.[36]

The notion of partnership established a new relationship between state and market that is central to the Third Way's political economy. In contrast to neoliberalism, this includes a strong notion of public responsibility in the economy. Similar to the way in which social democracy in the postwar period accepted a responsibility for the public good of the industrial economy in terms of investment in railroads, highways, education, and hospitals for a productive industrial workforce, in the knowledge economy social democracy accepts public responsibility for electronic superhighways and education and learning. The state effectively takes over investment for some of these things, with reference to providing access for all. In Sweden, the creation of a nationwide broadband network was subsidized by public investment.[37] In the United Kingdom, the wiring up of schools and the national grid for learning took place in public–private partnership with BT (British Telecom).[38]

In both countries, the state also uses its power over education and publicly funded research to steer resources to certain areas of research and training. Research funding has thus emerged as a new form of investment policy.

This adds up to the social democratic state imposing a specific definition of useful knowledge, that is, of what knowledge production needs to be prioritized and subsidized in the expectation that this knowledge, rather than other knowledges, will contribute to the public good. It is not really that different from old industrial planning. Both Swedish and British policies also include an emphasis on the role of public procurement as a way of steering demand for knowledge-intensive products and of supporting specific industries, for instance, information technology in the NHS in the United Kingdom or green technology in Sweden.[39] Indeed, this emphasis on the role of public capital for market innovation is one of the Third Way's notions of public value and public good. Further, the state assumes a certain responsibility for providing venture capital for research and development (R&D) and for the commercialization of new products. The fate of the Swedish wage earner funds is perhaps the best illustration of how these new forms of state intervention relate to old ones. Conceived in the 1970s by the labor movement's chief economic architect Rudolf Meidner as a way of increasing wage earner influence over long-term business decisions, the funds were a thorn in the side of the Swedish Right and were dismantled by the Bildt government. In the 1990s, the funds' means have been funneled back to business through the creation of a number of semiprivate R&D foundations and government agencies such as NUTEK (the Swedish agency for economic and regional growth) or Vinnova (the governmental agency for innovation systems).[40] The funds once designed to increase wage earner control over corporate profits have thus become the venture capital of the new economy. In addition, then, to setting frameworks, the state in both countries actually has a much more hands-on investment policy, one that effectively takes over investment decisions from the firm and steers the orientation of knowledge production. While entrepreneurship, innovation, and creativity are considered to take place in the market place of competitive ideas independent of intervention, Third Way policies give a very prominent role to the state for the creation of knowledge through investment in education, through new means to foster creativity or spur competition, for the commercialization of knowledge through the development of competitive products and services, and for the commodification of knowledge through strengthening intellectual property rights regimes that turn ideas into marketizable objects.

Hence, the Third Way is no laissez-faire Manchester liberalism but rather a highly interventionist productivism based on a new active role of the social democratic state in the economy.[41] We deploy "new" here in the way set out in the Introduction, "new" as in the sense that it draws on historic social democratic notions of the role of intervention but reconceptualizes these in relationship to new understandings of the economy and the process of value creation. As Alan Finlayson has put it:

> Where dogma driven neoliberals sought to liberate the market from the state, New Labour seeks to deploy the state in the name of the market, because it sees that the market itself has changed.[42]

There are important differences between the parties here in terms of their interpretations of the benefits and limits of the market, to which we will return. New Labour clearly believes that the market is a more efficient provider and more responsive to the individual consumer than the public; it also praises the role of profit as a driver of quality and efficiency. The role of the market in public services is a tension at the heart of the New Labour project; but, clearly, New Labour under both Blair and Brown insists on profit and competition as forces that spur creativity and innovation in the public sector.[43] The SAP has a much more ambivalent attitude to the role of the market in welfare state provisions, despite the fargoing privatizations that have taken place in the Swedish public sector. Education policy is a good example of the ambiguities in the parties' different stances. In both countries, education has come to be understood as a commodity in recent decades, a process that has been more blatant in the United Kingdom but has also structured education reform in Sweden. In the United Kingdom, despite a long-standing debate in the Labour Party on education as a public good, education policies have been steered by the strategic attempt to create a market for education, expected to provide for efficient delivery, choice, and diversity, as well as for crucial injections of capital in deprived areas.[44] In Sweden, the creation of a quasi-school market after the introduction of the voucher system is clearly one of the most dramatic changes of the Swedish welfare state. Social democracy initially opposed voucher schools and even promised to overturn the reform but has not touched the issue since. Private actors such as *Kunskapsskolan AB* have gained a strong bargaining position in the Swedish school system.[45]

Another illustration of the differences between the parties in their outlooks on the market is the attempts, in both countries, to introduce systems for competence saving or individual learning accounts (ILAs). The idea behind ILAs was to improve incentives for learning though a system where the costs for lifelong learning are shared among state, individual, and employer.

ILAs very clearly reflect the idea of knowledge as capital; it can be saved in a bank account like financial capital. ILAs were introduced in the United Kingdom in 2000. The policy failed because of the rapid emergence of a plethora of uncontrolled private providers and of corruption. In the British context, ILAs were framed in a discourse of individual self-improvement, with the idea that individuals would assume a greater responsibility for their learning and choice of provider.[46] In Sweden, a system for competence saving was part of the social democratic growth strategy beginning in the late 1990s, but it was framed in a discourse of universalism, addressed as a further extension of the rights of citizenship. There was a strong rhetorical emphasis on the historical institutions of the labor movement's self-education societies as providers, an emphasis that partly overshadowed the fact that the policy also anticipated the creation of a market of private providers working in partnership with local government.[47]

Socializing Capital: Politics beyond Conflict

Politics of partnership are clearly far from neoliberal in the role that they ascribe to public intervention and a strong state in the economy. Nevertheless, they also clearly differ from "old" social democracy in the way that they place the market at the heart of social relations. In the United Kingdom, the symbolic importance of the Clause 4 debate was that it firmly established that capital, through dialogue and partnership, can work for the common good, a common good that New Labour defined as "prosperity for all." Consequently, the market has been seen as a driver of social progress, introduced into education policies, social policies, and cultural policies, as a way not only of bringing in investment and financial capital but also of creating a "culture of aspiration" and fostering drive and entrepreneurship.[48] Social democratic policies have thus gained an element that is really about fostering market values as part, almost, of what it means to be social. This is not unique for New Labour. In Sweden, fostering market values are an active component of the new pension system.[49]

This logic of socializing capital—of making capital a part of the common good, not to be confused with socializing the means of production—is not new in the history of social democracy. Rather, as was set out in the Introduction, the specific historical project of social democracy is to make capital work in the interest of a particular definition of the common good. Swedish policies from the late nineteenth century onward contained a fundamentally procapitalist approach, which internalized industrial capitalism as the very meaning of "modernization," and the famous labor–capital compromise of the Swedish model was quintessentially about making capital work for the common good.[50] However, the Third Way's understanding of capitalism in the knowledge era is highly specific in the way that it denies notions of conflict or differences of interest between labor and capital, market and society, public and private good. Making the market a force for the common good by bringing it further into social relations and defining market virtues as fundamental drivers of social change is not the same as trying to discipline capital in the name of solidarity and equality, which is arguably where New Labour's notions of partnership and community differ from the idea of corporatism that laid the foundation for the Swedish model. It is important to make this distinction.

Certain specific presumptions as to the nature of knowledge as a nonrival good with positive externalities add to the Third Way's well-known emphasis on reconciliation and its appeal to politics beyond conflict. Knowledge is created through learning—and learning is a social activity, one that depends on communication and reciprocity.[51] The idea of a knowledge-driven economic expansion contains a reappraisal of trust, shared norms and values, partnership and dialogue—all things that stress interconnection and embeddedness rather than conflict or atomism. Economic dynamism in network production stems from partnership and dialogue rather than from asymmetries, hierarchies, and conflicts.[52]

The idea of partnerships has been described as a new form of competitive corporatism, where the production of surplus takes place in coproduction between state and market, through a new social contract where the state assumes an overall responsibility for creating the competitive environment for industry, while the firm assumes a certain responsibility for fostering social capital and encouraging learning. In this way, the firm—just like the family—becomes a provider of social virtues, trust, and learning in harmony with the surrounding community. The Third Way embraces this understanding of capitalism because it offers a way out of the conflicts and struggles of the 1970s while still escaping the dilemma of neoliberalism. It gives relevance to limited notions of stakeholding,[53] and it permits the Third Way's critique of the state, a critique it inherited from both the New Left and the New Right. The notion of partnership draws on the quintessentially Third Way claim that the new economy challenges both the old Left's and the New Right's understanding of the boundaries between market and state. The old Left, or so the New Labour story goes, thought that it could steer innovation and change and did not realize the individualism and private nature of creativity and entrepreneurship, while neoliberalism with its atomistic theory of economic man and free market did not see the fundamental social logic of processes such as learning and creativity. To that extent, the Third Way contains a firm rejection of socialism *and* neoliberalism, both with reference to knowledge as a good fostered in trust and not in conflict.[54]

It could be argued that the politics of partnership reflect a new historical compromise between labor and capital, similar to the one that laid the foundations for the Swedish model. Clearly, the historic corporatism of the Swedish model drew on an organic notion of the market very similar to the one that New Labour put in place in its rewriting of Clause 4, which is also why the changes in the Swedish party program in the last decade have been less controversial (although they caused conflict in Sweden, too). However, the corporatism of the Swedish model was based on the mediation of the differing interests of labor and capital, and it was also, arguably, a way of disciplining the market in the name of the wider social good.[55] The emphasis on partnerships seems, rather, to avoid the very problem that the historical compromise attempted to solve because it does not recognize the notion of a difference of interest in the first place. Politics of partnership presume that interests and norms are essentially the same among market, state, and citizen. In industrial relations, the notion of partnership is a reference to trust relations that will provide the basis for productivity and competitiveness in the interest of both employer and employee.[56] As Chris Howell has argued, the notion of partnership was the basis of New Labour's New Deal with business, a new "partnership for prosperity" based on mutual trust and collaboration, which also meant that New Labour continued on the path in industrial relations laid out by Thatcher, recognizing the role of unions to protect individual workers rights, such as the minimum wage, but remaining skeptical of collective action.[57] It is possible to see a similar development in Sweden. In the 1990s the SAP has been outspokenly critical of strikes, and Göran Persson is arguably the first social democratic leader to have defined the trade union federation, the LO *(Landsorganisationen)*, a vested interest, much as New Labour has applied the term to trade unions skeptical of the direction of change.[58] In 1997 the agreement on industrial development and wage formation *(industriavtalet)*, signed by Swedish trade unions and business, was seen as a reenactment of the famous *Saltsjöbadsavtalet* for a new era, but with an increased focus on the competitiveness of business.[59]

The notion of partnership established a new role for trade unions in the knowledge economy, which is not that of representing the interests of organized labor but one closer to the Japanese capitalism that was a source of inspiration for the debate on the new firm and specialized production in the period from the 1970s onward. As the Swedish historian Bo Stråth has shown, this understanding of capitalism gained in importance in Sweden in a shift, beginning in the 1970s, from discourses of labor capital conflict to discourses of stakeholding and codetermination.[60] In the Volvo plant in Uddevalla in the south of Sweden, Volvo experimented with a "Toyotaism," where workers and unions became more directly involved in the production process. As Ryner has suggested, this held the embryo of a different vision of the post-Fordist economy, one that gave way, however, with unemployment in the early 1990s that undermined the bargaining position of labor.[61] Worker influence in the knowledge economy's predominant conception of industrial relations is not primarily about influence but about making productivity gains through new forms of human resource management, where the role of labor organizations is to reintegrate skills into the production. This includes fostering trust, loyalty, and enthusiasm. Flexible production put workers and their attitudes at the heart of the production process. New forms of management, indeed of Taylorism, are directed at the rational management of the worker's inner self.[62]

We can take this argument one step further by contrasting the Third Way's conceptions of the relationship between private and public production with social democracy's historic notions of the public good. The knowledge era brings with it a number of challenges to the boundaries between private and public production and consumption because knowledge is often understood as a nonrival good with specific externalities, which give it important characteristics of a public good. In fact, it is hard to think of a resource that would more easily lend itself to a progressive theory of public good than knowledge.[63] Indeed, the Third Way has a notion of public good. Its appraisal of the market is matched by a discussion of the limits of the market in an age defined by the dissemination of intangibles, such as knowledge and information. But this is a different notion of public good from "old" social democracy. A theory of public good, for instance in learning and education, that follows from an analysis of what the market needs but cannot do is different from a notion of public good as what the public needs and what the market will not or cannot do because the latter implies a critique of key tendencies in capitalism. Social democracy's postwar notions of public good were informed by exactly such a critique of the tendencies of industrial capitalism. The mixed economy, for revisionists such as Anthony Crosland, was an answer to the dilemma of advanced industrialism. In Sweden, the expansion of the public sector drew on the notion of social balance put forth by the American economist J. K. Galbraith, who argued that affluence has to be steered by a greater emphasis on public consumption because consumption would otherwise lead to widening social gaps.[64] There is not, in the Third Way, such a debate on how to steer the results of production for the public good, or, even less so, for the creation of equality. Contemporary social democracy also lacks what might be called a public ethos. Social democracy's historic notion of public good was an ethos of solidarity that stated that there are goods in society that should be beyond the control of the market because their public value is of a character fundamentally in conflict with the idea of profit or even property. However, while the Third Way has a theory of the public good of knowledge because of its fundamental intangibility, which seems to make it necessarily part of the commons, this is a very narrow notion of public good, defined by ideas of market failure, as for instance in the double failure of the market to spread access to knowledge and to provide adequate property rights for knowledge. It is neither an ethos of solidarity nor a theory of public good as a limit to private consumption or a balance on the market. Its ethos, rather, is one of the good of market as provider of public value, for instance through more efficient delivery of welfare services but also through more complex matters such as the fostering of creativity and entrepreneurship through public private partnerships in schools and other public institutions. To that extent, its notion of public good is dictated not only by the limits of the market but by the recognition of the fundamental good of the market, of what might quite simply be called the market ethos. In education, then, the market emerges not only as the efficient provider but also as an injection of creativity, entrepreneurship, and best practice and, in the end, as the arbiter of which knowledge, skills, and creativity are useful in society. Policy inventions such as public–private partnership and public finance initiatives are based on the idea that public and private good can be combined in spheres previously protected from the market logic.[65]

The appeal to a political space beyond antagonism, defined not by ideology or social democratic principle but by what works, where notions of public good were replaced by notions of public value, is a central part of the ideology of the Third Way. What New Labour did in the 1990s was to reenact, albeit in extreme form, the SAP's Third Way experiment in the 1980s.[66]

Capitalizing the Social

In the previous pages, I have described the Third Way as an economic discourse construed around a new relationship between the macro and micro
side of the economy. This redrawing of macro and micro in the economic
policies of social democracy has, in turn, brought about a redrawing of the
boundaries between the economic and the social. While the logic of socializing capital informs contemporary social democracy's attempts to rearticulate
the market as a force for social progress, the Third Way's growth policies are
construed around the related but different logic of capitalizing the social, that
is, a logic that essentially capitalizes social structures and identifies social relationships and processes as the origin of the process of wealth creation. What
fundamentally sets the Third Way apart from neoliberalism is its framework
for political intervention in the social sphere.[67]

This capitalization of the social is a central part of the political economy
of the Third Way. In her 2000 article, Vivienne Schmidt argued that New Labour has continued Thatcher's neoliberalization of the economic sphere, but
in society.[68] The Third Way's economic theory is based on the idea that what
drives growth in the new economy are essentially innovation, curiosity, and
creativity—individual activities that cannot be induced or controlled by politics or collective action but that are dependent on certain social and cultural
frameworks that can be the creation of politics. Because knowledge is "out
there," the state's responsibility for ensuring a competitive, knowledge-fostering
climate contains an emphasis on social rationalization and social interventionism as an integral part of growth policies and economic regulation. This has
led to a new emphasis on the social structures and institutions that foster versus hamper the production of human capital and knowledge. To that extent, it
is not true that contemporary social democracy no longer takes an interest in
questions of inequality, unemployment, or poverty. On the contrary, the Third
Way takes a great interest in these things because it sees them as integral parts
of its growth policies. The Third Way is fundamentally interested in social relations because it sees them as producers of wealth. The difference—substantial
as it is—is that where "old" social democracy saw inequalities as the effects
and outcomes of a specific regime of capital accumulation, the Third Way sees
them as the starting point of accumulation.

The capitalization of intellectual and social resources is central to endogenous growth theory with its idea of human and social capital. The term
human capital refers to the aggregate level of knowledge, talent, and skill—

hence, the sum of the knowledge-potential embodied in the individuals of a society. It is capital that "resides in individuals."[69] Most importantly, human capital comprises not only educational levels and skills: It is also composed of individual dispositions such as motivation, the aptitude for teamwork, the capacity to make ethical value-based judgements, problem solving, and self-discipline. It is quite simply about a certain knowledge-fostering, reflective, innovative individual personality.[70] *Social capital,* in contrast, refers to inter-relational capital, the kind of capital that resides in the social relations among people. Social capital is created through social interaction—it is about values, norms, and trust. These are the central resources that provide the individual with access to a social network that encourages norms of learning, interaction, and reciprocity. These norms, in the discourse of social capital, are considered to be productive. Social capital, like other forms of capital, creates a surplus, in the form of social norms that make up an efficient market economy.[71] In a seminal article, the sociologist James Coleman argued that the creation of human capital is dependent on social capital. In other words, the growth of knowledge depends on the quality of our social relations. Consequently, our social relations become objects of economic intervention.[72]

The notion of social capital has attracted great interest in the United Kingdom. Indeed, the notion of modernization, in New Labour discourse of the mid-1990s, took on a very specific meaning as the modernization of the human and social capital of the British people, through policies aimed at changing the quality of social networks, people's behavior and attitudes, and the skill levels of the workforce. Another significant factor is that human and social capital can be expanded, through policies such as learning or social investment strategies, in a way that physical capital cannot. Nevertheless, the limit of an economic expansion driven by human capital is also the limit inherent in that capital, which means that it is ultimately defined by individuals and by the knowledge and ability to learn that they possess. In this way, the individual and his or her capacities are, as Michael Freeden has argued, located at the heart of the social democracy's neo-Keynesian project, subject to investment, expansion, and capitalization, a resource to exploit, potential to be tapped.[73] The investment politics of the 1970s have been replaced by what are known as the social investment policies of the 2000s, policies designed to change attitudes and dispositions and invest in the human capital of people.

There are important differences here between the parties, to which we will return in later chapters. While the SAP's supply-side policies fall back on a historic productivism, which was at times highly socially interventionist, its modern language is far from the blunt social economism of New Labour. The 2001 party program even rejects the commercialization and commodification of social relations, and there is very little mention of the term social capital in Swedish discourse.

Conclusion

The political landscape has changed in such a way that our labels may no longer apply to the mesalliances and compromises that are the outcome of the struggle between Left and Right in the last three decades. The Third Way is hard to define because in its appeal to a conflict free zone of pragmatic politics it borrows freely from more or less all political currents of European modernity. But there is nothing neoliberal about contemporary social democracy if by *neoliberal* we mean an economic and social philosophy based on the free market and free individuals, both postulates that contemporary social democracy rejects. There is more to be said for the term *illiberal liberalism*, as Desmond King has suggested, that is, of a morally conservative kind of social engineering that attempts to make coldhearted winners of all.[74] The Third Way does draw on important elements of neoliberalism, particularly the idea of competition as driver of social progress and the notion of the market as quintessentially creative. But it fuses these ideas with a social democratic productivism, in which wealth creation depends on collective responsibility. In the new economy, this responsibility is extended to new areas and thereby also reasserted. To this extent, the Third Way contains a distinct interventionism that goes well beyond that of "old" social democracy because it goes further than economic policy and into the social sphere. Indeed, the object of regulation is not the economy, but the "soft" or "wet" capital located within the knowledge worker, his or her very attitudes toward learning, employers, and the community at large. In this respect, many aspects of Third Way policies are closer to social utopian discourses in social democracy's own history than they are to neoliberalism, indeed, to a Fabian concern with the cultivation of the perfect character in all.

3 Defining Old and New Times: Origins of the Third Way

The origins and trajectories of Swedish and British Third Way policies are strikingly different. The very meaning of modernization has different connotations in Sweden and the United Kingdom. From British perspectives, the central element of Third Way discourse has often been identified in the emphasis on radical newness and discontinuity.[1] Modernization, in New Labour discourse, was synonymous with the term *renewal*, a term intrinsically related to ideas of pervasive economic and technological change. In the mid-1990s, renewal was, at times, a breathtakingly futuristic modernization narrative, a vision of a Britain that did not "shuffle" into the new millennium afraid of the future, but that "strides into [the future] with confidence."[2] To Swedish social democracy, from their first experiment with a Third Way in the early 1980s to the restructuring and retrenchment policies of the 1990s, the key metaphor was not "renewal," but "safeguarding" (*slå vakt om*).[3] These different outlooks on the process of change established the framework for the parties' understanding of the knowledge economy—in the United Kingdom as a revolutionary transformation, a great tide that, "unless we start preparing for it will simply roll over us, leaving us stranded in its wake," while in Sweden, as a relatively peaceful process of transformation in line with the evolution of the Swedish Model.[4]

Renewal and safeguarding contained two radically different political approaches to the knowledge future. These different future visions, in turn, were dependent on the different pasts of Swedish and British Labour and of the recent political history of Swedish and British society. The New Labour project was a reaction against both Thatcherism and the "old" Left, both neoliberalism and the 1960s rights revolution. Contemporary political history in Sweden is, with the exception of the polarized years of the 1980s and early 1990s, marked by the absence of radical opposition. There is in Sweden a relative hegemony around the welfare state and its values, a hegemony that is often overstated by foreign observers but that has nevertheless resulted in "the most success-ful Social Democratic Party in the world," and the entrenchment of the val-ues of the welfare state in national culture. This element of social democratic hegemony—the creation of a value consensus around its historical edifice of the People's Home—is a mixed blessing. It protects the welfare state from ideological attacks but also ultimately strengthens a self-image of the SAP as managers of the past. The central political problem of Swedish social democ-racy, which has grown in importance throughout the postwar period, is how to be *"stolt men inte nöjd"*—"proud but not satisfied," how to find strategies of reform that do not break with the past but protect it and yet allow the party to appear in touch with change.[5] The constant reassertion of the values of the People's Home is arguably one of the explanations behind the party's lack of ideological debate in the 1990s and its noticeable silences on important aspects of policy change. Where articulation and, some would say, spin have been so important to the political project of New Labour, silence and the construction of continuity form a central strategy of the SAP. History is one of its most im-portant ideological assets.

This aspect of hegemony as a kind of national consensus around social reformism has tainted the legacies of both Left and Right in Swedish political history. There is a long-standing critique of welfare statism in Swedish politi-cal history, a critique that goes back to the late nineteenth century and runs parallel to the development of the welfare state. Over time it has included ori-entations such as ethical socialism and the "Third Ways" of mutuality and cooperative movements, both cultural radicalism and cultural conservatism, neoliberalism and pro-Europeanism, but it has rarely questioned the founda-tions of the Swedish model. There is a marked reluctance in Swedish social democracy to take in new intellectual currents, sometimes along with an ex-plicit mistrust in intellectuals.[6] This is a legacy of its famous pragmatism. New Labour's naissance in the critical currents of post-Marxism, post-Fordism, and postmodernism and the British Labour Party's ongoing struggle with a legacy of the Left are strikingly different from the way the last decades seem to have been marked primarily by the absence of debate in Sweden.

This chapter traces the contradictory and complex origins of the Third Way in Sweden and Britain from the early 1970s onward. It is concerned with the conceptual and ideological heritages of the Third Way, what might be called a genealogy of its predominant narrative of the new economy. In particular, it looks at how social democracy has understood and conceptualized change and the drivers of change and what distinguishes new times from old ones.

Politics of Safeguarding

In its appeal to individual preferences and choice, its decentralization of core welfare services, and its managerial approach to public spending, New Labour's Third Way reenacted many of the themes that entered Swedish social democratic ideology in its Third Way experiment in the early 1980s.

The trigger of the Swedish Third Way was the SAP's second electoral defeat in 1979, which was interpreted by important groups on the party's right flank as social democracy's failure to modernize its ideological postulates to adapt to what seemed like a radically altered economic reality. The party's 1981 crisis program, entitled *A Future for Sweden*, laid out a Third Way between the then-existing alternatives in European politics, Thatcherism and Mitterand-style Keynesianism. The aim was to protect industrial jobs while cutting costs in the public sector.[7] While this marked the end of the 1970s attempt to use expansionary politics out of recession, it also contained something more fundamental, namely the idea that the transformations of the economy in the wake of the 1970s recession required a principled reconsideration of the organization of the Swedish welfare state. The core of the 1981 program was the notion of safeguarding. Defending the historical achievement of the SAP—the welfare state or the People's Home—in a time of economic turbulence required a fundamental reconsideration of social democracy's means.[8] The new means stood in stark contrast to postwar social democratic ideology and led to the split between the "modernizers" in the Ministry of Finance and "traditionalists," mainly in the trade unions, a tension that in new constellations has remained at the heart of Swedish social democracy.[9]

The SAP was one of the first social democratic parties of Europe to embark on what was by the mid-1990s unanimously referred to as the Third Way. In Britain, Labour's lost election in 1979 saw a move to the left and the consequent split of the Labour Party as modernists such as Roy Hattersley and David Marquand left to form the Social Democratic Party. The 1983 manifesto called for a renationalization of the utilities privatized under Thatcher. It was the 1983 election defeat that triggered the revisionism of Kinnock's policy review, a process that introduced many of the themes that would become New Labour. However, the Labour Party had already, under the Callaghan governments in the mid-1970s, left Keynesian deficit spending and introduced the wage controls that brought about the Winter of Discontent and paved the way for Thatcher.[10]

The impetus of the SAP's revisionism was economic crisis, and the Swedish Third Way was dominated by a pragmatic search for new economic ideas for welfare reform. Influences for these new economic ideas were found in Margaret Thatcher's Britain as well as in Ronald Reagan's United States, cases that social democracy studied with interest from the late 1970s in its attempt to also thwart an increasingly aggressive Swedish Right. When the SAP regained parliamentary power in 1982, it put in place a new framework for public spending and a program of decentralization under the banner of freedom of choice. In the mid-1980s, the party began to consider privatizations and decentralization, foreboding the large-scale privatizations in the Swedish public sector that were to come during the conservative years in the beginning of the 1990s.[11] In the process, the SAP broke with many of the core tenets of its economic philosophy around the welfare state, developed by party theorists such as Ernst Wigforss and Gustav Möller, in particular the notion of the productive role of public spending. In the mid-1980s, it is fair to speak of a new Third Way ideology in the Swedish welfare state.[12]

This 1980s revisionism meant a final break with a very different Third Way in the 1970s, which consisted of a more radical equality agenda, economic democracy, and wage earner funds. It was influenced by the rise of a Swedish New Left critical of the SAP's historical compromise with capital. As Jonas Pontusson has shown, the wage earner funds and the investment politics of the 1970s marked the limit of the SAP, as they also led to the end of corporatism and the "fall" of the Swedish model when Swedish business left corporate agreements.[13] In the subsequent years, the party started to marginalize former influential left-wing intellectuals, including Rudolf Meidner. The party's interpretation of economic crisis as a call for renewal meant that the ideas of the generation of the 1960s lost out to the very influential group of young economists who wrote the crisis program and came to set forth the modernization agenda. In the 1990s, the members of this "Chancellery Right" became senior members of government and of the Swedish administration.[14]

New Times

Swedish political debate in the 1960s and 1970s was more concerned with the crisis of the advanced industrial society than with ideas of an emerging new order. Conceptualizations of structural and long-term perspectives fell back to an economic managerialism that is strikingly different from the origins of British modernization discourse in the New Times debate, which channeled important aspects of the New Left's ideas into a debate about the changing nature of capitalism. The New Times debate started outside the Labour Party, in a nebulous group of thinkers around the review of the British Communist Party, *Marxism Today*, in the late 1980s. Members of the group were the post-Marxist and postcolonial intellectual Stuart Hall, the editor of *Marxism Today* Martin Jacques, the sociologist David Held, the historian and Labour Party intellectual David Marquand, and the Swedish Marxist sociologist Göran Therborn. In addition, two younger members of the group, Geoff Mulgan and Charles Leadbeater, would later become closely involved in the New Labour project.

The New Times debate was concerned with a vague but tangible impression of crisis in a range of areas of economic, social, cultural, and political life, adding up to what it suggested was a critical conjecture in the life of capitalism. The metaphor "new times" sought to capture what the group did not quite know how to describe, as the "dawn of a new age," or merely "the whisper of an old one." Globalization, flexible specialization, and computerization seemed to challenge fundamental characteristics of industrial modernity. The direct impetus behind New Times was the rise of Thatcherism. To the New Times group, Thatcherism signified much more than a temporary rise in neoliberal populism; it saw Thatcherism as the successful hegemonic articulation of a new politics in a world in which complex phenomena loosely labeled post-Fordism, postmodernism, and individualism seemed to add up to a pervasive crisis of the Left. To the New Times group, the Labour Party was a deeply conservative cultural force, stuck in its historical logic and its blueprints for economic and social progress. The 1945 settlement that had created the basis for British Labourism in elements such as the male breadwinner, the imperial state, and the Cold War had eroded. Changes in Western economies since the 1970s, characterized by underinvestment and faltering growth, had caused growing social conflict. The sexual revolution, the pill, the punk assault on middle-class sensibilities, and the protest against racial discrimination had brought about a revolution of identities and undermined the social contract. Finally, as it put an end to the collective utopias of socialism, 1989 had redefined the world. Socialism no longer offered a viable alternative to capitalism; instead, the Right had emerged as the provider of the radical alternative.[15]

The New Times debate argued that post-Fordism meant the crisis of assembly-line production. "Benetton Britain" was characterized by production

processes based on computerization and new employer–employee relationships. These new patterns of production were paralleled by new patterns of
mass-consumerism, reflecting a search for individual identity. It was these
forces that Thatcherism usurped. The New Times debate was influenced by
the works of Alain Touraine and André Gorz on the coming end of the working class and by postmodern theories of articulation. Grand narratives were
dead, and working class identity had no obvious role in the present.[16]

In retrospect, the New Times debate stands out as a tension-ridden intellectual and political project, and it imploded over Blair's Third Way in the
1990s. The New Times debate was a critique of what it saw as key tendencies
in modern capitalism—and an attempt to articulate a progressive response to
them. It did not praise post-Fordism or globalization. It concluded that there
was nothing in post-Fordism that led toward increased equality; rather, it saw
wide-scale social exclusion and the drive toward a two-tier society as fundamental characteristics of New Times. In fact, the New Times manifesto contained an explicit warning to the ongoing policy review in the Labour Party,
a warning to a revisionist Labour project to remodel itself as a moderate force
within the new parameters set by Thatcher and produce, not a progressive
analysis of New Times but a

> brand of new times that adds up to a slightly cleaned up, humanised version
> of the radical Right. Such would be the inevitable consequence of two things:
> a pragmatic adjustment of the Left to the collapse of its previous visions and a
> failure to generate its own new historic project.[17]

It is the historical irony of the New Times debate that, in its attempt to
provide a new platform for Leftist debate, it introduced the themes that in
the mid-1990s became the platform of New Labour. The Marxist origins of
the New Times debate meant an emphasis on production forces and technological change that, despite the theories on articulation and radical politics
provided by Stuart Hall and others, leaned toward a highly determinist account. It came close to a description of change as a binary logic of old and
new and an interpretation of change as driven by the revolutionary forces of
technology. Most importantly, it dismissed social democracy as a project that
had outlived its time and was fundamentally flawed in a world dominated by
dynamic flows of information and identity. It came close to the hand of history language, which would later echo from New Labour as it established that
history, culminating in the events of 1989, had overtaken socialism.

One of the more problematic paradoxes was that the New Times debate identified class as a question of political representation and rejected the idea of socioeconomically determined identities and interests. This, indeed, seemed to be the only way to understand the appeal of Thatcher's anti-working class populism to precisely that working class.[18] But in so doing it identified the individual subject as the core of a reborn Left. Collective projects were dead. Instead, the New Times group proclaimed a kind of social vision of individualism, a vision of decentralized mutuality that Geoff Mulgan later brought into the communitarianism of New Labour.

There was nothing inevitable about this development, and Eric Hobsbawm, Martin Jacques, and Stuart Hall became vociferous critics of the New Labour project as a simplistic continuation of Thatcherism.[19] Mulgan and Leadbeater became policy advisors, producing visions of a future driven by ICT. In Mulgan's 1997 book *Connexity*, the future was driven by three laws of network technology: Moore's law of the silicon revolution, whereby computer power doubles every twenty-four months; Metcalfe's law of the growth of the network, where the value of a network increases exponentially relative to the square of the number of people using it; and Kao's law, which states that the creativity embedded in a network is dependent on the diversity and divergence of the people using it, hence the sum of networked intelligence.[20] In such a world, there is no place for collective utopias because knowledge constantly changes everything:

> I mean I think that the idea that you describe an endpoint towards which you get, which was the popular idea of utopias in the 17th century, 19th century and so on, is simply incompatible with any society where knowledge plays a big role, because the nature of knowledge is to be dynamic, continually changing and transformative, so there can't possibly be a vision of an endpoint, there can only be a vision of some of the processes that are controlling how that evolution happens. One of those is democracy, one of those is widespread access to education, one of them maybe the market economy . . . all you can have a vision about are the means of knowledge to constantly change everything else.[21]

A Postmodern People's Home

The preoccupation of Swedish politics with safeguarding and social democracy's break with the legacies of the New Left in the 1980s meant that there was little of the sophisticated analysis of New Times in Sweden. There was little concern with changing production orders or the nature of contemporary capitalism, other than a growing worry, dating back to the late 1960s, with the difficulty of protecting the export-dependent Swedish economy in an increasingly volatile world economy. Rather than grand theories of post-Fordism, Swedish interpretations of changing times were concentrated to a very Swedish perspective on rising individualism as a threat to the collective solidarity of the welfare state and as a force associated with egoism, commercialism, and social fragmentation.

The theme of individualism was taken up by the SAP in the years following the crisis program in 1981, as the party put freedom of choice at the heart of the agenda for welfare state restructuring. In 1984, the then–Minister of the Future Ingvar Carlsson, subsequently Prime Minister, drew up a program that appealed to a new social democratic utopia, that of the individual.[22] In a speech the same year, Olof Palme described the People's Home as an outdated social vision and argued that the historic role of social democracy was freeing human potential—not locking it into the bureaucratic structures of the state.[23] Individualism was also the main theme of the SAP's program for the 1990s, 90-talsprogrammet. Written in the year of the Velvet Revolution and three years before economic crisis hit the material foundations of the Swedish welfare state, it saw the main threat to Swedish society in a widening gap between what the program termed "material welfare" and "spiritual poverty." The social democratic welfare state had wrapped people in the warm blanket of material well-being, but in this house of material security there were growing feelings of alienation and growing groups of people who felt they did not belong. The program saw this as a problem of values. The historical strength of Swedish social democracy, the program argued, was that it had combined a pragmatic program for material reform with an ethical argument based on values of the good society, of vision and ideals that had given meaning to the collective project. In the late 1980s this project seemed to have exhausted its role as mobilizing future vision. In contrast to how the debate New Times saw things, the problem was not a breakdown of the social democratic project. There was no question of the continued relevance of social democracy in Swedish society. On the contrary, the problem was that progress had led to a point where the SAP's historic articulations seemed exhausted. The program described a development in which Sweden in the course of a few generations had developed from an agrarian, poor, isolated country to a technologically advanced economy with close links to the surrounding world. Trends in culture and consumerism increasingly influenced Swedish society. This was not a good thing. There was a growing fear in Swedish society, the program argued, of the rapid pace of technological change. Genetic research and computer technology advances turned the old, familiar world upside down. This sent people longing for ideals, "for something lasting beyond the timed existence of each and every one of us." Politics seemed to lack the answers to the big questions: [24]

> The feeling of a common historical mission—building the People's Home—was a powerful and cohesive force far beyond the ranks of the labor movement. But now that feeling is growing weaker, and the ideological consensus is thinning out.[25]

In the Swedish society of the 1980s and 1990s, there were no longer any self-evident mobilizing goals such as building the welfare state. Populism and possessive individualism had led to fragmentation and egoism, "a weakening of our common values." The diffusion of knowledge meant that people lost belief in authority and claimed new channels of participation. Postmodernism was an expression of this fragmentation in the realm of culture and ideas—"a multicoloured and multifaceted surface, where the once so stable, common inner nucleus is cracking." Fragmentation and diversity might turn out to be dynamic forces for the future, but they also meant insecurity, fear, the erosion of trust and solidarity, and worry over the long-term itinerary—"feelings of spiritual poverty in our material welfare."[26]

In contrast to how social democratic revisionism in the 1980s moved toward neoliberal language, the 1990s program was more clearly anchored in a longer continuity of social democratic thought, going back to ethical socialism. The late-1960s themes of alienation and social exclusion were strongly present in the program. It warned of a social democracy more attuned to institutions than to people and implied that the SAP had become a conservative force as it rhetorically asked what had happened to the Labour movement's old view that the emancipation of the working class must be its own creation and not the creation of some avant-gardist elite. "The mission is to free people's creative potential—not lock it in . . . It's about freeing commitment, not suffocating it."[27]

The program put forward a vision of a social individualism that was not unlike the one of the New Times debate, although it appealed to a specific Swedish tradition of social individualism and mutuality. The program spoke of the existence in Swedish society of a particular ethos, based in the strong social movements and worker organizations that paved the way for the labor movement in Scandinavia at the end of the nineteenth century and that were organized around self-education and mutuality, the *folkrörelse*. This was an ethos based on mutuality, voluntary cooperation, fraternity and solidarity, and the recognition that "it is together that we grow." The *folkrörelse*, in the program, was the opposite of the government, the *myndighet*, and the program suggested that maybe this ethos of solidarity and mutuality had been squeezed out during the decades of the expansion of the welfare state. It now ought to be revived, as "a social ethos for the advanced service economy," for a society well equipped with things material but in need of ideals.[28]

The means of revival of this social individualism was a kind of cultural revolution, a push forward in the realm of cultural policy and education designed to bring back those instinctive feelings of reciprocity and self-improvement in Swedish culture. Culture was, the program said, a great liberating force, a route both to individual emancipation and to rebuilding trust and values in Swedish society. The program tied this discussion of a new cultural policy to the expanding role of knowledge in society. In a society where material welfare had been achieved, the growth and potential of people must be put at the heart of politics. Freeing people's creative potential was the main task for social democracy in the 1990s.[29]

The Young Country: The Workshop

The New Times debate contained a critique of capitalism that went missing even though several of the themes of the New Times debate—the new economy and individualism—became core tenets of New Labour ideology. As Alan Finlayson has argued, the interpretation of post-Fordism that underpinned New Times was gradually stripped of its critique of the new production order in favor of a technologically determinist "technofuture," where adaptation to information technology and globalization became the central element of modernization.[30] New Labour's platform, in the mid-1990s, was construed around themes that had been introduced in the Policy Review and that took over some of the themes of the New Times debate but within the parameters of Labourism. The Policy Review saw the genesis of a modernization narrative that centered in on the role of labor skills and education and the growing importance of ICT.[31] In the New Labour manifesto in 1997, this had become an assertive imperative around the knowledge economy as a dramatic third industrial revolution, where national survival depended on adaptation to the logics of knowledge and information. The future success of Britain depended on its capacity to exploit the new opportunities offered by this and to claim a new historical position as prime mover in a new race for global markets—to "make Britain the electronic workshop of the world."[32] Globalization was a race, a worldview of a fiercely competitive world order, where some would win and some would fall behind,

> and it is because nations will rise and fall at speed because no nation can ever take its future prosperity for granted, and the race will be won by the skilled, the flexible, the enterprising and the creative . . . [33]

The workshop of the world is a Victorian notion, coined by Disraeli in a House of Commons debate in 1838, and a metaphorical expression of the Victorian pride in industrial growth, urbanization, and the temples of capitalism.[34] The historian Tristram Hunt writes:

> Industrialisation and urbanisation went hand in hand to shatter practices centuries-old and crown Britain the workshop of the world decades before her commercial and military rivals in continental Europe or North America. Britain was the first. The horrors, the wonders; the isolation, the excitement; the inequality, the opportunity of the city all appeared in their modern guise for the first time in Britain.[35]

To New Labour in the mid-1990s, the knowledge economy represented the chance to restore this glorious past of industrial greatness. The electronic workshop, or the "knowledge factories" that Gordon Brown has spoken of, were metaphorical expressions of particular notions of improvement and advancement found in a Victorian world of entrepreneurship and innovation.

New Labour's platform drew on a pervasive narrative of crisis and decline, where the United Kingdom's former position as the leader of the industrial world had gradually crumbled. Thatcherism had waged war on British society and caused unemployment and poverty. Decades of underinvestment in business and services had caused industrial decline and a national failure to keep up with a world that had already left coal and steel behind. British engineering and manufacturing were losing out to Indian and Chinese ingenuity. The ERM debacle, the United Kingdom's failure to keep to the European exchange rate mechanism, became a symbol of the eroded confidence in that foremost British institution, the pound sterling. The decision to give independence to the Bank of England immediately after the takeover in 1997 was deeply symbolic, not only for the prudence and credibility of a new, economically responsible, Labour Party but for reviving a national institution that occupied a central place in the historical consciousness as the heart of the Empire.[36]

"Renewal" was to break with this crisis-ridden past and to build a new British future in an era dominated by the forces of information technology and globalization. Renewal set out an agenda for building "a better Britain," "a Britain confident of its place in the world." This new Britain was a new and rejuvenated country, full of drive and purpose, "convinced that its best times can lie ahead."[37] From the onset, renewal was a vision that was firmly rooted in ideas of the new economy, and it established the knowledge economy and information technology as the basis of the modernization strategy. The young country was one that embraced technological and economic changes and accepted the challenges of globalization, just as Britain had done so successfully throughout history. The 1997 manifesto stated that Britain was "a great country, with a great history." The British people were a "great people."[38] In his 1998 Mansion House speech, Gordon Brown spoke of

> a modern Britain, founded on lasting British values, the values of the British people, built on a determination to make Britain a more prosperous country for all its citizens, driven forward by a new generation willing, like our predecessors, to reject failed dogmas and to modernise and reform—a Britain ready to fulfil its role in the new world and to realise the potential of its people.[39]

In this way, New Labour put forth a vision for renewal that fell back on notions of specific British values and that anchored the process of modernization in a specific past of greatness. This emphasis on *Britishness* has been an integral part of New Labour's project of modernization and its approach to governance as the governance of culture and identity. The reform agenda in economic, social, and labor market policies was thus praised as one that "realises, for a new world, the great British qualities—the virtue of hard work, creativity, and openness."[40] Globalization and the knowledge economy have been conceptualized as being particularly befitted to British values of creativity, flexibility, and entrepreneurship. In the speeches of Gordon Brown, the Britons were a nation of islanders, forged by "the tidal flows of history" and hardened by successive experiences of invasion. This oceanic existence has created an "openness" that in Brownian terms means a readiness to embrace globalization and its competitive pressures. The British are innovative and entrepreneurial, from the agricultural revolution to the new economy.[41] In a 1997 speech Brown spoke of the "British genius," a play on Orwell's wartime notion of the English genius:

> If you ask the British people what qualities they would identify as distinctly British, they will tell you the British are inventive, creative, and adaptable, they work hard and learn fast. The British have a strong instinct for fairness— for opportunity for all. And the British, at their best, are outward looking and

international in outlooks and tolerant to new ideas and cultures. These are the traditional, historic, permanent British qualities. They are qualities that have been making the British character over centuries, making up what George Orwell once called the British genius. These qualities—inventiveness, adaptability, hard work, love of learning, fairness and openness laid the basis for success in the 19th century. And they are precisely the qualities that are required for a country to succeed in the 21st century. Global markets and the information age call for inventiveness and creativity, adaptability in face of ever more rapid change, a culture of learning and a belief in opportunity for all . . . We need to reaffirm these values, to rediscover the British genius.[42]

Orwell's notion of the English genius was of a resilient Englishness that would not be defeated by war but also one that would not accept the injustices of inequality and privilege. In fact, it was a plea for socialism.[43] Gordon Brown's praise of the British genius was, rather, a plea for global capitalism. The endurance and national pride of the British, he argued, were lost in the period of decline but could "help us tackle the biggest challenges we face and place modern Britain at the forefront of an era." The British way was not to fear change but to embrace it, confident in the knowledge that the British people had the innate capacity to "master change and turn it to our advantage." The British genius was a kind of instinct for modernization, a willingness to embrace inevitable, constant, and "relentless" change. The British genius could make Britain one of the global success stories of the new world economy.[44]

In this appeal to national unity and the historic values of the British people, the Victorian era emerged as a past utopia of national unity, social harmony, and industrial success. To Brown, it was an era of social integration and of commitment to collective improvement. It was "entrepreneurial vigour coupled with responsibility and mutuality," a shared sense of national purpose. What was missing from contemporary British culture could thus be found in history. In the third industrial revolution as in the first, the philosophers of the Scottish Enlightenment were advocates for the moral benefits of capitalism. In Brown's reading, John Locke's treatise on liberty became a defense of the moral standing of the New Labour rights-responsibilities agenda in welfare policy. Adam Smith's ideas of the moral sentiment were, in Brownian terms, the hard work that would extend opportunity in an era of skill.[45]

In this manner, the knowledge economy was linked to a specific past of industrial progress. The values of Britishness—industriousness, flexibility, and creativity—became historical values, forged in the historical experience of the

Empire. Thus, creativity, invention and adaptability were defined not as new demands required by the new economy but as natural, integral features of the British people, elements of a national character that made Britain and the British particularly suited to the task of "rising again." In this way, the notion of modernization became utterly essentialized as a process not pushed on the British people by markets or forces of economic and technological change but as a process that stemmed from the true character of the British. This was a highly strategic discourse, which made modernization into the process of re-discovering what, in fact, the British already truly were and not into the threat of dramatic change. Modernization became a simple question of bringing these British attributes out from their hiding place somewhere in the depths of the British consciousness and banking on them, of indeed, as Brown put it, *exploiting* the British genius.[46]

The Old Country: The Library

Swedish politics are not less stuck in history, but the referent to the past is different. Whereas in the British case the way to the future went through the Victorian workshop, in Sweden it went through the People's Home. Where in the United Kingdom the new economy was vested with references to British values of flexibility and entrepreneurship, in Swedish discourse, the knowl-edge economy was anchored in particular values of Swedishness: solidarity, equality, and security.

In Swedish social democratic discourse of the last decades, there were none of the British calls for a rupture with a traumatic past or adaptation to a third industrial revolution. Swedish notions of modernity and modernization draw on continuity and on an idea of modernization as a more or less continuous historical process of economic and social reform. This has partly to do with the context of the 1990s. New Labour's narrative of renewal and its emphasis on a third industrial revolution that would change the face of Britain forever was informed by its general need to break with the past and portray itself as a new historic project with a fresh future. In Sweden, discourses of radical transformation came from the Right. To the Bildt government in the early 1990s, ICT and knowledge were part of a narrative of epochal change in which everything would come undone, not least the welfare state and the corporat-ism of the Swedish model.[47] Thus the idea of the knowledge economy was part of a neoliberal project of systemic change, but to social democracy it needed to be anchored in the tradition of the Swedish model.

The Swedish interpretation of the knowledge economy falls back on the particular ideas and tropes that historically were the building blocks of Nordic modernity. As the Polish historian Kasimierz Musial has shown, the very notion of the Nordic, Scandinavian, or Swedish model has strong connotations to a "blueprint" Third Way in the form of a quintessentially progressive middle way between socialism and capitalism, a rationalist culture of social reform and democratic institutions rooted in the strong social movements of the past. The notion of a Scandinavian model or progressiveness is informed by an idea of a certain moral quality, a uniqueness of being, the idea that "in Scandinavia there exists a certain frame of mind, a mental capacity by virtue of which a change for the better comes to be regarded as inevitable."[48]

This idea of virtually embodying modernity has been part of the mythology around the Nordic countries since Marquis Childs's famous observation of Sweden as a middle way between capitalism and socialism in the 1930s, but it is also a pervasive self-image of Swedish social democracy—a self-image that is thus that of owning the instinct for rational reform.[49] This self-image faltered in the mid-1990s as unemployment hit levels Sweden had not seen since the 1930s. Almost overnight, Sweden went from the role model of the world to the punching bag of gleeful observers in the pages of the *Wall Street Journal* and the *Financial Times*.[50] Former Prime Minister Göran Persson has repeatedly described that deeply humiliating moment when, as the leader of the advanced industrial nation of Sweden, he had to travel to Washington to defend the postulates of the Swedish welfare state to a group of young International Monetary Fund (IMF) economists.[51] The first years following social democracy's return to power were blighted by tough decisions regarding budget cuts and clashes with the trade unions. But in the mid-1990s, as the budget deficit was dealt with and all curves were pointing in the right direction, memories of crisis seemed to fade rapidly, and the 1990s became a kind of glitch in a social democratic success story. Consider Göran Persson's metaphorical description of the Swedish welfare state as a bumblebee to the party's conference in Sundsvall in 1997:

> Imagine a bumblebee. With its heavy body and its frail wings it shouldn't fly. Yet it does. Every summer it returns and makes the impossible possible on its way among forget-me-nots and daisies. This is how the so-called analysts look at the Swedish economy. We revoke the law of gravity. We have high taxes and a big public sector—and yet Sweden flies. And we fly in a way that many look upon with envy.[52]

In social democratic debate, the late 1990s marked a decisive moment when crisis management finally seemed to be a thing of the past and the party could start looking forward. A series of conferences and seminars were devoted to the social democratic future and to the ideology that would carry the new millennium.[53] In sharp contrast to New Labour's futuristic narrative of renewal, this took the form of a return to the past in, at times, highly nostalgic accounts of past achievement and affirmations of the validity of a Swedish *sonderweg*. Social democratic texts of the 1990s tended to begin with the attestation "Sweden is a good society to live in":

> Step by step, Sweden has developed from an unfair and poor society to a country with a unique combination of great equality, excellent welfare and world-leading multinational companies. This is a development we can be proud of. This progress has been made while a strong sense of solidarity and cooperation has developed, a sense that meant that unions and employers created uniquely good relations, that the public sector and business have been able to cooperate, that no one has to fear illness or old age, and everyone has access to education and self-improvement. Democracy is deeply rooted in all parts of our society. Our faith in the possibility to deal with the challenges of the future together has guided us through this century. Now we stand before a new century with new and equally great challenges. . . . It is on the basis of democracy, cooperation, fairness, and solidarity that social democracy wants to build the future. Together we take the step into the next millennium.[54]

In this process, many of the things that the party had broken with in its 1980s Third Way came back into party discourse, and the notion of the People's Home, a notion the party shunned in the 1980s, came back as a pervasive future metaphor for the knowledge era. It is illustrative that this return to the "classical" social democratic heritage did not take place through a dramatic break with the 1980s Third Way, nor through conflict and debate. Rather, it was a process of rearticulation that happened as a silent return to past ideologies, a process wherein postwar values were quietly brought in through the back door. More than anything, this change was rhetorical. While rhetoric started to echo the Erlander years, there was remarkably little debate on policy change and how a newfound People's Home rhetoric related to the party's Third Way policies and welfare state change. Nor was there much analysis of the state of Swedish society during or after crisis. At the 1997 Conference, a disenchanted participant voiced his confusion over this discrepancy between social democratic rhetoric and a Swedish society in change:

Our beautiful welfare society, which we have been so proud of, has become a bit worse for wear in recent years. How should I put it? In some strange way we seem to be heading toward a kind of poor law society. The poor have become poorer, and the rich have become richer.[55]

Social democracy had very little to say about such impressions of economic and social change in Swedish society and even less about its own role in the process. Instead, it resorted to discourses of continuity in which the experiences of the 1990s were silenced and marginalized. In this manner, the idea of the knowledge society became part of a social democratic narrative of a resurrected People's Home. Where New Labour spoke of the knowledge economy as a return to the workshops and factories of Victorian times, Swedish Social Democrats, from former party leader Ingvar Carlsson to Persson, described the knowledge economy as firmly anchored in Swedish political history and the rise of the social democratic state. Thus, the knowledge society was portrayed as a logical continuation of the self-education movements that spread literacy in the late nineteenth century and were an important base for labour mobilization. The creation of regional colleges in the 1990s was compared to the historical forging of a literate and politically aware working class in the study circles of early labor. The study circle was praised as the model organization for the knowledge society—a model of education where all help to lift each other up by joining knowledge and sharing experiences. In Sweden, the equivalent of the description of the knowledge economy as the British Imperial workshop was the public library, *folkbiblioteket*, the people's libraries that began as ambulating book carts and eventually became central institutions in each town.[56]

In this way, the knowledge future became conceptualized as something integral to a long-standing Swedish tradition of democracy, solidarity, and equality. The next millennium, it was understood, would be judged by the ability to preserve these particularly Swedish historical achievements for the future. This fell back on a notion of modernity as a continuous sense of reform and improvement and on ideas of knowledge as a tool for a specific reformist rationality. In contrast to the way in which the knowledge economy, to New Labour, stemmed from British instincts of industriousness and competitiveness, in Sweden it was literacy, the spread of democracy, and working-class solidarity that would lead to the liberation of everyone in the knowledge age. Knowledge was not a competitive good in a zero-sum race for global competitive advantage but a good for self-fulfillment and a happier, more democratic, and solidaristic society, one inhabited by individuals with an understanding of the principles of the universal welfare state. Knowledge was a means for human growth. Knowledgeable and educated young individuals would grow, be strengthened by their insights, not only with diplomas but with commitments to society, with interest in the world, and humility for the "values that we share in this country":

> Knowledge frees man and gives him new horizons. Knowledge gives man power and deepens democracy. The strength of reason leads away from superstition . . . , it leads to fact, truth and empirical knowledge. When we se reality as it really is, we also see how society can be improved and developed. In this way, the knowledge of man urges on creativity and strength. Love and solidarity is developed. Solidarity and cooperation gain in scope. Through the development of knowledge we understand how to explore the infinite potential of people.[57]

Knowledge was thus not conceptualized as a driving force for economic modernization but as a means for the safeguarding of the principles of the People's Home.

This contained a historical construction of Swedishness that was no less pervasive than the construction of Britishness that informed New Labour's idea of modernization, but where modernity was defined by literacy, democracy and solidarity. Swedes are, said Persson in the late 1990s, the world's most knowledgeable people. "We could read more than others could." Linked to democracy and literacy in this success story were the successes of Swedish multinational companies such as Ericsson, historically seeking world markets for knowledge-intensive, value-added products, "turning our natural resources into innovations and technological change." In addition, Swedish trade unions have always been on the side of modernization, willing to embrace technological change and adapt to structural changes in the economy. Therefore, the ability to constantly change and modernize was a historical asset that paved the way for the future.[58]

Through these constructions, modernization became something that emerged from within, an instinct embedded in the Swedish psyche. While modernity, in British political culture, was defined by the markers of prosperity and competition, in Sweden modernization was a process of extending solidarity and cooperation; but the function of this modernization discourse in both countries was similar, namely, that of providing legitimacy to one way particular forward, rather than another.

Conclusion

The call to people, nation, and even national character in social democratic ideology in the period following the 1990s is a curious phenomenon. It is clearly influenced by the need to fend off populist articulations in the political field and by the rise of anti-immigrant sentiment and racism in social democracy's core constituencies. New Labour's notion of Britishness clearly reflects a legacy from Thatcher's appeal to Middle England. In Sweden, the nostalgia of the Persson years contained a romantic construction of the values of the welfare state as the natural values of the Swedish people. The appeal to nation and people is not in itself new in social democratic ideology, but the function of the themes of Britishness and Swedishness in contemporary social democratic ideology is different from the way in which social democracy once translated working-class preferences to the national level. In the present, discourses of national identity are part of a reinvention of the political project around notions of ethics, morale, and national identity—values beyond the scope of political struggle. The appeal to national unity is a way of silencing conflicts around change. History becomes a source of legitimacy for a process of economic change that is potentially disruptive and damaging for many groups. New Labour's fiercely modernistic futurism and the SAP's People's Home nostalgia were, despite the different approaches to change that they contained, indications of the same phenomenon. In addition, the knowledge age places a premium on trust, identity, and culture as forms of competitive advantage, which seems to strengthen these nationalist expressions. We will return to this problem in coming chapters.

4 Capitalism?

As we have seen, a central element in the idea of the knowledge economy as a progressive economy is the idea that because knowledge is capital within, located within workers, it also makes workers the owners of capital and that there is something inherent in a capitalist stage organized around knowledge that defies the Left's conventional understandings of the conflict between labor and capital. To Gordon Brown, writing in the mid-1990s, the knowledge economy was the point of departure for a "new economic egalitarianism," an "opportunity economics," because it is people's potential that is the driving force of the modern economy.[1]

This conception of the order of things has led to two dominant interpretations of contemporary social democracy. The first one, discussed in the previous chapter, is the idea that because of the fundamental intangibility of knowledge capital in a global era, politics must strengthen the strategic role of human capital. This is the postulate that informs the political economy of the Third Way and emphasizes the role of state and public intervention for the creation of prosperity. From this presumption of the strategic role of human capital follows a second conclusion, namely, that the knowledge economy is somehow detached from the logics of capital accumulation and that there is something inherent in a capitalist order that works for the development of human potential. To the optimists, the knowledge economy seems to be a nicer kind of capitalism, a more social economic order, one that draws on human potential instead of destroying it. To Charles Leadbeater in his 1998 account, the knowledge economy was the promise of a postcapitalist utopia, a world where toiling in mills and mines was replaced by the power of imagination and creativity.[2] As the French economist Daniel Cohen has argued, the knowledge economy could be the era of human capital, a fundamentally more humane variety of capitalism in which exploitation is replaced by emancipation through processes of self-exploration and learning.[3] To that extent, the Third Way contains a notion that might be described as the end of capital, the presumption that an economy driven by potential will also finally bring the realization of the old socialist notion of freeing potential.

The realization of potential, or the freeing of individual talents fettered by capitalism, is social democracy's classical notion of emancipation. It reflects the social democratic idea that unregulated market capitalism leads to a deeply inefficient society where the potential and talents of some inevitably go to waste. The rhetoric of freeing potential has been central to both the British and the Swedish labor movements, from early Chartism and ethical socialism to postwar debates on the mixed economy. In Third Way ideology, however, the presumption of the new economic power of potential has led to a thorough rethinking of problems previously associated with capitalism. An opportunity economics would, arguably, be one that frees opportunity for people to grasp and gives them the means with which to realize their inherent potential. The Third Way's notion of emancipation is this idea of everybody's freedom to fully realize his or her potential, to "bridge the gap between what we are and what we have it in us to become."[4]

However, emancipation does not seem to be the dominant feature of the knowledge economy. There is sufficient analysis of the post-Fordist production order to suggest that while it might hold the potential for emancipation for some, it also brings new forms of exploitation for others, a relationship that is obvious and yet poorly understood in both politics and social science. The tension between emancipation and exploitation in the knowledge economy might be thought of in terms of the dilemma posited by Daniel Cohen— if the era of human capital is, on the one hand, a promise of a more humane form of capitalism, it also brings with it, on the other, a highly economistic understanding of human potential and human beings as a form of capital. Conceivably, rather than representing the final end to the labor capital conflict, the knowledge economy could be the ultimate commodification through the exploitation of the worker's inner self.[5]

To be sure, there are many aspects to the new economy that would suggest that the idea of knowledge exploitation is worth considering. Critical writers on the knowledge economy have argued, for instance, that information technology and flexible specialization do not empower workers but rather take the division of labor one step further, as they dissolve the links between employer and employee and extend responsibility over time and space. ICT is not necessarily the liberating technology that connects people but also a technology of alienation. Flexible specialization is a mode of production that displays contradictory tendencies because it concentrates responsibility for a multitude of tasks on the individual employee while also making him or her exchangeable in the chain of production.[6] As Darin Barney suggests, reducing our brains to "wetware" is ultimately also an economic philosophy of "people as bits."[7] Such a philosophy has consequences and social effects. The American sociologist Richard Sennett, one of the key interpreters of the social and cultural effects of flexible production patterns, speaks of the corrosion of character—the breakdown of self-worth and self-esteem as talent, skill, and craftsmanship are destroyed by outsourcing, consultancy cultures, and short-termism.[8] This is a dramatic perspective on the knowledge economy. Rather than fostering knowledge and skill, Sennett argues, the new economy extinguishes skill, as the education system turns out young, educated, but unemployable people whose dreams of self-fulfilment clash with the realities of the decreasing value of knowledge and potential in the information revolution. The returns of individual investment in education are unpredictable and volatile. Narrow definitions of flexibility and employability lead to the hollowing out of potential and talent, as these become standardized goods. The depreciation of talent and skill, Sennett suggests, creates a spectre of uselessness: large groups of people whose place in economy and society is primarily defined by their lack of talent and knowledge.[9] The contrast to Brown's assumption of an opportunity economics might be that the skills economy may need only an ever-smaller knowledge-owning elite, that opportunity is not abundant, but scarce, and that its distribution is less than optimal. From this perspective, lifelong learning policies take on a new meaning, as policies of disciplining, rationalization and even standardization, equipping knowledge workers for lives in knowledge factories and reducing potential to exchangeable skill.

These are dismal prospects for social democratic politics, and we should not judge the Third Way by them entirely. The Third Way's articulations of skill and potential are the expression of a social democratic aspiration to give a progressive potential to the knowledge economy. In doing so, however, social democracy seems to silence important elements of its ideological past. This chapter examines how contemporary social democracy conceives of contemporary capitalism and of its own role in it. In the 1990s and 2000s, both parties rewrote their constitutions to adapt to knowledge and the World Wide Web. The different constitutions express very different understandings of what capitalism is today and how social democracy should respond to it. This is due to the different historical legacies of British and Swedish Labour around capitalism and to prevailing differences in understandings of the relationship between the market and society.

The End of Capital

Let us go back to Gordon Brown's suggestion that because knowledge is capital located "within," that is, in the head of the knowledge worker, the knowledge economy makes the worker the owner of capital, and therefore the knowledge economy marks the end of the conflict between labor and capital. Gordon Brown's argument on the opportunity of the new economy can be found in the pamphlet "The Politics of Potential" in the manifesto for a new politics of the Left, *Reinventing the Left*, which was a central text in the construction of the New Labour platform in the mid-1990s. In this article, and in his following Fabian pamphlet "Fair is Efficient," Brown laid out the central tenets of New Labour's revisionism. Indeed, Brown's contribution was intended as a dialogue with the central modernizer of the Labour Party, Anthony Crosland, key interpreter of the class dynamics of the industrial society.[10]

Anthony Crosland's famous 1956 argument on the future of socialism was that capitalism had gone through a fundamental transformation in the twentieth century to the extent that it was questionable whether one could really speak of capitalism at all. He saw this process as triggered by technological changes, the diffusion of ownership in the joint stock corporation and the rise of a managerial class, changes that had led to the virtual disappearance of the old capital-owning elite. To Crosland, this meant that it was time to rid social democracy of certain dogmas, particularly the principle of the nationalization of the ownership of the means of production. In modern capitalism, the central problem was no longer the question of ownership but democratic influence and social justice in a mixed economy.[11]

In Gordon Brown's interpretation, the knowledge era takes Crosland's revisionism one step further. Network production is the end of managerial capitalism because the employee emerges as the owner of capital.

Brown asserts that the objective of socialism is the "realisation of potential." The politics of the Left must aim at stopping the waste of potential that takes place in an unregulated capitalist society and "enable people to bridge

the gap between what they are now and what they have it in themselves to become."[12] However, the realization of this age-old objective, in an era in which
individual aspirations and skill are greater than ever, must be different.[13] Liberating potential can no longer be about protecting people from change, but
it has to be an "enabling vision"—a vision of how to give individuals control
over their own lives. The challenge of potential, in a time in which potential
seems to have a new bargaining position against forces of exploitation, requires a rethinking of market and state because in the modern age it is not
only the structures of the economy that lock in potential but also the structures of the state. The old Left did not see that the institution and bureaucracy
of the state could become a vested interest that locks individual potential in or
that "power can concentrate at the expense of individuals within the state as
well as within private capital." Potential requires new forms of social organization, forms that promote its realization. This gives socialism a new role:

> The unique contribution of socialism is that we know that the strength of
> society—the community working together—is essential not only to tackle the
> entrenched interests and accumulations of power that hold ordinary people
> back, but also positively to intervene to promote the realisation of potential.
> In other words, the power of all of us is essential to promote the potential of
> each of us.[14]

Thus, the idea of an opportunity economics created strong links between the
notion of potential and the notion of community, and in doing so it also established that the market was a central means to free potential. "Controlling the
means to life in the interest of enhancing individual freedom" is about controlling the whole environment of which the economy is only a part. In Brown's
interpretation, two fundamental postulates of the Left were thus wrong—the
first that emancipation stems from controlling the means of production and
the second that the public interest conflicts with the existence of markets:

> The socialist answer to the exploitation of labour by capital was, a hundred years
> ago, to advance the public interest by abolishing, or at least controlling, private
> capital. Now most would accept that the real answer to capital exploiting labour
> in the interest of a few is to create the circumstances not in which capital is
> somehow abolished but in which labour can exploit capital in the public inter-
> est. Indeed where the success and failure of an economy depends on access to
> knowledge more than access to capital, individual liberation arises from the en-
> hancement of the value of labour rather than the abolition of private capital.[15]

Fundamental assumptions of socialism are therefore false in the era of po-tential. In the modern economy, the "real answer to capital exploiting labour in the interest of the few" is not to abolish capital but to create the circum-stances in which "labour can exploit capital in the public interest." This was the ideological justification of the politics of partnership, as a new form of mixed economy for the knowledge era. Hence were "the values of freedom to be liberated from old leftist dogma."[16]

The final revision of Clause 4, a process begun under Gaitskell, recognized the market as a central part of the community and a central actor for freeing individual potential. The old Clause 4, written by Sydney Webb and adopted in 1918, said

> To secure for the workers by hand or brain the full fruits of their industry and most equitable distribution thereof that may be possible upon the basis of the common ownership of the means of production, distribution and exchange, and the best obtainable system of administration and control of each industry or service.

The new Clause IV, adopted in 1995 for an era in which, as Blair later put it," we compete with brains, not brawn,"[17] says

> The Labour Party is a democratic socialist party. It believes that by the strength of our common endeavour we achieve more than we achieve alone, so as to create for each of us the means to realise our true potential and for all of us as a community in which power, wealth and opportunity are in the hands of the many, not the few. Where the rights we enjoy reflect the duties we owe. And where we live together, freely, in a spirit of solidarity, tolerance, and respect.[18]

The old socialist emphasis on the ownership of the means of production was replaced with the emphasis on community and the assurance that the old conflicts of capitalism were no longer of any relevance.[19]

In its revision of Clause 4, the Labour Party followed the revisionist road that European social democratic parties had long since taken, albeit in a rather extreme form. The notion of community contained an explicit appeal to national unity, drawing on the values of Britishness discussed in the previ-ous chapter. This appeal to national unity was a central part of New Labour's repositioning of laborism as a project beyond fractionary class politics, its ap-peal to the Middle England voter, and its occupation of the political center. A core element in the idea of renewal was the explicit break with ideology and with socialism as a worldview. The New Labour journal *Renewal* appeared with the word hyphenated into *idea-ology*, to denote a set of ideas defined not by the values of social democracy but by a pragmatic outlook on "what works." The project of modern governance launched by New Labour and its creation of "new politics" built on this rejection of ideology in favor of a national common good. Community, with its claim to occupy a political space beyond the Left–Right divide, was a key metaphor of new politics. As the concept of the Third Way was launched by Blair in a Fabian pamphlet in 1998, and subsequently in the web-based Nexus debate, it was explicitly positioned as a political project that went beyond political polarization between Left and Right.[20] The 1997 Manifesto claimed to have liberated values from outdated ideological dogma and doctrine and applied them to the modern world. It promised to appeal to the people "of all walks," people who "work hard," "play by the rules," and "pay their dues"; in essence the Middle England that was old Labour's problem. It was an appeal to a common good in the national interest, a "shared sense of purpose." It was social, but it was not socialism.[21]

This rearticulation of Labour values as national good is a striking parallel to the historic Swedish notion of the People's Home, which was also a vision of national renewal and which also sprang from pervasive notions of crisis.[22] In the interwar period, continental social democratic parties chose a reformist path, which appealed to national unity and the values of the people. In Sweden, the metaphor of the People's Home was the expression of the SAP's successful reinvention of itself from a party of fractionary class politics to a national party. The notion of the People's Home was a fiercely modernist notion, one that promised to break with the past and portrayed social democracy as the carrier of the future and "prosperity for all." In its 1930s policies, the SAP set out an agenda for economic and social rationalization and modernization. In 1938, it signed a new deal with Swedish business and promised peace in industrial relations, just as New Labour in the 1990s promised a new deal for British business. The New Labour Manifesto promised to set out a covenant with the British people, just as the SAP, in the 1930s, promised to build a home for all Swedes.[23]

Knowledge Capitalism

In the interwar period, Swedish social democracy abandoned nationalization and chose pragmatic reformism as the route to radical transformation.[24] It reaffirmed its market-friendly approach in a series of historical compromises throughout the twentieth century. During the radical decade of the 1970s, it stopped speaking of workers and instead began speaking of "coworkers" or indeed "stakeholders."[25] Paradoxically, the revisions of the party program in the period from the 1990s have seemed to bring a new emphasis to anticapitalist themes in party ideology, perhaps as a concession to the critics of modernization. In striking contrast to Brown's discussion of the emancipatory logic of potential, the SAP speaks of the knowledge economy as an essentially capitalist order: "In a capitalist production order, profit is elevated above all other interests, regardless of how it is achieved and of the costs it brings to society, environment, and human beings."[26]

Just as the Industrial Revolution led to great social conflicts, the knowledge economy is a new production order, which in some ways strengthens the position of human capital and labor but which also leads to sharper clashes between labor and capital. The power of capital has increased because it is no longer dependent on physical production factors and national boundaries. Hence capital is set free of the control of the interests of labor and social democratic governments. This strengthened position makes the "inherent incapability of capitalism to rationalize and sustain resources as obvious as its inherent tendency to create economic and social injustice." The social consequences of this, to the program, are devastating. In the countries of the Western world, the interests of capital have put a large part of the labor force outside production as unprofitable and unemployable. Further, the rationalization of production that follows the introduction of new technology has also injured health and capacities of those in employment. Politics and culture have become imbued with the "capitalist idea of worth," and this "power over thought" serves to strengthen capital interests. Money becomes the benchmark for all that is good. The result is a cold, harsh society without trust and solidarity. The program asserts that the SAP is anticapitalist, in the sense that it rejects the right of capital to exert power over economy and society; in the sense that it rejects a process of change wherein capital interests and the market dominate the direction of progress and the commercialization or commodification of human, social, and cultural relations; and in the sense that social democracy, in the conflict between labor and capital, is on the side of labor.[27]

There is thus not the New Labour idea that the new economic stage leads to some magical transformation of the fundamental forces of capitalism; but, rather, the SAP sees a transformation of the capitalist tendencies for exploitation in the knowledge economy. The program contains a long discussion on class, which departs from social democracy's traditional emphasis on the distinction between those who own capital and those who own labor. The new production order changes this relationship, but it doesn't abolish it. It is, thus, a double-edged change that both sharpens the distinction between capital and labor and strengthens the importance of labor against capital in other ways. Importantly, the program argues that globalization has weakened the relationship between ownership and responsibility. Capital has become anonymous, detached from social responsibility. Short-term capitalism increases the pressures of production on employees while it reduces employer responsibility. Theoretically, the increased importance of knowledge could mean that the control of labor over production is strengthened, but this does not seem true for growing groups more or less permanently outside of new labor markets. These groups do not appear empowered but rather increasingly subordinated to the power of capital. Indeed, there is a concern with a growing group of nonproductive outsiders in Swedish society. In contrast to Brown's assertion of the end of managerial class divisions, the Swedish program speaks of a new triad in class relations: a class that owns both financial and knowledge capital, a knowledge-owning class, and an underclass of outsiders—the people who do not own knowledge, a kind of knowledge proletariat.[28]

In Swedish interpretations, this leads to conclusions about the role of politics that are fundamentally different from the new politics of New Labour. Change does not simply produce opportunities for realizing individual potential; the transformation of capitalism also leads to new social conflicts, just as industrial capitalism led to the mobilization of organized labor. In the long run, the program states, the inequalities brought on by new technology will themselves be a force for change. This, in Swedish discourse, is "opportunity":

> The power in the opportunities that the new order of production creates is then and now too strong for the interest of the few to resist. Today's displacement of power to the interests of capital is not the unavoidable and unchangeable consequence of globalization. It can be breached through politics.[29]

This interpretation of what constitutes opportunity seems almost diametrically opposed to the interpretation of New Labour. Opportunity is not something that is thrown up by the new economy; rather it resides in the risks and conflicts that the new economy creates. Change is not an economically determined process but one determined by the social reactions that it triggers. The program thus retains a notion of conflict; the interests and social reactions that once shaped social democracy and the welfare state will also determine the fate of capitalism in the future. Change is human-made.

It would be mistaken from this to think that the SAP holds on to a Marxist legacy that it has long left behind. In 2001, the party finally dropped the ownership clause from the party program.[30] Hence the old clause stating the nationalization over the means of the production (*bestämmanderätten över produktionen och dess fördelning ska läggas i hela folkets händer*) was changed into the new formulation of a "democratic production order," where the principle of ownership is replaced with the principle of democratic control. This seems like a mere formalization of the party's traditional revisionism dating back to the interwar period; but, in the 2001 program, it was represented as a vision of socialism in tune with a modern conception of democracy, particularly, as Göran Persson said to the Conference, in the era of the World Wide Web:[31]

> All power in society has to come from the people who together constitute society. Economic interests can never be allowed to rein democracy in; democracy sets the conditions for economy and market. . . . Social democracy wants to create a social order where people as citizens and individuals can influence development and social change. We seek an economic order where every person as citizen, wage earner, and consumer can change the organization of production and the distribution of its results and the conditions of working life. Social democracy wants to let these democratic ideals structure society as a whole and the relations between people in society. Our goal is a society without class differences, without gender segregation or ethnic divides, a society without prejudice and discrimination, a society where all are needed and all have a place, where all have the same right and the same worth, where all children can grow into free and autonomous adults, where all can control their lives and in equality, solidarity, and cooperation strive to create the social solutions that benefit the common good.[32]

A crucial element in the party's rewriting of the nationalization clause was the distinction between the market and capitalism. In a democratic order of production, the market and its entrepreneurs are accepted as vital parts of a democratic society. The market, the 2001 party program argues, is acceptable because, in contrast to capitalism, which is a system of exploitation in the interest of capital (not acceptable), the market is simply a system for the efficient exchange of goods and thus an acceptable mechanism of redistribution.[33] Moreover, the market provides the necessary material resources for the Swedish welfare state. Thus the market is neutral and not a cause for ideological concern. Part of the definition of a democratic production order, however, is the recognition that there are fundamental social interests in society that are not compatible with the market interest, for instance the idea of a common good. In Swedish discourse this common good is defined not by prosperity but by solidarity:

Freedom and equality are about individual rights and collective solutions for the common good, which is the basis of individual potential. Individuals are social beings who develop and grow in interaction with others, and much of what is important for the welfare of the single person can be created only with others. This common good presupposes solidarity. Solidarity comes from the realization that we are all mutually in need of each other and that the best society is built on mutual consideration and respect. All must have the same right and possibility to influence our collective solutions, and all have the same responsibility to them. Solidarity does not rule out individual advancement and success but the egoism that allows some to use others for their own benefit.[34]

While this paragraph has clear similarities with the community paragraph of New Labour, there is also a fundamental difference. Solidarity and the common good are, in Sweden, values that are in opposition to the market and that act as a control on the market. The program states that market worth and human worth are in conflict and that social democracy is against the commodification and commercialization of social, cultural, and human relationships:

> Social democracy rejects a development where capital and market are allowed to dominate and commercialize social, cultural, and human relationships. Market norms must never be allowed to determine the value of human beings or the shaping of social and cultural life.[35]

Because the market is not capable of recognizing the existence of key social interests it cannot be an acceptable norm for the provision of what the program refers to as "social goods" (*sociala nyttigheter*). Social goods are key welfare services, goods that must not be guided by principles of profit or supply and demand mechanisms but by the principle of need. It would thus seem that while the party does not deny the role of the market as a provider, it does reject the market ethos, which it sees as distinct from the public ethos. However, *social goods* is a neologism that avoids the problematic term of public good (*kollektiva nyttigheter*), arguably because the party has embraced the market in key services that it formerly considered to be essential public goods to be kept away from the logic of the market, for instance child care, hospitals, education, and housing. This is an indication of the highly ambiguous stances of the SAP toward the market. While it says that a democratic production order poses limits on the market, the party remains vague as to what these limits are. Indeed, in the next paragraph, the program states that the provider of services should be chosen on the basis of "what works," a wording that falls back on the principle not of public good but value for money.[36]

Socialism and Equality

In the postwar period, social democracy's answer to the dilemmas posed by affluence was to attempt to reconcile social mobility with equality through the welfare state and the mixed economy. A "revolution of rising expectations" and an increasing diversification of need and preferences in the affluent society seemed to challenge social democracy's notions of equality, but it was met with the ideas, of revisionists Crosland or Wigforss, namely, that through equality, individual freedom could be reached. Affluence required more equality, not less, to balance the effects of growing private consumption. In this way, there would be no conflict between the principle of equality and diversity, nor, indeed, freedom of choice. In contrast, social democracy in the 1990s argued that equality is at odds with affluence. It saw the creation of prosperity as dependent on the just reward of merit and achievement, and it argued that rising individual expectations for choice and diversity in services challenge collective and universal solutions, not least in the crucial area of education.

This has led to a rethinking of the principles of egalitarianism and the balance between equality and diversity. Allegedly, the individualism of the knowledge era, along with the emergence of individual talent, potential, and skill as key drivers of prosperity, calls for a rethinking of egalitarianism to make room for individual differences. Therefore, Social Democrats have shunned the notion of equality in favor of a notion of equality as equality of opportunity, a notion that shifts the focus from the structures that determine potential to the opportunities available for individuals to realize their potential. The notion of equality of opportunity has often been seen as a natural evolution of ideological postulates in an age of knowledge, as an era where the exploration of one's talents is more important for individual self-fulfilment than disparities in income and socioeconomic position, and where, allegedly, the economy produces opportunities in the form of flexibility, career advancement, and education. In a capitalist order organized around potential, people must be allowed to pursue their individual potential and different talents even if this creates differences in economic and social outcomes. This is what Anthony Crosland once called "the rent of ability." Such a reward for the development of individual talent and achievement was legitimate, he argued, because anything else would be an intolerable infringement on the individual right to develop. In the affluent society, the objective of socialism could no longer be equality of outcome but rather giving everyone the chance to succeed because destitution and material want were no longer the most pressing concerns, and the industrial economy seemed to provide opportunities for advancement and mobility.[37] Ernst Wigforss also believed that the reward of merit was a justified ideological principle, as long as it did not further entrench class differences.[38]

Meritocracy has a new relevance in social democracy's contemporary ideas of the knowledge society where, on the one hand, it is argued that in a competitive knowledge economy there must be a premium not only on individual investments in education but also on individual talent, while on the other, the pressing need for the potential of all also revokes an egalitarian ideal.

The rearticulation of the concept of equality to equality of opportunity in the United Kingdom was informed by this postwar debate on the relationship between affluence and equality. The notion of equality of opportunity reflected New Labour's ideas of a new governance, where the central role of the social democratic state was to foster opportunity and leave individuals to explore their life chances. Equality of opportunity, in New Labour's interpretation, was a positive notion of freedom, one that allowed for active individuals capable of fulfilling their potential. It was a concept of equality that allowed for aspiration, advancement, and achievement, and that recognized the different talents that exist in society.[39] It drew not only on Crosland but also on the arguments of philosophers such as John Rawls and Ronald Dworkin on social justice, specifically, that inequalities in outcome are acceptable if they create a situation where the poorest are better off, or if inequalities result from the pursuit of talent rather than the unjust inheritance of privileges and resources. As we will see in upcoming chapters, it was also strongly linked to the notion of responsibility and, above all, to the individual's responsibility to seize opportunity.[40]

Equality of opportunity is potentially a very radical notion, one that puts life chances, aspiration, and self-realization at the heart of emancipatory politics and sees individuals as competent, autonomous individuals. It recognizes the unfair distribution of opportunity in society. Equality of opportunity, in contrast to the emphasis on material redistribution of the notion of equality, contains an emphasis on the role of politics to foster and redistribute opportunity, extend it over the life cycle, and distribute it among social groups, as, for example, in the emphasis on raising skill levels or on extending access to the social networks of privileged groups. Arguably, life-long learning, understood this way, could be a very radical agenda for equality.

To New Labour, equality of opportunity represented an attempt to put in place a more meritocratic notion of equality and break with "the leveling down" of old laborism. Equality, to New Labour, was a strangling notion, one that crippled individual initiative. Equality was "putting everyone in the same mold" and a stranglehold on creativity. As such, equality was on a par with the notion of common good as defined as prosperity for all because prosperity, to New Labour, is seen as emanating from the entrepreneurship and creativity that comes from differences in talent and ability. In a virtual turnaround of old social democratic postulates, in an economy of opportunity, it was the drive for equality that led to the waste of potential. To New Labour in the mid-1990s, equality of opportunity fit into a narrative around the competition, entrepreneurship, and market logic of the new economy. Its inclusive elements were downplayed in favor of a stress on individual survival and the individual capacity to seize opportunity and increase his or her competitiveness on the ladders of the knowledge society. This was directly related to its interpretation of the knowledge economy as a cornucopia of opportunity for individuals to grasp. The central element of equality of opportunity was competition, the competition that New Labour sees as the driving force for the fulfilment of human potential.[41]

New Labour's dismissal of the notion of equality stemmed from its stereotypical representation of "old" social democracy. Equality has not, in the social democratic project, been primarily about the socialization of the means of production and absolute equalities in outcome. Rather, the importance of the notion of equality to social democracy historically has been that of a central motivation for what might be termed the good society. *Equality* is a utopian aspiration of the realization of the equal worth of all in society. Arguably, this is where New Labour's notion of equality of opportunity differed from the notion of equality of opportunity of Crosland. While Crosland did argue that absolute equality of outcome was not a desirable principle in a society of welfare statism, he also believed that the principle of equality of opportunity was not enough and that it would lead to a fiercely competitive, wasteful society, where potential would not be freed but eroded:

> Whereas in a hereditary system competition is limited, in meritocracy it becomes general. And as the area of competition and the scope for self-advancement are increased, so the rate of failure to opportunity must increase. A hereditary society, denying the opportunity to rise, avoids also the sense of failure at not having

risen, but if all had the opportunity, and only 10% succeed, 90% are conscious of having failed and suffer a loss of self-esteem. And the more unequal the rewards, the greater will be the frustration from failure, the more ruthless the competition, the more bitter the intolerance shown to rivals . . . acquisition is intensified . . . Such is the society—restless, insecure, aggressive, and acquisitive, that results from the pursuit of equality of opportunity . . .[42]

Hence, equality of opportunity was not enough as the guiding principle of socialism. To Crosland, the importance of equality as aspiration could not be replaced, precisely because it was not a means to an end but a defining principle of social democracy. Crosland recognized that differences in achievement and the pursuit of talent constituted the foundation of a prosperous society. But he could see no reason why intelligence should be elevated above other forms of capability or merit in society. Indeed he warned, in *The Future of Socialism*, of a society strictly organized after the principle of intelligence.[43]

The SAP still holds on to a notion of equality that includes references to outcome. The Swedish notion of equality—*jämlikhet*—is different from the liberal tradition because it does not see equality as being on a par with efficiency and dynamism; rather it sees it as a prerequisite for these very forces. The notion of *jämlikhet* is strongly linked to notions of security, solidarity, and freedom. In its discourses on the knowledge society, the SAP has thus argued that equality is a prerequisite for individual creativity. The party program states that free and equal individuals are the goal of socialism.[44] Freedom is the right to develop as an individual, control one's life, and participate in the shaping of society. This freedom is dependent on equality and incompatible with big disparities in rewards because these break down the solidarity that is the basis of freedom. A democratic order of production thus presumes the fair distribution of the results of the production.[45]

However, just as New Labour's new community paragraph also saw the redefinition of the concept of equality into the neologism of equality of opportunity, the SAP's 2001 program included a rewriting of the concept of equality, which opened up for differences in individual talent and achievement and seemed to lead away from class analysis. Class, it was said, remained relevant, but it was insufficient for an analysis of inequality in new times of creativity and diversity. Equality, Persson said in the conference debate, had to celebrate difference, because "our difference is what is so fantastic."[46] This effectively shifted the focus from outcome to opportunity. According to the program, equality meant giving all individuals, despite their different individual starting points, the same opportunities (*förutsättningar*) to shape their own lives and participate in the shaping of society. The precondition for this is the right to choose and develop differently from one another, as long as these differences do not lead to new social hierarchies and gaps in power and influence.[47]

As this follows in the footsteps of Wigforss and others, the rewriting of the notion of equality as the objective of social democracy in the 2001 program is a less radical departure from egalitarianism than New Labour's break with the principles of socialism. Nevertheless, in Swedish social democratic politics the notion of equality has also effectively become compatible with the notion of freedom of choice, which was introduced in social democratic ideology in the 1980s and has since been the ideological basis of a thorough restructuring of the Swedish welfare state. In the 1980s, the party's rethinking of the principles of the People's Home included a careful evaluation of the neoliberal concept of freedom, which was introduced, into party ideology, as *valfrihet*, freedom of choice. *Valfrihet* was an ambiguous notion because it played—just as New Labour plays on Crosland—on the revisionist notion of freedom of choice of Erlander in the 1950s. In a number of texts outlining the ideas of the Strong society and the principles of solidarity in the welfare state, Erlander argued that equality and freedom of choice went hand in hand because the expansion of public services and the universal welfare state was what, for the great majority of people, made choice possible.[48] Freedom of choice thus required a public commitment to equality and to the solidarity institutionalized in the welfare state. In the 1980s, freedom of choice was no longer about public responsibility but about the individual consumer's right to choose between a variety of providers and services in the Swedish welfare state. The formulations in the party program in 2001 can be seen as the culmination of a long process of rethinking the relationship between the universalism that underpinned the development of the Swedish welfare state and demands for diversity. There appears to be a fundamental conflict between the emphasis on equality in party rhetoric and the principle of freedom of choice that was the guiding star of welfare reform in the 1980s and 1990s. There is no better example of this conflict than the issue of voucher schools, to which we will return.

Conclusion

The Third Way's 1990s revisionism can be seen, on the one hand, as the apex of previous processes of revisionism in the history of social democracy. The values of social democracy have never been stagnant; rather, as Moschonas puts it, the history of social democracy is the history of its modernizations.[49] In history, periods of structural economic change have led to new attempts to assert and interpret social democracy. Nevertheless, the Third Way does mark a fundamental break with social democracy's past because it argues that core values of social democracy—above all the value of equality—were means to other ends and that their standing as means should be seen as specific to each time. Equality was not a suitable principle for an era of diversity, information flows, and the constant dissemination of knowledge. An economy driven by human potential and creativity demanded that social democracy recognize differences of talent and achievement as legitimate organizing principles of society. Equality, to New Labour, was utopia gone astray, a "socialist nightmare."[50] The rewriting of Clause 4 was a tormented process; and, since then, many Labour voices have called for a reinstated notion of equality.[51]

In Sweden, revisions of the SAP's political program have been much more frequent in history, and the changes in the 1990s and 2000s were thus less radical, maybe even just a formalization of changes already naturalized in social democratic ideology. However, the rewriting of the party program was not less about the soul of social democracy and the links between its role in the present and its past heritages. The program's most radical stances—"social democracy rejects a development where capital and market are allowed to dominate social, cultural, and human relationships"—stand in sharp contrast to the marketization that has taken place in core policy areas in the last decade. It is conceivable that the partial radicalization of language and ideology in the 1900s is exactly what made these policy changes possible, glossing over gaps between rhetoric and policy and asserting that the values of social democracy were but the same.

5 Politics of Growth

In Chapter 2, I discussed the political economy of the Third Way as construed around a new concept of capital, a kind of capital that, in the form of knowledge, skill, and potential, is defined by its location within people and its creation in social and cultural relations. Third Way discourse can be understood as an economic language construed around the capitalization of knowledge, a capitalization that leads to an understanding of individual potential, talent, and creativity as the key assets, indeed the raw material, of the new economy: "Human capital is the 21st century equivalent of the 19th century dependence on natural resources. Modern enterprise and wealth creation depend upon the development of people."[1]

The key to growth in the new economy is the transformation of these assets into marketable goods, thus turning knowledge into capital and value. In other words, growth depends on the development of people.

Let us consider briefly the fundamentally ambiguous notion of growth. Growth is a powerful notion of progress because it implies a direction toward a better state of affairs, an accumulation of some kind of surplus, a growing of something into something better or at least *more*. To us, it is often silently presumed to mean economic growth, but growth could, of course, have many other meanings, and it has also had many other meanings in the history of modernity. To that extent, *growth*, like *capital*, is a historically specific concept, one that changes meaning with social and economic change and with changing definitions of what is considered to constitute strategic value at every given point in time. In consequence, growth policies—the political activities aimed at promoting value and prosperity—reflect definitions of what value is and what is considered to be improvement. The modern definition of growth as economic growth, that is, of capital accumulation and aggregate national income, standardized in the quantitative gauge of GDP, is more recent than we care to remember. It originated during the immediate postwar period and the reconstruction of European economies under American influence. The notion of growth as a process of linear economic expansion is a conceptual invention of industrialism, which replaced notions of the economy as an organic and ecologic system.[2] Linked to this reconceptualization of growth was a move, in socialist debates, from conceptions of growth as culture and human development to economic prosperity as the foundation of working class advancement.[3] Notions of individual improvement and human growth became linked to industrialism, and industrialism itself became understood as a culture of improvement, contrary to the way in which utopian socialist thinkers saw industrialism as the destruction of individual—and cultural— growth. Industrialism became equated with progress, not least in the productivism of Swedish social democracy.[4]

The Third Way draws on these tensions in debates on growth in socialist history, from utopian thinkers such as William Morris and Raymond Williams in the United Kingdom and Rickard Sandler in Sweden, to the theoreticians of industrial affluence such as Anthony Crosland, Ernst Wigforss, and Tage Erlander. However, it also draws on the legacies of the last decades. The Third Way contains continuities from the critique of affluence of the late 1960s, as well as from a neoliberal concept of growth, linked to freedom and entrepreneurship.

These different strands of thought are reflected in the specific meaning of the concept of growth in the knowledge economy. Because growth stems from the expansion of human capital, which occurs through processes of learning, the notions of growth and learning become almost synonymous. As such, learning is conceptualized not only as the cultivation of individual character but as a process of economic expansion. There is de facto a double bind in the contemporary notion of growth, where the term *growth* refers both to a process of economic accumulation and to a process of individual growth. Growth discourses of the Third Way are concerned not only with notions of productivity and profit but also with notions of self-improvement and self-fulfilment. These economic and individual processes are presumed to be frictionless and virtually identical.

This double bind is mirrored in almost all key metaphors of the value production in contemporary economic discourse. It is also clearly expressed in the rise of education as a central means not only of social but of economic reform, indeed as a new form of industrial policy.[5] Modern education policies are the means for both economic and social rationalization and for the self-exploration of curious, innovative individuals. The same is true for cultural policy, which also emerged as a new form of growth policy in the 1990s.[6]

This double bind of growth is not new in the history of social democracy, nor is it new in the history of capitalism. Rather, the idea of industrial progress, throughout the history of social democracy, has also taken the form of disciplining individuals, of the political creation of industrial man, a process that can be seen as the accommodation of values of self-fulfilment with the demands of technology and economic modernization. There is a central tension in social democracy's notion of modernization between connotations to industrial change and to individual development. Indeed, social democracy's notion of emancipation is inherently related to its notion of efficiency. Its various modernization discourses have emphasized the relationship between improvement on the individual level and the aggregate effects in terms of economic and social progress. Consequently, there are strong links in social democratic discourse among the elements of improvement, growth, emancipation, efficiency, and even culture. In Third Way discourse, it is these tensions that are reflected in the parties' rhetoric of freeing the potential of all and in growth policies aimed at turning this potential into productive capital.

Exploring Potential

In both countries, the period beginning with the mid-1990s has seen the creation of growth strategies organized around human potential, knowledge, and creativity. The SAP came back to power after the 1994 election with a new growth program for the knowledge age. In this program, the concept of economic growth (*tillväxt*) was redefined as human creativity (*skapande*) and represented as a natural process of human growth and fulfilment. Indeed it was conceptualized with the term *växande*, which means human growth, as if human growth and economic accumulation were the same process. Growth was a question of humankind wanting to "dream, think, and create." It originated in "the human thirst for knowledge."[7] In the United Kingdom, policy spoke more bluntly of the economic necessity of "tapping the potential of all." The Competitiveness White Paper of 1998, *Our Competitive Future*, argued that the route to competitiveness in the new economy lay in "the way we exploit our most valuable assets: our knowledge, skills, and creativity."[8] In this way, human potential and creativity came to occupy a central position in a new social democratic strategy for the creation of prosperity, as, indeed, new forms of goods to exploit and put to use. While Swedish discourse was more romantic—"together we explore the infinite potential of humanity"— the message was the same, namely, making the most of national brainpower to be competitive in the global race for knowledge. The Swedish Innovation Strategy, in words that echoed the European Lisbon Strategy, spoke of making Sweden the most competitive knowledge-based economy in Europe by 2010:[9]

This redefinition of growth as a question of creativity, potential, and talent has led to new framings around education and learning as policies as part of the growth strategy aimed at bringing out the productive potential of the people. The process of innovation begins, as the Swedish Innovation Strategy puts it, in innovative people. Because growth policies must foster innovative minds, policies for education and early learning have become increasingly charged with teaching creativity and fostering young people's capacities for original ideas and actions with, as it were, bringing out the talents of every child.[10]

In the knowledge age, to "leave no child behind" is not just a moral but an economic imperative: "A nation the size of ours simply cannot afford to waste the abilities of any child, discard the potential of any young person, leave untapped the talents of any adult."[11]

In Sweden, the old institution of the preschool, *förskolan*, has gained new emphasis because it is now seen as the first stepping-stone in lifelong learning. Thus preschool education received its first curriculum in 1998; the aim of early learning was defined as fostering a culture of learning, through play, pedagogical instruction, and fun, thereby also fostering creativity. It is through children's play that vital processes of creativity and interaction, the social dispositions of learning individuals, are created. In social democratic rhetoric, the objective of reform of preschool education was described as to help children grow and develop their talents. Traditionally, Swedish social democracy rejects what is called the commercialization of childhood, and this position was also echoed in the 1990s, as it was stated that early learning must "let children be children" and should not apply the demands of working life on the youngest.[12] Meanwhile, the Swedish Innovation Strategy included the organization of a national program for entrepreneurship, from preschool to high school, for the purpose of teaching creativity and fostering positive attitudes toward entrepreneurship and risk taking. In early learning, this strategy was oriented toward the stimulation of problem solving through children's play, whereas in high school it allowed students to set up small companies of their own.[13] In this manner, preschool education was directly linked to growth and entrepreneurship.

Creativity, potential, and talent are all notions that take on a very specific meaning in the growth discourses of the Third Way. In both countries, creative thought is defined as the capacity to think critically and make a difference, see new solutions to problems, and come up with original ideas. Creativity is risk taking, initiative, and the ability to see new combinations of knowledge. Creativity is what gives pupils the opportunity to become innovative, enterprising, and capable of leadership, all qualities that are ultimately defined by the entrepreneur. Policies aimed at fostering creativity are about helping young people gain self-esteem and helping them pursue their particular interests and talents—helping them grow as individuals. In Sweden, there was a new focus on children's culture in the 1990s, with government investments in art and literature for children as something that would help children grow and give them the means with which to realize their innermost ambitions.[14] But "growing" here referred to the highly ambiguous process of both individual growth and economic growth, a process of learning wherein children were to become creative, not only for their own sake but also in the hope that they will grow up to become the next generation of competitive entrepreneurs. In the United Kingdom, putting creativity on the national curriculum was first suggested in the Business Manifesto in 1997. It was then taken up in the Schools White Paper in 1997 and resulted in the creation of a national curriculum for creativity. In the famous words of Blair, "entrepreneurship doesn't begin in the boardroom, it begins in the classroom."[15]

Entrepreneurs are the crucial link in the process of wealth creation in the knowledge economy because entrepreneurs are those individuals in society who turn the amorphous and nebulous mass of original ideas into useful knowledge, that is, knowledge that can become market commodities in the form of competitive products or services. As with other raw materials, the potential value of talent and creativity depends on finding the applicability and use that turn individual creativity into gold and allow nations to move up the ladder of value-added production. The contemporary notion of creativity is one that is inherently related to the idea of use and applicability. As such, it reflects a highly normative idea of what knowledge and creativity are. It is not creativity in itself that is at a premium but those forms of creativity that can be put to use. The ultimate meaning of this is that the process of human growth is defined by market applicability and commercialization.

This is a notion of creativity that is explicitly informed by the notion of innovation in the new economy, that is, a notion of development that is no longer that of invention, hence the process of thinking up new ideas or products, but rather the process of constantly finding new uses and new applications.[16] Creativity denotes a kind of economic expansion that is about the constant development of new ideas and new uses. This is a reflection of the understanding of modernization as a process of constant, accelerating change. In a world of perpetual innovation, competitive advantage has to be reasserted constantly, and the skills of the workforce need to be continually upgraded; otherwise, competitiveness will decline. Therefore, the meanings of *creativity, talent,* and *potential* are intrinsically related to the needs of the new economy and to a specific notion of useful knowledge in the knowledge economy. Ultimately, creativity is about fostering creative workers who are capable of thinking up new opportunities for themselves in a changing world:[17]

> Pupils who are creative will be prepared for a rapidly changing world, where they may have to adapt to several careers in a lifetime. Many employers want people who see connections, have bright ideas, are innovative, communicate . . . and are able to solve problems. In other words, they want creative people.[18]

Learning and the Cultivation of the Mind

These changes in the notion of creativity to a kind of individualized modernization process—where the purpose of originality is to be risk taking, entrepreneurial, and use-minded—reflect the new mode of governance, discussed in previous chapters as the governance of culture, attitudes, and dispositions. The emphasis on early learning and children stems from the perception that learning is not primarily about acquiring skills but about aptitudes or even cultural norms, and as such it needs to be forged in the individual from its very early years. This is a very specific understanding of improvement as a process that takes place within people, in the form of individual adaptation to changing demands for skills and attitudes. Learning, in the United Kingdom, is "a culture of continuous self-improvement," the "continuous education and development of the mind and the imagination."[19] This is a rhetoric that falls back on historical legacies in social democracy's ideas of education as a tool for the cultivation of competent, educated citizens. But it is also a perspective that seems to run counter to important strands of thought in the history of social democracy—to do with equality and democracy.

The Third Way gives new relevance to a central tension in social democracy's outlook on education between education as a utopian ideal concerned with self-fulfillment and autonomy, on the one hand, and a technocratic orientation that sees in education a means with which to create productive workers, equipped with the skills and competences needed for the more efficient functioning of capitalism, on the other. In the history of social democracy, both of these strategies have an emancipatory bearing but in radically different ways—the former acts as a critique that rejects an education system and a concept of knowledge that reproduces the values of the prevailing production order, while the other identifies the improvement of that very order as the route to reform. To socialist thinkers, such as R. H. Tawney or Rickard Sandler, education was the process of discovering a more fulfilled self and of fostering a radical ideal of equality. Education was a means for fulfilling potential in the sense of escaping the fragmentation of the mind caused by industrialism and the alienation of the worker by the machine, that is, of restoring the self.[20]

In Sweden, the tradition of *folkbildning*, the self-education movements and study circles of the early labor movement, stemmed from just such an egalitarian ideal, even if this also merged with a strong disciplining emphasis on the creation of the socialist self. A key to educational debates in the history of Swedish social democracy is the tension between the notions of *bildning* and *utbildning*. *Bildning* lacks an English translation but could be translated as cultivation or civilization and is close to the German term *Bildung*, which signifies a process of self-exploration and self-cultivation. It identifies learning and knowledge as the tools with which to understand the world, and it has strong historic connotations to high culture and elite education. *Bildning* stands in contrast to *utbildning*, education, particularly in the form of skills and vocational training. *Folkbildning* came about historically as a rejection of this divide between academic studies and vocational training and drew on radical discourses of knowledge as the tool with which to understand the power structures of society and participate in its shaping. *Folkbildning* was built on principles of mutuality and freedom; it was turning workers into socially and politically aware citizens. The self-education movement remains an important institution in Swedish society.[21]

The notion of knowledge in the social democratic tradition is, thus, deeply associated with self-cultivation as a form of emancipation, as the process of becoming aware of social and economic structures in society to be able to question them. Education was part of a social democratic critique of the capitalist economy and the privileges of power in capitalist society. This conception of education as a radical tool started to change in the postwar period, as social democracy increasingly identified education as a means with which to create a skilled, suitable workforce adapted for economic and technological change and capable of delivering the productive economy.[22] The expansion of education, under Erlander in Sweden and Wilson in the United Kingdom, was linked to a human capital argument, in which the "cultivation of the mind" was essentially the process of creating skilled workers for the industrial economy. In the 1950s and 1960s, extending educational opportunity was part of social democracy's project to create the industrial economy. As the Norwegian historian Francis Sejersted points out, the productivism and growth orientation of Swedish social democracy implied a deeply technocratic outlook on knowledge. Human capital theory was a strong component of the creation of comprehensive education in Sweden in the 1960s, a project later dismissed by a radical generation as the "knowledge factories" of standardized learning.[23]

This productivist streak around education mirrors in contemporary social democratic notions of competence, employability, and life-long learning. New Labour's outlook on education clearly draws on such a technocratic strand in British laborism going back to the Webbs, Crosland, Wilson, and Callaghan. To Wilson, education was about the creation of an educated working class for the scientific age.[24] To New Labour, lifelong learning is the creation of knowledge man, the constantly learning, flexible, entrepreneurial person. Policies of lifelong learning are about creating "a well educated, well-equipped and adaptable labour force," capable of a life in the knowledge economy.[25] Part of New Labour's skills strategy was the creation of a University for Industry, modeled on the Open University. The latter was created in 1967 as part of a White Heat attempt to create a university based on distance learning to compensate for workers being denied access to academic education. The purpose of the University for Industry was to use ICT and wireless learning to provide the skills needed by business and "change attitudes to learning and acquiring skills in the new century."[26]

In Sweden, the expansion of higher education in regional colleges in the 1990s was motivated by the need to fight unemployment and increase the competence of the workforce.[27] At the same time, the idea of the knowledge society brought about a renaissance for alternative notions of education and the tradition of *folkbildning*. In social democratic discourse of the 1990s and 2000s, the ethos of *folkbildning* as that of fostering alternative values of education was declared more important than ever in an era of rapid technological shifts and increased need for critical thinking. *Folkbildning* was thus seen as part of a public responsibility to guarantee the prevalence of an alternative radical ethos to the commercialization and marketization of other areas of education but also as an alternative path for individuals who had fallen out of the mainstream education system.[28] With the emergence of a social democratic growth narrative in the period from the mid-1990s, the notion of *bildning* also saw a remarkable resurgence, viewed as the route to personal advancement through new means, such as competence saving, lifelong learning, and employer-led training courses. The expansion of higher education through the creation of regional colleges and the government drive for improving the skills of the long-term unemployed in the *kunskapslyftet* were defined as policies for *bildning*. However, this was a new and treacherous notion of *bildning*, which increasingly focused on marketable skills, employability, and entrepreneurship and thus seems closer to technocratic ideals than to the radical ideas of *folkbildning*.

In this manner, when social democracy today speaks of the freeing of potential and the liberation of selves that stem from learning and education in the knowledge society, it silences a central conflict in the history of social democracy—the conflict between radically different interpretations of the real meaning of "the cultivation of the mind." The Third Way, with its references to growth as human growth and its emphasis on education as a dual process of economic and individual improvement, ignores such tensions in notions of knowledge and education and presumes that self-improvement and economic improvement are the same thing. When New Labour speaks of creating a culture of self-improvement, the idea of self-improvement that this contains is, despite the emphasis on love of art, music, and poetry, essentially an idea of improvement that is about acquiring the dispositions in demand in the new economy. To "equip ourselves with knowledge and with understanding" is linked to innovation and entrepreneurship. The richer life that the arts can bring is instrumental to "developing the intellectual capital that is now at the centre of a nation's competitive strength." Fostering an enquiring mind and nourishing the soul creates added value for business. Learning breaks vicious circles of underachievement and builds confidence and independence, the tools for individual achievement and success on the labor markets of the new economy.[29] In this manner, Tawney's radical notion of self-exploration becomes merged with a Fabian idea of productivity because the Third Way presumes that individual self-fulfillment and market efficiency ultimately lead to the same goal, namely, a more knowledgeable society made up of learned individuals.

Politics of Competitive Advantage: Branding Identity

In both countries, the growth discourses of the new economy tie into narratives of British and Swedish identity because the values of national identity are also defined as economic values and sources of growth and prosperity. Thus, discourses on creativity go one step farther than hitherto discussed; creativity is not only something that resides in people and can be fostered and brought out by politics, but it is also something that resides in the common cultural heritage of the nation-state and is rooted in collective memory and history. Creativity is defined in both the United Kingdom and Sweden as something particular to British and Swedish identity—a national inclination toward thinking up new and good ideas. Swedes are a "creative and curious nation." The United Kingdom is "an island of creativity." This is, in fact, an integral part of the competition strategy. Because both countries rule out the possibility that European countries can fend off the competition from "Chindia" with low wages, they must compete on the higher part of the value-added chain by being original, creative, and novel; by the ability to "lead and not take after others."[30] There are clear assumptions in this of a new global division of labor, where the European creativity legacy is a competitive advantage. The specifics of an Enlightenment heritage in European culture become sources of growth.[31]

In this manner, the cultural heritage becomes a kind of bank of creativity that can be put to use in the new economy, a virtual pool of knowledge into which one can tap. Third Way growth policies have brought about a new interest in the historic heritage, architecture and design, and libraries and museums as national creative resources and sources of learning. Just as the understanding of education as a central means for growth has brought about new affinities between education and economic policy, the development of new growth policies has also meant a rapprochement between policy areas such as culture and trade and the creation of a plethora of new institutions such as councils and task forces for design and the creative industries. Swedish and British art, design products, and music are exhibited at world fairs as markers of progress, just as, at the dawn of industrialization, it was industrial success and sophisticated social policies that were on display.[32] In the intangible world of the new economy, appearance, form, and the values associated with a specific brand are key to competitive advantage. Following this logic, national identity and attributes have also become integral parts of growth strategies. Today, creating a national brand name is a strategic concern for governments increasingly engaged in something that might be described as a capitalization of national stereotypes, a process in which these are also constantly reasserted.

Part of New Labour's strategy of national rejuvenation was the renewal of the British trademark and the image of the United Kingdom. In the 1990s, New Labour tried to represent itself as a youthful political project not only through the celebration of pop music and a trendy art scene but also through its economic appraisal of the creative industries—the successful export commodities of Britpop, Britart, British cuisine, and British fashion.[33] Much of this is remembered as "Cool Britannia." Its more opportunistic expressions, such as the famous Downing Street receptions where the prime minister mingled with pop stars and artists, have been much ridiculed, but they were part of a wider reappraisal of the role of culture in contemporary capitalism.[34]

The origins of Cool Britannia were in a 1997 Demos report entitled *Britain TM: Renewing Our Identity.* Its message was that the British trademark was in a sad state. During the decades of decline, the very notion of being British had gone from that of a nation proudly ruling the world to a "backward-looking has-been, a theme park world of royal pageantry and rolling green hills, where draughts blow through people's houses." As such, being British had become a major liability to British industry in a time when appearance was at a premium. The solution was bluntly put as "rebranding." It was necessary, for reasons of competitive advantage, to rethink the very meaning of Britishness into something more modern and dynamic. The United Kingdom was a trademark that needed careful managing, just as corporations manage their brand names and labels. A well-managed national identity has positive externalities for national firms and is, therefore, a task for government, part of social democracy's reinvented role of state and its responsibility to create the best conditions for business.[35]

The idea of Cool Britannia drew on a curious mix of the postmodern historian Benedict Anderson's notion of imagined community, as it spoke of the need for new shared stories, and a crude management approach that was directly borrowed from the corporate sphere.[36] History became a source of images and narratives about the common past, which could be turned into a competitive label. Rebranding, to Demos, had to be about a new fit between elements of the historic narrative of Britishness and the future. This new fit was somewhere between the Empire, cricket, and multiculturalism. Diversity and the postcolonial legacies of Empire were thus made part of the notion of creativity as a national attribute, through the celebration of British writers, artists, and designers such as Salman Rushdie, Nitin Sahwney, and Oswald Boateng.[37] Diversity, however, also gave rise to core tensions in the project. It proved difficult to airbrush collective memories of Britishness from less marketable experiences of Empire. The Demos report's naïve suggestion that a successful rebranding of the United Kingdom might require a "tour of the Monarch of all sites where there is still bitterness about Britain's past—from Ireland to

Iran" was repudiated by the report of the British Commission on the Future
of Multi-Ethnic Britain, which stated that the "Rule Britannia mindset" was a
major problem in the rethinking of the imagined community of Britain:

> Britain seems incapable of shaking off its imperialist identity. The Brits do
> appear to believe that "Britons never never never shall be slaves" . . . But it is
> impossible to colonise three-fifths of the world . . . without enslaving oneself.
> Our problem has been that Britain has never understood itself and has stead-
> fastly refused to see and understand itself through the prism of our experience
> of it, here and in its coloniser mode.[38]

This tension between attempts to accommodate the colonial past and turn
it into competitive advantage, on the one hand, and more critical notions of
diversity on the other resurfaces regularly in New Labour's debates on Britishness, testifying to the contested nature of identity and the fine line between
progressive identity politics and populism.[39]

Diversity is a highly contested issue in Sweden and, more than anything,
Swedish creative industries seem concerned with the reproduction of images
of Sweden as a country of green forests and blond women. Nation branding
emerged as a central part of the growth strategy in the 1990s in connection
with a new emphasis on export commodities such as pop music or Swedish design. In 1998, a government bill on design identified design policies as
crucial to selling Swedish products, by giving them a particularly Swedish
identity. Swedish design had a competitive edge that had to be associated internationally with something called "the image of Sweden," *Sverigebilden*.[40]
In 2004, the Swedish Innovation Strategy defined the projection of a positive
image of Sweden abroad as a crucial part of the innovative strategy, part of a
government strategy to "make Sweden visible, highlight the values the country stands for and the opportunities it offers."[41]

What then is the image of Sweden? Paradoxically, it is the values defined
in the Party's 2001 Program as values in conflict with commercialism, which
are the components of the brand name of Sweden. As in the case of the Cool
Britannia debate, attempts to brand Sweden depart in understandings of particular Swedish assets and Swedish particularity. In Sweden, these are the values of Swedishness—solidarity, cooperation, and equality. In a speech on the
image of Sweden, the Minister for Culture Leif Pagrotsky spoke of the legacies of Olof Palme and Anna Lindh as traditions that "evoke respect and add
to the positive image of Sweden." More than anything, the image of Sweden

draws on the famous model of welfare, which, "even when some find it loath-some, distinguishes us from Swaziland or Switzerland."[42]

Gender equality, solidarity, and democracy are all parts of the brand name of progressive Sweden, one that no longer connotes the crisis-tinged notion of Sweden in the early 1990s but is, rather, a fundamentally positive asset. Profiling Sweden, then, is about banking on the values of the People's Home and its symbolic value as the role model of the world, "the decent society":

> Sweden needs profiling. Profiling means to be different, to have a profile that stands out and does not blend in with the wallpaper: to go against the tide, to dare to take a different course and express different values. We have in Sweden a number of values and opinions that get much attention. For instance, we put a lot of money in soft, human values in our society, things like equality, the environment, children's place in society, family policy. We are a society that in other countries is often seen as a more humane society. This is nothing we should be ashamed of, and we should not try to adapt to others . . . we need to stand up for the fact that this is the way that we have decided in Sweden that we think a decent society should be organized. . . . this is very efficient, very powerful . . .[43]

The progressiveness of the Swedish model—its solidarity, equality, and decency—is, thus, not just a role model in terms of economic and social justice but a marketing strategy for Swedish industry as well.

The rise of nation branding is a good illustration of the turnaround in the political consciousness in both the United Kingdom and Sweden in the decade from the mid-1990s to the mid-2000s, from the humiliating and painful attempts to regain the confidence of international capital for debt-ridden national economies to managing the brand names of success stories. Perhaps Leif Pagrotsky expresses this best when he says "In the 1990s, I sold government bonds, now I'm selling Sweden."[44]

The Value of Culture

In growth strategies of the 1990s, culture became part of a concept of growth having to do explicitly with economic accumulation. This has a particular relevance as seen from within the history of social democracy because culture, as Raymond Williams once pointed out, is a notion of improvement that, in the history of social democracy, is inherently related to self-fulfilment and happiness—"wholeness"—and on a par with the fragmentation and disruption caused by the division of labor that separated the workers from the products of

their work.[45] From its very early history in worker's guilds and Chartism, social democracy has contained a cultural critique of capitalism as the destroyer
of the harmonious working class self. These articulations have varied from the
nostalgic, for instance in the arts and crafts movements and the ideas of William Morris or the socially conservative aesthetics of Swedish arts and crafts,
to the radical, such as Raymond William's genealogical critique of culture and
economy or the egalitarian ideas of *folkbildning*. The Third Way, in its articulations of a cultural growth policy, seems to break with these historic notions of
culture as an alternative order of value and to transform it into a market commodity like other commodities.[46]

The emphasis on the creative industries in the United Kingdom has been
paralleled in Sweden in the development of a new social democratic cultural
policy that has increasingly identified culture, design, and music as crucial
export commodities. In 1995, a government White Paper on culture argued
for the role of culture in the new economy as part of the innovation strategy.[47]
These ideas went back to the 90s Program (*90-talsprogrammet*), which called
for a radical cultural policy; however, they also seemed to mark an important break with social democracy's ideological legacies around culture. The
SAP's first cultural policy program, drawn up in 1952, came about as a reaction against the commercialization of popular culture and the emergence of
new culture markets, a tendency that the party rejected.[48] This was strengthened in the 1970s with the development of a social democratic cultural policy,
the role of which was to protect cultural expression as a realm beyond the
market.[49] This rejection of the commercialization of culture was reiterated in
cultural policies in the 1990s, and the party's 2001 Program explicitly rejects
the commercialization of cultural expression, "a development whereby capital
and market dominate and commercialise culture."[50] Culture is not a means of
market making but a means of personal growth and autonomy: "Knowledge
and culture give people the opportunity to grow and broaden their perspectives, free people's thoughts and their creative abilities. This is a crucial balance to the constant attempts of economic and social elites to grasp power
over thought." However, it is also a means of economic growth: "Knowledge
and culture are the tools for human freedom and growth or social progress
and economic growth."[51]

This reflects the ambiguity in the contemporary notion of growth, and the
rejection of commercialization is also, interestingly, at odds with the SAP's
own economic policies. Nevertheless, Swedish social democracy is troubled

by the adverse effects of commercialization on the cultural access of under-privileged groups, and it warns against the market as a threat to the diversity of cultural expression.[52] In contrast, New Labour, in line with the way that it sees the market as a driver of creativity and consumerism as an expression of identity, has identified the commercialization and marketization of culture as means of democratization and of spreading cultural access to the underprivi-leged. New Labour links culture as commodity with democracy and access, which, as we shall see, is also the case in education. Its celebration of both pop culture and pop art clearly contains such an idea of marketization as a way of spreading culture to the masses. This has led to what critics see as a kind of ob-jectification of the "masses," where cultural policies also draw on ideas of the cultural preferences of the "people."[53]

Social democracy's identification of culture as a commodity clearly draws on legacies from the neoliberal policies that, in the 1980s, exposed cultural institutions to market models based on principles of supply and demand. But the Third Way also seems to contain a much larger notion of cultural value as something that is fundamentally about individual happiness and social pro-gress. In Sweden, design is not just an export commodity; it is also about indi-vidual welfare through better homes and work environments. Design "for all" is about enabling and empowering weak groups. In this sense, good design becomes a means not only for competitive export products but for reconciling economic and social change, making sure that physical planning takes into account the needs of disabled groups.[54] In the United Kingdom, culture has gained importance for the fostering of strong communities and civic renewal. The cultural secretary Tessa Jowell repeatedly emphasized culture as having a distinct value on its own terms. Culture was "a way of daring to aspire to the future." Culture was a "hug of love," a way of "finding one's place" in times of rootlessness and alienation. In both countries, culture is stressed as source of stability and identity and of an intangible feeling of belonging. [55]

This emphasis on culture as a means of forging trust, social cohesion, and identity stands in a rather obvious but highly complex relationship to impres-sions of pervasive economic and technological change and their disruptive ef-fects on individual lives and collective identities. Culture emerges as a means of holding us together in a time when allegedly everything comes undone. The collective memory, heritage, history, libraries, and archives become part of an identity politics that seems to contain a reassurance of stability in a changing world. Policies for promoting access to the collective memory, for instance in the digitalization of archives or the opening up of forgotten museum collections, are a way of strengthening the ties between individual and society. Ironically, the heritage of the old industrial society—old mills, factories, and manufacturing plants—acquires a new role in this, as the remnants of working class culture that somehow constitute the link between a past of manual work and the electronic future.[56] In postindustrial cities like Glasgow, Newcastle, Malmö, and Göteborg, culture is a source of regeneration. In the United Kingdom, this process of urban transformation has been compared politically to the way that, in Victorian times, architecture and design were the means to forge a public ethos and create public spaces that transmitted a sense of grandeur and hope for the future.[57] As Minister for the Creative Industries James Purnell put it, "Once we were the workshop of the world, now we have to become the world's creative hub."[58]

This reflects a search for order in which economic and cultural values merge. Like education, culture becomes a means for both industrial success and the creation of happier individuals with a stronger attachment to economy and society. This is an ambiguous process. Contemporary social democracy seems to partly appreciate the radical potential of culture, perhaps in the absence of other, political utopian visions. Its economic policies represent not only the commodification of culture but also an attempt to give it value. Cultural policies in the 1990s broke with decades of chronic underfunding.[59] But the couching of the cultural in economic terms also leads to a process in which cultural value becomes economic good, and the role of culture in social democratic ideology changes fundamentally. The approach that the Third Way takes to culture, as the source of a new creative industrial revolution, is potentially devastating for the idea of culture as critique. The Third Way's most radical cultural articulations define culture as an expression of individualism and as a kind of self-fulfillment that is instrumental to finding one's place in the new world and becoming a full citizen. These are definitions and statements that, today, are very close to labor market discourse because the Third Way sees productive participation as the primary definition of self-fulfillment. To "find one's place and purpose" is a rhetorical construction very close to the idea of finding a use of one's talents and skills, which reflects the ideas of applicability that underpin the new economy. Ultimately, these values are connected to the economic. Hence, the British Young Roots Program, designed to give young people a way to connect with their heritage, is also motivated by its effects on fostering creativity and entrepreneurship. Beyond its importance for our sense of identity, the historical heritage is also a new industry, "mine in an era when other mines are closing."[60]

In this manner, while the Third Way embeds its notion of culture within its larger narrative of economic and social improvement, it silences its potential role as a reaction against the effects of new production orders and new technologies. William Morris's ideas of beauty are no longer a radical argument for equality and social transformation but an argument for the commercialization of marketable products, just as design, in Sweden, despite the political insistence on its role in a welfare society, is ultimately about competitive export commodities. Industrialism, with its mass production and erosion of craftsmanship was, to Morris, incompatible with art, and culture, to Morris, was a radical emancipatory ideal. Only from the equality brought about by socialism could art and culture spring.[61] In the same spirit, Swedish social democracy embarked on large-scale projects of the democratization of culture in the postwar period, for instance through its attempt to put art in public spaces such as the *tunnelbana*, the Stockholm subway. To contemporary social democracy, cultural values and market values are virtually the same. This stands in sharp contrast to Raymond William's notion of culture as a reflection on what values in society are valuable to us. In William's words, culture is "the court of appeal in which real values are determined," in contrast to the "fictitious" values of the market.[62]

There is also something inherently nostalgic in the Third Way's approach to culture, which seems to defuse its potential as utopian critique in social democratic ideology. The idea of Cool Britannia came about in a distinctly postimperial moment with the end of the lease on Hong Kong, a moment, moreover, of millennium spleen.[63] New Labour's grand cultural project for the millennium was the Millennium Dome, built as a museum of the future in the London borough of Greenwich, through which the Prime Meridian runs. The Dome stood as a curious monument to the new economy, in an explicit flirtation with the world exhibitions of the Victorian era.[64] In Sweden, the design strategy of the 1990s was intimately concerned with memories of the People's Home, through constant revocation of the aesthetic legacies of 1920s and 1930s functionalism. The recent, massive interest in Sweden in the interwar period has led to the reestablishment of social engineers Alva and Gunnar Myrdal in Swedish political culture, cast in the 1990s as dangerous social utopians, rethought in the 2000s as legitimate advocates of rational social change and creators of a modernist aesthetics.[65] The 1990s saw a virtual gold rush for functionalist objects in Scandinavian and international auction houses. The successes of Swedish design as an export commodity draw on these images of Sweden as a rationally planned society of continuous social reform. Inherent in this is a nostalgia that goes back to the Swedish idea of modernization as a process of safeguarding glories of the past.

Conclusion

As the Swedish example testifies, social democracy's contemporary appraisal of culture is ambiguous, and its debate on the role of culture, creativity, and identity is a contested field, one that perhaps is best described as a field of competing discourses around the value of culture. There is a fine line between appraising and evaluating in the sense of giving value to the noneconomic, intangible, and immeasurable values of culture, on the one hand, and turning cultural expression into commodities, on the other.

New Labour's infatuation with the pop music scene ended when the New Musical Express rejected the New Deal for the young unemployed because it took away the unemployment benefits that had created the conditions of survival for young musicians in postindustrial areas.[66] Pop music was appreciated as an important source of urban regeneration and a successful export product but not as a political expression. Ironically, many of the successes of the British creative industries emerged from unemployment and social marginalization in cities like Manchester or London and were also important sources of political expression, indeed, critics of Thatcherism. Although its cultural policies have embraced postmodern culture, they have done so in terms of individual consumerism and not as political critique. New Labour drew very selectively on the critical cultural studies that came from the British New Left in the late 1960s. It understands cultural representation as an appeal to individual consumerist preferences but not as a way of challenging power structures. As Timothy Bewes puts it, this is a cultural policy, where the relationship between culture and politics is defined by the absence of any cultural or ideological vision distinct from the economic one and where culture per definition affirms the values of the capitalist world.[67]

6 Knowledge Societies

Just as the industrial economy brought with it ideas and discourses on the industrial society, the idea of the knowledge economy brings with it new ideas of the knowledge society. Part of the notion of modernization, in contemporary politics just as in the politics of the past, is the idea that technological and economic change must be matched by a corresponding process of modernization of the social sphere. The idea of the knowledge society, as it has existed in social science and politics since the 1970s, is clearly an analogue of the idea of the network, just as the understanding of the industrial society was modeled on the ideas of the social hierarchy of the industrial factory.[1] Ideas of information technology and network production lead to a social structure consisting of interconnected individuals. The idea of post-Fordist production as flat and ahierarchical is mirrored in notions of a society of stakeholders who are equals. As we have seen, the consequence of this is a breakdown of the idea of class and collective interests as the foundation for political action and, thus, a rethinking of the very role of social democracy in the process of change. Old ideas of social change as driven by "mechanistic" change, by the dialectics of interest mediation and class struggle, is replaced, in knowledge capitalism, by ideas of social change as evolutionary and harmonious, a process of organic growth and inclusion.

Social democracy is intimately involved in this reconceptualization of the social. The idea of the knowledge economy has important implications for its understanding of social needs and of the relationship between individual and collective advancement. The idea of poverty, in an era of knowledge, learning, and individual self-fulfilment and drive, becomes the New Labour notion of a poverty of aspirations, the individual lack of hope and ambition. Structural social inequalities, considered in relation to an organic idea of the social fabric, become a question of in-exclusion. Redistribution, in an economy driven by opportunity, is the redistribution of the opportunity that the new economy is presumed to produce. [2]

These social articulations are all ambiguous. While they are overwhelmingly individualistic, focused on individual attributes, they also contain a certain structural, indeed, social emphasis. The notion of a poverty of aspiration, for instance, or the problematic concept of equality of opportunity focuses on individual dispositions and capacities, such as the capacity to seize opportunity. However, they also contain a certain emphasis on the structural constraints that determine opportunity—the social structures that "lock in potential." The Third Way tends to translate these social problems in cultural terms, in line with its cultural approach to political economy. Social policies become cultural policies, aimed at the behavior and dispositions of individuals. [3]

Social democracy's idea of the networked, learning society is clearly a reaction against neoliberalism in its emphasis on the interdependence of the social and the economic. As discussed in previous chapters, the Third Way embodies a rapprochement between social and economic policies. Learning and education, in Third Way discourse, are not "just" social issues; they are directly concerned with economic growth. On the one hand, this means that social democracy brings back, after decades of neoliberalism, a serious concern with social inequalities and social justice because it sees them as the core of a rational organization of society and economy. On the other, there is something in the Third Way's social discourses that seems to turn the postulates of welfare capitalism on their heads. [4] The conceptual invention of the social in the mid-nineteenth-century debate on the social question was linked to the rearticulation of social problems and poverty as processes beyond the control of the individual and as consequences of economic transformations. Competition, market liberalization, free competition, and the elusion of social responsibility in industrial capitalism had destroyed the social organization. Consequently, the relationship between the social and the economic was deeply antagonistic. Social policies that intervened into the organization of production were a means to restore efficiency. This is the meaning of the European notion of welfare capitalism: state-led intervention into capitalist structures to bring about a more efficient organization of economy and society. It is different, of course, from liberal notions of welfare capitalism. The latter are linked to philanthropy and corporate social responsibility, to notions of mutuality, self-help, and market liberalism. Indeed, the nineteenth-century European debate on a social economy was a reaction to the variant of laissez-faire politics, which was then termed Manchester liberalism because it was controlled by the market interests of British cotton manufacturers.[5] New Labour is a child of these liberal legacies.[6]

New Labour's notion of the social as "community" was a reaction to an "old Left" vision of society as something mechanistic and violent, created by a social struggle that it saw as historically specific to the industrial society. In Sweden, social policies seem to stand in continuity with legacies of the People's Home and the SAP's postwar ideas of a Strong Society. However, the notion of society—*samhälle*—has, arguably, been one of the very central points of change in Swedish political culture from the late 1970s onwards. While the SAP in the 1990s returned to rhetoric from its past ideologies, the relationship between society and market became a growing fissure below the surface.

The next chapter deals specifically with contemporary social democracy's ideas of the welfare state. In this chapter, we are concerned with how the parties understand the social sphere and the relationship between the knowledge economy and the knowledge *society*. In short, what kind of a social vision is the idea of the knowledge society to contemporary social democracy?

Community

Part of New Labour's modernization project was the attempt to rethink the social sphere and domesticate or settle the chaos of social life into something more coherent and organized. The notion of community, which it placed at the heart of Labour ideology with the rewriting of the Labour Party constitution in 1994, captured this quest for social harmony.[7]

Community is a concept with complex historical legacies in British political culture, from the ethical socialism of Tawney to elements of liberalism, social democracy, and social conservatism. The concept might best be described, as other parts of New Labour ideology, as a number of subplots, ideologies, and counterideologies ranging from the socially authoritarian in discourses on crime and asocial behavior to radical and even utopian discourses on the transformative role of architecture in the city landscapes of Glasgow and Liverpool or increased citizen participation in politics and services through the use of ICT.[8] However, while the notion of community has complex origins, New Labour's communitarianism has drawn very selectively on some elements in the communitarian tradition, thus silencing others. As the philosopher Sarah Hale has pointed out, New Labour leaned on Tawney's fraternal notion of community but silenced his critique of affluence and his call for socialism in favor of an approach to communitarianism that drew on governing individual behavior in the name of the common good.[9]

New Labour's platform was the idea of a widespread social crisis. Its very first policies in office—the New Deals for the unemployed, working families and communities, and the creation of the Social Exclusion Unit in Downing Street—were attempts to counter social degeneration. New Labour framed this social crisis in specific terms, which departed from social democratic class analysis. From the outset, New Labour put in place a framing around social problems that was distinctly cultural and, in important parts, familiar to American discourses on poverty.[10] As many critics of New Labour have argued, its ideas of the social came with a stereotypical dichotomization of individuals into deserving and undeserving and with pervasive notions of the poor as deviant, dependent, and dangerous. The cultural emphasis on breaking with vicious circles of exclusion by creating a culture of learning and aspiration carried with it a deeply disciplining approach to individual deviance and policies explicitly designed to change individual behavior and attitudes. To New Labour, social crisis was not only the result of economic decline, Thatcher's attack on society, and decades of underinvestment into crucial public services but also the result of the erosion of fundamental social values. It was a crisis narrative explicitly concerned with social order and with a social fabric "tattered and torn."[11]

Communitarianism made a direct appeal to the moral virtues of citizenship, defined by the duties and obligations we owe each other as morally and socially responsible individuals. Social virtues—such as the work ethic, a love of learning, and the sense of obligation—were seen as being fostered in reciprocity and recognition, in the trust relationships that create social order and that provide the basis for a prosperous economy. The central element of the notion of community was the rewriting of the social contract around the strengthening of the responsibility side of social citizenship, in order to break with the individualistic legacies of the late 1960s and the 1980s. New Labour's individualism was thus not a vision of unfettered individuals—but of people enabled by the social web and the historical bonds of virtue. The process of civic renewal came from this revocation of the virtues of citizenship, and the freeing of individual potential stemmed from the realization of fundamental obligations to the community.[12]

At the core of the notion of community was a rethinking of the relationship between individual and collective advancement. In contrast to neoliberalism, New Labour saw individualism as a force for the common good. In this manner, individualism and competition became forces for the good of the community, forces that transcended individual utility (but nevertheless originated in the search for individual utility).[13] The notion of solidarity that underpinned "community" was a solidarity based on the competitive instinct—the instinct that would lead to "prosperity for all." Community became a vision of the social as driven by the quest for self-improvement while, at the same time, recognizing the role of social interdependence for that improvement. The market was at the core of the notion of community. The market, in communitarian terms, must be socially embedded—not so much to keep it from having disruptive effects on the social, nor to steer profit for social causes, but because it is considered crucial for the fostering of the virtues of competition and for the cultivation of aspiration and creativity and the "continuous drive for improvement." Policies such as social entrepreneurship programs and public private partnerships create this culture of improvement by giving the market a social role.[14]

Community was a highly organic view of society. It was a curiously apolitical concept, reflecting New Labour's rejection of conflict. Community was construed as a locus beyond politics, governed by consensus, harmony, and the inculcation of shared values.[15] It saw social change as a quintessentially harmonious process of spontaneous evolution. Community was a self-correcting organism, made up of individuals in "self-help," "self-government," and "mutuality." These bonds of reciprocity, liberated from the disruptive role of state intervention or public bureaucracies, constituted the common good.[16] In the emphasis on mutuality, reciprocity, and interdependence, there was a clear analogy between the notion of community and the idea of the computer network. The American philosopher Amitai Etzioni, whose variant of communitarianism was an important influence on New Labour, frequently defines the social as a web. In his 1997 book *Connexity*, the Downing Street advisor Geoff Mulgan, who was the one to bring Etzioni to New Labour's attention, defined community as individuals striving for self-expression but dependent on their inclusion into a social network for the full realization of their being. To Mulgan, "connexity" was a logical stage of the evolution of social life and a social structure similar to other organic systems, such as the *Gaia*, the biosphere or the electronic network, all systems built on complex interdependence and dependent on order for their survival.[17] The New Labour frenzy around the Internet and information technology as means of governance was an expression of the desire to create new forms of interconnectedness and thus restore the social fabric.[18] This was radically different from social democracy's traditional notions of social struggle. A web, defined by inclusion or exclusion from the network, grows organically. Society, in New Labour ideology of the mid-1990s, was a mechanistic notion, driven by organized interests and labor–capital conflict, a sphere of strife and crippling class interests. Correspondingly, the public, in New Labour discourse, was a sphere controlled by the vested interests of the professions. In contrast, the idea of community represented an organic whole. Trust and mutual feelings of obligation were central social virtues but, and this is equally important, also virtues that had a direct role for the creation of a specific kind of (social) capital.

New Labour's concern with social order was motivated not only by concerns of social cohesion but also by the understanding of economic dynamism as a process that begins in the social. Community, in New Labour thinking, is where aspiration and opportunity are founded. The role of community is to foster the "love of learning," which, in New Labour discourse, is the primary driver of social mobility and economic dynamism. The opportunity economy, therefore, is dependent on intervention into the social to create and redistribute these goods. The preoccupation with the social fabric was a concern not only with social harmony but with the social fabric as the de facto fabricator of human and social capital.[19] As such, there were strong links between the notion of community and the notion of capital.

The term *social capital* had a remarkable impact in political discourse in the 1990s, following the American political scientist Robert Putnam's work.[20] Putnam argued that the social networks of civil society were a crucial factor for the fostering of economic innovation, property rights, and collaboration. His argument that the United States was witnessing the rapid erosion of social capital had a strong influence on the Clinton administration and was an important impetus behind the rise of communitarianism. The concept of social capital has much deeper origins, however. It can be traced back to an American debate on public education in 1916, during which the importance of federal investment in the social capital was likened to the role of capital investment in factory production.[21] Thus, social capital was about the economic interest in rational social organization.

The economic argument around social capital in contemporary economic and political discourse is that it provides the individual with access to a social network that determines the access to opportunity: "It is not what you know, but who you know."[22] It is in social institutions such as the family, the community, and the company, all consisting of mutual reciprocal trust relationships, that aspiration is founded and that the norms of the social contract, such as the sense of duty and the love of learning, are created. As a result, New Labour family policies have contained an emphasis on the role of parents to foster social capital and imbue children with the values of citizenship and commitment to the common good because the family is where the crucial, first, early steps of learning take place.[23] Next to the two-parent family, the company was also seen as an institution crucial for the creation of social capital because it supposedly fosters cooperation and builds trust and loyalty.[24]

The notion of social capital fit in with the Third Way's argument regarding the close relationship between social cohesion and economic efficiency. In many ways, the concept seemed to stand in continuity with a social democratic tradition of marrying the economic and the social and with social democracy's historic notions of the waste generated by social inequality. For instance, the debate on social exclusion was quickly framed as a question of social capital. The notion of social capital was, however, also indicative of the tensions within the Third Way. It attempted to bring social issues into the sphere of economic reasoning. In this sense it contained a kind of social democratic critique of neoliberal economics, similar to the way in which Fabian economics once provided a critique of laissez-faire economics. It was even argued that social capital was a public good.[25]

Social capital discourse contained an important critique of the British class society, particularly the "old boys' network" of public schools and Oxford and Cambridge. Still, the notion of social capital was oddly detached from notions of class or equality. Its emphasis on intervention into social networks tilted toward an authoritarian logic; if social capital is created in networks and social norms, there must be sanctions against those forms of social networks that create bad social capital or destroy social capital. This has led to new means of intervention such as the ASBOs (asocial behavior orders) and to the creation of a socially conservative Respect agenda, institutions that criminalize deviant behaviour.[26] Market virtues were a central aspect of the notion of social capital. Policies such as asset-based welfare have played crucial role in social capital arguments because owning assets is seen as fostering virtues such as being financially literate, entrenching a culture of saving, and cultivating a feeling for property. ILAs and baby bonds, the latter of which are potentially a radical policy of redistribution, have thus been framed within the logic of building social capital.[27] The notion of social capital also failed to provide a theory of public good. Social capital is a concept that falls back on notions of individual good and thus on an individual and economic utility preference. Ultimately, social capital is an individual resource, which provides for individual competitiveness in social hierarchies. In this manner, the notion of social capital illustrates the tension between social democracy's contemporary strategies of socializing capital or capitalizing the social. The notion of social capital clearly contained an embryo for a social critique of capital. However, it was also a distinctly economistic approach to the social, one in which social relations effectively became forms of capital. Despite its socializing tendencies, social capital discourse has been less concerned with the creation of a more social form of capitalism than it has been with finding new ways of creating economic efficiency.[28] The social capital debate also highlights New Labour's unease with ideas of equality, redistribution, and social justice. The framing of social issues within the logic of community has clearly been a strategy for New Labour to address issues of redistribution without speaking of equality, and, indeed, without a critique of capitalism. The emphasis on community has meant that there has been less emphasis, in New Labour politics, on structural factors of society and social problems; rather, it has dismissed "structures" as part of its critique of public responsibility, described as destroying the spontaneous social organization of community.

Society

Communitarianism has not wielded nearly the same influence in Sweden, where political discourse in the 1990s and 2000s was primarily be concerned with universalism and public responsibility. When Amitai Etzioni visited Stockholm in the 1990s, the reception was very different from the one that he had received in Downing Street. There was little understanding from Swedish perspectives of the good in philosophical abstractions around what, to a Swede, are obvious norms of behavior, particularly when these abstractions came from an American. The then–Prime Minister Ingvar Carlsson was, says Etzioni, cold as a fish.[29]

Meanwhile, many similarities exist between the contemporary communitarianism of New Labour and the social philosophy of modern Swedish politics. There is in the Swedish social democratic tradition a reluctance toward more intellectual reasoning around the social contract, a phenomenon linked to the way that the values of the Swedish welfare state are seen as deeply rooted in tradition and history and as a kind of entrenched ethos in the Swedish psyche. This silent presumption of the naturalization of the values of the welfare state is in itself rather close to the postulates of contemporary communitarianism, and it shares many of its limitations, primarily, the appeal to history as common experience and shared identity. In their 2006 book, much discussed in Sweden, the historians Henrik Berggren and Lars Trägårdh argue that the Swedish welfare state resides on a specific notion of Swedishness, a historically rooted sense of the values of solidarity, equality, and individualism as part of the national identity.[30] Exactly such an outlook on the values of the welfare state as the natural values of the Swedish people is an important part of the ideological strategy of Swedish social democracy. Many of social democracy's key ideological elements, first and foremost the notion of the People's Home, were elements that it usurped, in the interwar period, from conservative discourses on national unity and social order.[31] It was this "natural" social democratic order that was questioned in the turbulent and ideologically polarized decades of the 1980s and the 1990s, and the resurgence of the notions of Strong Society and People's Home in social democratic discourse from the mid-1990s must be seen as a way of trying to recreate a kind of hegemony around its social philosophy as if it were truly the values of the people. The former Prime Minister Göran Persson has flirted with communitarian themes in his writings, echoing themes of duty and obligation to the common good and often citing Blair.[32] The return of the notion of the People's Home in the 1990s is also a clear a reaction to a growing debate on multiculturalism and a social and cultural diversity, which social democracy has tended to see as a threat to the overarching community of the welfare state.[33]

The notion of *samhälle*, as it was shaped in Swedish political history, was influenced by German institutionalism, the deeply conservative *Kathedersozialismus*. Historically, it stood for a highly organic relationship between market and society, in which social rationalization was understood as necessary for capitalist efficiency, an understanding that united thinkers as diverse as the conservative economist Gustaf Cassel and the socialist Gunnar Myrdal.[34] This organic approach led, in history, to a sometimes far-going social interventionism in the name of the common good. *Samhälle* is also a concept of the social that theoretically makes no distinction between state and civil society. Rather, the notion of *samhälle* drew on the ambition, beginning in the late nineteenth century, to bring together market, state, and citizens into an organic whole.[35] This is not dissimilar to communitarianism's postulates of the constitution of community in a social context of tradition and historically defined virtues and to its understanding of the market as part of the common good. However, there are important differences between the historic meanings of *samhälle* and the contemporary communitarian notion of community, particularly in the role given to the market.

The idea of *samhälle*, from the late nineteenth century but particularly with the development of the Swedish model from the 1930s onward, was based on controlling the market and its forces of competition and profit in the name of the common good. As such, it was about disciplining market capitalism and keeping it from having devastating effects on the social. Social democracy's idea of the Strong Society in the 1950s and 1960s drew on this notion that a sophisticated market society required increased social responsibility. Arguably, this was not so much a market ethos to society as a social ethos to the market, and as such it underpinned the development of the Swedish Model of labor market and welfare policy. Moreover, the notion of *samhälle* appeals to a fundamentally different notion of reciprocity than the one assumed in contemporary communitarianism. The Swedish notion of society does not draw on a contract metaphor, of the idea of a contract between state and citizen, or indeed, between rights and responsibilities; rather, it draws on a notion of reciprocity that is defined in terms of the mutual recognition of need. This is expressed in the metaphor of the People's Home, as a source of inclusion and belonging. In the Swedish tradition, it is not the obligation side of social citizenship that constitutes the common good; instead, the constitution of the common good is dependent on the active exercise of fundamental democratic and social rights. Individual and collective advancement are fundamentally interrelated notions, and in the social democratic tradition the notion of advancement is closely linked to ideas of universalism. To that extent, the notion of *samhälle* draws on an idea of social change as a process driven by the rights side of citizenship.[36]

It is this conception that is mirrored in the SAP's insistence on knowledge as a kind of democratic capital, a tool for protecting the values of the universal welfare state. The SAP's 2001 Program defines the knowledge society:

> Giving all access to knowledge is crucial to breaking down patterns of class. Knowledge and competence are more and more the means of production that determine the opportunities of the individual in working life. Differences in access to these means increase social differences and shape society. A high level of knowledge and competence breaks down barriers of class. . . . The new order of production that is currently emerging is built on information. Infor-

mation flows have never been as important as they are today, and modern information technology brings with it a real democratization of knowledge. But the power that knowledge brings is not just about the access to information but also about the ability to independently interpret and evaluate information, see social contexts, and distinguish fact from values. Only through these abilities is a democratization of knowledge possible. The task of social democracy is to create a real knowledge society, built on knowledge and education, open and accessible to all on equal terms.[37]

In this way, knowledge is a tool for building a social democratic society made up of solidarity and universalism and based on people's capacity to think critically. These virtues are understood as controls on the market. While New Labour makes strong links between the notions of community and the notion of capital, the SAP speaks of society as a sphere defined by democracy. This reflects in the notion of social capital. While the notion of social capital is rarely mentioned in Swedish discourse, when it is mentioned it is with reference to the self-education movements, *folkbildning*, as a means of creating a strategic social capital made up of democratically aware citizens.[38] This is also the meaning of the Swedish notion of competence, *kompetens*, or indeed *social kompetens*, that is, the skills and knowledge necessary in the knowledge society.

The notion of competence became important in the early 1990s with the Bildt government's economic strategy.[39] However, as social democracy started to articulate a narrative around the knowledge society in the mid-1990s, the notion of competence became vested with ideas of democracy and individual empowerment. Upgrading and strengthening individual competence through lifelong learning and competence saving were articulated as rights of citizenship and as further steps in building the universal welfare state. In Sweden as well as in Britain, then, competence was framed as a crucial question of individual advancement and competitiveness in the new economy, with the difference that in Sweden this was linked to the risks of the new production order and to the importance of upgrading everyone so that no one would fall behind. Moreover, in social democracy's interpretation, the notion of competence became a question of citizenship and individual awareness of the problems of information and technology. Hence, competence was capital in the sense of empowerment and political resources, including the individual capability to articulate a critique of the market.[40] However, this is full of contradiction. Social competence, ultimately, is part of a labor market discourse in which it has become closely linked to the concept of employability; the individual possession of the skills

in demand on post-Fordist labor markets. This reflects a gradual shift from notions of social competence as citizenship competence to market competence
and a reconfiguration of the role of social democratic politics from that of fostering democratically aware citizens to that of making people competitive.

In addition, the notion of social competence has a very clear cultural component. Just as social capital in the United Kingdom is related to ideas of industriousness, duty, and fair play—all part of the definition of *Britishness*—the notion of social competence, in Sweden, draws on values presumed to be rooted in
the common historical experience of the People's Home. Social competence has
thus tended to be defined as "Sweden-specific" knowledge that includes knowledge of the Swedish language, of Swedish habits, and particularly, of the culture
and work practices of the Swedish model. Part of this Sweden-specific competence is the ability to "make one's voice heard" and to be able to protest in
the workplace and thus influence patterns of production. Immigrants seeking
employment are often seen as lacking these skills. For this reason, the notion of
social competence has been viewed as being part of the problem of structural
discrimination in Swedish labor markets because it identifies noncompliance
with the specific demands on competence as disabilities and shortcomings, not
unlike the emphasis on deviance in the notion of social capital. Through its appeal to values as culturally specific, the term *social competence* becomes exclu-
sive, dependent on references to a specific national and cultural community.[41]

Knowledge and the Virtues of Citizenship

New Labour's notion of community is a vision of the social sphere where the cement of the social contract consists of responsibility and duty. The central virtue of citizenship is not the awareness of rights but the feeling of obligation and
the attachment to a greater common good through prevailing notions of duty.
Next to work, education is the primary means for fostering feelings of duty,
for creating "competent and respectable citizens."[42] This process begins with
children. Since the mid-1990s, English curricula have emphasized the teaching
of obligation and duty to the surrounding community as part of citizenship
education. This stands in contrast to how, after devolution, curricula have been
adopted in Scotland and Wales that emphasize the role of education to foster
individuals aware of their rights. In Scotland, responsible citizenship is defined
as "the ability to examine matters critically and to develop informed views,
including views that challenge established conventions and the status quo," a
phrasing clearly influenced by the curricula of the Scandinavian countries.[43]

The English emphasis on education as a way of forging a culture of obligation can be contrasted to the Swedish case in which education, beginning with preschools, is seen as a means of forging a culture of belonging through knowledge of the rights of citizenship and awareness of the needs of others. Citizenship, in Sweden, is about having the knowledge necessary to influence the structures that shape society, in the workplace, in politics, in the local community, and in schools. In that sense, the notion of education in Swedish social democratic discourse is traditionally closely coupled with the notion of equality and to citizenship as process of fostering equal individuals, as expressed, for instance, in Alva Myrdal's Equality Program for preschools.[44] Today, SAP programs on early learning see it as the strategic way to give children from different backgrounds and conditions an equal start in life, confront them with the awareness of the situation of others, and teach them the importance of working together.[45] The National Curriculum for preschools says

> Early learning is the foundation of democracy. Its task is to forge the democratic values of our society. The sanctity of human life, individual freedom and integrity, the equal worth of all individuals, equality between the sexes, and solidarity with the weakest are the values that preschools should teach children. The rights of myself and others are to be emphasized.[46]

This emphasis on early learning as a means of creating democratic and solidaristic citizens falls back on the long tradition in Swedish political culture of viewing learning and education as means of citizenship and as radical emancipatory tools for working-class rationality. We have seen how the idea of *folkbildning* gained new importance in ideas of the knowledge society. *Folkbildning* is also seen as a means of integration, creating solidarity with groups in society that fall outside the mainstream education system. While the notion of community emphasizes social change as evolutionary and harmonious, the notion of society sees change as driven by a quintessentially social process where interests are merged and balanced. Knowledge is a strategic tool, indeed, a kind of critical social capital that, just as in the history of the labor movement, is about using democracy and insights in society and economy to influence the very direction of change, *samhällsutvecklingen*.

Equality and Meritocracy: The Lift and the Ladder

Meanwhile, some developments in Sweden seem to challenge exactly this notion of knowledge as a good for equality and democracy; and, arguably, it is exactly this idea that has to take a backseat when knowledge and education become commodities in the growth policies of the Third Way.

There can be no doubt that democratizing access to knowledge and education was at the top of social democracy's agenda in the 1990s. Both countries have made substantial investments in education in the last decade and drawn up ambitious political objectives, such as the Swedish objective to increase the number of PhDs to 10 percent of all students who begin a university education.[47] In a sense, this is the next step of those social democratic policies that, in the 1960s, sought to transform education from the privilege of a small elite to a comprehensive education for the working class.

Depending on the different institutional legacies in the education system, the scope for social democratic reform of education differs greatly in Sweden and the United Kingdom. The divide between grammar schools and comprehensives and the importance of elite "public" schools are defining characteristics of British class society. The issue of comprehensive education versus forms of selection by aptitude and ability is a standing debate in the history of the Labour Party, and it may also be one of the real limits of British Labourism. While the party has often questioned the existence of grammar schools, it has never managed to abolish them, due in part to their importance to the British middle class and in part to Labour's own reluctance to challenge these middle-class privileges.[48] Grammar schools were theoretically abolished under Wilson in 1965, but the implementation was vague and came to a halt under successive Conservative governments, with the result that, in reality, grammar schools and selection of students at eleven remain in parts of Britain. Blair's emphasis on "education, education, education" to the party conference in 1996 was deeply symbolic, raising hopes on the Left for a thorough reform of the school system.[49] Ten years later, it is clear that New Labour has continued many of the important themes of Thatcherism, above all the reverence for the role of the market in education and the celebration of choice and diversity, seen by the party's Left as a badly disguised reinvention of selection by ability. In 2005, the party faced a revolt of backbenchers over its education bill.[50]

Sweden's starting point for egalitarianism in education is a better one. Until the introduction of the voucher system under the Bildt government in 1992, private schools played a minor role in Sweden, limited to a few boarding schools that catered mainly to the children of foreign diplomats and of the small Swedish upper class. These schools did not play anywhere near the role in determining individual careers as do U.K. public schools. Since 1842 Sweden has had a system of basic schooling accessible to all, *folkskolan*, providing historically for exceptionally high levels of literacy in the Swedish population, and since 1962 Sweden has had a single system of comprehensive education. It was followed by reforms of higher education in the late 1960s that aimed at extending access to further education and providing the expanding welfare state with educated civil servants.[51] A further step on the road to the abolition of the vocational–academic divide was taken by the SAP on its return to power in the 1990s, when it included theoretical elements in all vocational programs and created one unified baccalaureate with the idea of qualifying all pupils for higher education. This abolition of vocational training programs has been much criticized as leading to an erosion of standards. Many students fail to keep up with theoretical studies, but when it lost power in 2006 the SAP's election campaign included promises to further strengthen the academic status of vocational education and apprenticeships.[52]

SAP policies reject meritocracy in favor of a highly egalitarian approach that stresses the collective boost of educational opportunity and rejects the idea that some should be allowed to rise above others. The SAP's flagship reform in the 1990s was *kunskapslyftet*, the "knowledge lift," designed to shift large numbers of people from unemployment benefits to adult education and provide them with the skills to succeed in the new economy. Other reforms included the creation of regional colleges in nonurban and suburban areas to recruit new groups to higher education and counteract segregation. These reforms were framed in the same egalitarian rhetoric of "the lift," informed by the notion of *alla ska med*, of everyone coming along, which became the election slogan in 2006.[53] This has a somewhat hollow ring in light of the dramatic changes that took place in the Swedish school system in the 1990s following the introduction of the voucher system, which has effectively opened the door for thoroughgoing specialization and competition among schools.[54]

Voucher schools were introduced by the Bildt government in 1992, influenced by Thatcher's attempts to create a market for education in the United Kingdom and by ideas of diversity, parental choice, and market specialization. In opposition, social democracy promised to undo the reform on their return to power, but in government the party has chosen not to. The introduction of a voucher system has led to a plethora of semiprivate "free schools" that compete for students with public schools. Voucher schools are now a central feature of the Swedish school system, and the SAP is deeply split over the issue; indeed, this is one of its loudest silences.[55] Meanwhile, voucher schools represent one of the few reforms that senior Social Democrats will refer to as an example of ideological change because they allow for middle-class parents to take their children out of public schools and entrench social and ethnic segregation in suburban areas.[56] For party modernizers voucher schools are, rather, a necessary concession to more individualist times. [57]

Many "free" schools are schools with special pedagogy, such as Waldorf or Montessori, which appeal to many Social Democrats and also seem to be in tune with alternative notions of education in the history of social democracy; others are high schools that specialize in sports, dance, or music; others again are faith schools. The party opposes the latter because it is not comfortable with the idea of a religious component in education.[58] Meanwhile, value-based components have gained in emphasis in national curricula. The 1980 curriculum stated that the role of education is to foster a "critical and active role in shaping society and working life," and it also spoke of solidarity with the surrounding world. In the curriculum implemented by the Conservative government in 1994, this emphasis changed into a more individualistic one, that drew on a liberal concept of freedom and on a Christian ethic, "allow[ing] each pupil to find his or her own particular talent, so that they can participate in social life in responsible freedom."[59]

The changes in the Swedish school system, from one based on comprehensive universalism to a system based on choice and vouchers, are dangerously at odds with principles of equality and solidarity. Specialization means that schools are allowed to compete for students, leaving municipal schools in tough areas with increased needs and fewer resources. This seems to go against the party's idea of education as a meeting point and a celebration of different talents and abilities. These changes add up to a transition in Swedish notions of education from an old ideal of knowledge as a democratic resource and a fundamental public good to education as a market commodity. Just as in the United Kingdom, the prerequisite of the system is a process of standardization through national tests, which allow parents to follow the results of pupils and schools. [60]

Nevertheless, the SAP's insistence on the knowledge society as a collective lift, whereby advancement must continuously be based on the values of universalism, stands in sharp contrast to the way New Labour sees change as a process of competitive strife. British metaphors of the knowledge society are, as already discussed, the "race" and the "ladder," both reflecting a fiercely competitive idea of social change, where some rise and some fall behind. The ladder is a fundamentally meritocratic notion, where advancement depends on the successful nurturing of one's innate talents and where differences in individual success are not the unfair outcomes of capitalist structures but the just rewards of these talents. The "ladder of opportunity" is a metaphor with origins in Fabianism. To Sydney Webb, the ladder of opportunity stood for the managerial division of social classes according to skill, where workers were shuttled into systems of vocational training and apprenticeships, while theoretical education provided pathways into the civil service for the best brains.[61] This duality in the British education system between vocational training and academic study has endured, and New Labour has also continued the emphasis on vocational training and apprenticeships as routes into the labor market at the expense, many have argued, of the creation of a high-skill strategy. This is unfair because there has also been an important emphasis on increasing the standards and value of vocational studies, but the predominance of the notion of the "ladder of opportunity" reflects the central role of meritocracy in New Labour ideology.

Meritocracy is a deeply ambiguous concept in the history of social democracy. A meritocratic social order is one that promises individual advancement based on merit and not on inherited privilege and, thus, the breakdown of the class privileges that historically held the labor movement down. As such, it is a deeply radical notion, concerned with profound social transformations. However, as Michael Young warned in his book *The Rise of the Meritocracy* (which was initially published during the 1960s debate on comprehensive education), meritocracy is also a social order wherein differences in intelligence and talent are recognized as legitimate sources of inequalities and placed at the heart of societal hierarchies.[62] From this perspective, meritocracy represents the threat of the rise of a knowledge-owning class that governs masses stripped of the tools to question and understand the power structures of capitalism. This is meritocracy as social order, not social change. The self-education movements of the early socialists, such as the Swedish *folkbildning*, were reactions against meritocratic education systems and their reproduction of a bourgeois elite.[63] However, social democrat education policies in Sweden have also been informed by a kind of human capital argument that sprung from the historic growth orientation of the SAP. The Swedish debate on comprehensive education included a discussion of meritocracy and a fear that equality in schooling might hold back the best brains; "it could be unfortunate if the working class, in the name of equality, were robbed of its best talents and potential political leaders," but the party solved this dilemma through its appeal to universalism as a strategy for making the most out of all available brains.[64]

New Labour has embraced and even praised the principle of meritocracy. Some of its arguments—the idea that the economy needs not a knowledge elite but the creativity of all the people or that the challenge is to create a culture of self-improvement for the many and not just the few—reflect an egalitarian aspiration that is motivated by human capital arguments, as it were, "finding the use of every child."[65] Since 1997, substantial investments have been made in educational allowances, in buildings and ICT, and in teacher's wages. New Labour's emphasis on standards has focused the spotlight on the quality of teaching and the democratization of outcomes and placed more importance on basic skills and literacy. But when it redefined the notion of "equality" to "equality of opportunity," New Labour effectively replaced a vision of an egalitarian social order with a vision of a meritocracy. Education policies have contained a very strong meritocratic component, reflecting the idea that the route to competitiveness lies in encouraging the full realization of individual talent, which is understood as being at odds with the principle of equality. From the first Schools White Paper, prepared in opposition, education was framed in a language of excellence, where strict standards for monitoring progress were introduced and underachieving schools were faced with the prospect of being closed. The role of government shifted from steering education to control, including sanctions of underachievement and implementation of what was called a "zero tolerance for failure," a notion that has primarily applied to schools and teachers but even to individual pupils. [66]

Zero tolerance of failure is a metaphor imported from the sphere of policing, and it put in place a highly authoritarian discourse of excellence where failure was to be punished in "inverse relation to success." The language of excellence is firmly meritocratic in the way that it applauds differences in talents and closely monitors both schools' and individuals' performances. Former Downing Street education advisor Michael Barber says in an interview that standardization and the monitoring of excellence are prerequisites for creativity because they drive everyone's progress up.[67] Excellence is also directly related to marketization and competition. In the controversial Academies Programme, failing schools can be taken over by the market for injections of creativity and drive. Schools, in New Labour policy, have also been encouraged to specialize to become competitive on the education market, attract the best students, and pursue excellence. This has been praised as a "postcomprehensive principle," a principle that allegedly brings the comprehensive ethos further by actively promoting the pursuit of different talents. Diversity, a keyword under

Blair, is about making sure that no child falls behind—through extra support for underachieving students but also through special tracks for the brightest.[68]

Hence, meritocracy is an organizing principle of contemporary education policy. In fact, the appraisal of meritocracy is key to the Third Way's renegotiation of the relationship between equality and individualism and to New Labour's vision of social order. Meritocracy has become a defining characteristic of a new social democratic project, part of its new political space:

> Our aim, explicitly, is to combine the drive for excellence, often associated with the right in politics, with the insistence that opportunity be open to all, the basic principle of the political left, in a public service system where the relationship between the government and people is one of partnership, not central control or laissez faire.[69]

Learning Societies: Conclusion

In the history of social democracy, meritocracy was a notion that called for radical social change in the name of equality and that brought about a critique of the structures of capitalist society as being what held individuals back. Meritocracy was a vision of equality, one that recognized achievement—and not original talent—as a legitimate basis of social hierarchy. To contemporary social democracy, meritocracy is a vision of society as organized around individual talent. This is informed by a human capital argument wherein the differentiation of people according to talent is motivated by the economic desire to make the most of the "best brains." Education policies under New Labour, despite their emphasis on access and spreading excellence, have been more concerned with social order than with social change, more with the social fabric than with mobility, more with "tapping potential" than with equality. While social democracy rejects inherited privileges as inefficient and wasteful (and has also attacked hereditary privilege with means such as asset-based welfare), it seems to praise the social order of talent that Crosland and Wigforss explicitly warned us against.[70] Moreover, as Richard Sennett has argued, there is something inherently meritocratic in the very notion of potential as something that lies latent within us, waiting to be discovered and extracted because this approach disregards circumstance and presumes that with access to the right opportunities, individuals can cast off their chains and free the potential hidden within.[71] This is a social vision defined by the economic. Indeed, New Labour speaks more of the knowledge economy than of the knowledge society.

In contrast, the SAP rhetorically seeks to promote a social vision of an egalitarian knowledge society where all groups have a real opportunity to influence the process of change and where key social values, above all the common good of solidarity, are protected by the social democratic state. Its vision of society is that of a social organization made up of classes and divergent interests, interests that are merged together through a democratic process wherein knowledge plays a crucial role. But in its proud proclamations of this social vision, social democracy speaks as if Swedish society were still the society of Per Albin Hansson and Tage Erlander and as if its own policies were still those of the 1950s. It is a discourse that is oddly detached from reality. The period from the 1970s, historian Francis Sejersted argues, can be seen as a process of disintegration of the notion of *samhälle*, a process in which the notions of civil society, market, and individual have entered Swedish discourse as autonomous and even rivaling spheres.[72] Privatization policies in Sweden, such as the voucher schools, clearly draw on this conception, pitting individual choice against collective solutions. The institutional changes in the Swedish welfare state in the 1990s have put in place policies that appeal not to the solidaristic citizen projected by social democracy in speeches and pamphlets but to a utility-maximizing individual. The values reproduced by policy are not solidarity but choice and competition. Voucher schools are part of an emerging new concept of society that is at odds with the principles of the People's Home.

7 Investing in People

A quintessential feature of Third Way discourse is its claim of reconciling seemingly irreconcilable alternatives and finding a Third Way path or compromise between them.[1] This applies particularly to the notorious dilemma of efficiency and social justice, which the Third Way claims to solve through its pragmatic attitude to welfare state intervention. This is not new in the history of social democracy. As discussed in the first chapter of this book, it is a fundamental of social reformism that it tries to reconcile seemingly irreconcilable alternatives, particularly the dilemma between capitalist efficiency and equality. From the postwar period onward, social democracy saw the welfare state as the means not only of intervening into the market for the creation of social justice but also of creating economic efficiency, a tool not only against the market but for the market.[2]

In the 1990s and 2000s, both parties, much in line with the changing approaches to social citizenship and welfare state intervention in the European context, emphasized the positive relationship between economic efficiency and social justice as part of their modernization strategy. Beginning in the mid-1990s, New Labour argued that what is fair is efficient and that there was no trade-off between social justice and efficiency. Indeed, this claim was a central element of its repositioning of Labour in the center left field, between the "exhausted" alternatives of state socialism and neoliberalism. In 1997 it promised a "new deal"—a break with the postwar Beveridge model to create new synergies between economic and social policies and lay the foundation for a new "active" form of welfare state intervention.[3] In a sense, this process has been reminiscent of the Swedish model, which drew on just such a close relationship between economic and social policy and an active supply-side orientation.[4] The language of Swedish social reformism is historically construed around exactly the kind of reconciliatory elements that have made up the platform of New Labour, first and foremost the idea that economic efficiency and social justice go hand in hand. This reflects the way that the welfare state, in Sweden, has been seen not only as a means to correct negative consequences of the market but as a productive investment into the economy and a precondition for growth. These historic articulations are echoed in the SAP's contemporary insistence on the welfare state as the prerequisite for successful economic transformation and what leading Social Democrats refer to as "security in change."[5]

However, there are important differences between these seemingly similar modernization discourses—differences that can be brought back to different discursive legacies around the social contract and the welfare state in the social versus the liberal model. A central part of these differences are, I argue, different approaches to efficiency, to ontological and ideological perceptions of how society and economy should be organized, and to definitions of what constitutes an efficient society. At the core of these notions are the different understandings of social citizenship.

Costs and Investments: Social Investment Strategies and Productive Social Policies

New Labour's understanding of the social as a sphere for the production of a specific kind of capital, social capital, has led to the emergence of new means of governance designed to invest in that capital, namely, social investment strategies.[6] The idea of social investment was a central part of its modernization strategy narrative and its call for investment in fundamental British capabilities. Physical investment into the machines and capital of British industry was to be coupled with social investment in the social capital of the British people.[7]

The rise of social investment strategies in European welfare states in the last decade are part of an emerging concept of state that is clearly linked to the rethinking of the principles of political economy discussed in Chapter 2. The core purpose of the role of welfare state intervention in the "social investment state" is to use public spending and state intervention to "invest in people"— not to protect them from the market but, on the contrary, to give them the skills and opportunities needed to succeed in the knowledge future. In particular, this applies to those in society who can most easily be molded for the future. The idea of social investment has thus brought with it a shift in the prioritized activities and groups of the welfare state—a shift that specifically targets children as the crucial future social capital of the nation. The substantial emphasis on children and family policies in the 1990s—possibly New Labour's most important achievement—was motivated as a strategic investment "in the potential of every child."[8]

New Labour's social policy agenda has in many ways been radical, for instance in the pledge to end child poverty, the creation of the national day care strategy, or the Sure Start program, designed to prevent future social exclusion by intervening in the early years that statistically are highly significant for an individual's future life course. These programs have signified a break with the liberal philosophy of welfare that has dominated British political culture because for the first time children have been made a public responsibility and a central area of reform.[9] However, social investment strategies reflect a changing governmentality around social intervention, with direct reference to a new economy built on human and social capital.[10] The idea of social investment was part of New Labour's economic narrative of social justice, a narrative that effectively turned social policy into a new form of economic policy and established a framing around welfare as motivated by its economic returns. This economic language clearly had a highly strategic function. It was a pragmatic argument for an egalitarian agenda and not a moral or ideological one. As such, equality became compatible with the common good and possible within the parameters of the values of "Britishness." However, it also led to a highly utilitarian discourse around social justice and equality, as if these were economic principles.

This economistic approach to social justice has led to a fundamental transformation in understandings of social citizenship. As Jane Jenson and Denis St. Martin have suggested, social investment strategies are indicative of a changing time dimension in social policy, where it is not the security or welfare of individual citizens in the immediate here and now that is most pressing but the supposed future rentability of welfare subjects.[11] And as Ruth Lister has persuasively argued, the rise of the social investment state signifies a shift in our outlook on children, from "child-citizens" to "citizen-workers of the future."[12] The dominant focus of policy is not to invest in children to give them a better childhood and help them lead more meaningful lives, even if this is an integral aspect of the rhetoric of the social investment state, but to invest in the strategic future brainpower that they represent. Children become a de facto capital investment.

Seen from within the long history of European welfare capitalism, New Labour's economic discourse around social policy is not new but, rather, a contemporary variant on the investment discourses that have followed the development of modern social policies. The idea of social policy as an economic means for the efficient allocation of social resources is an integral part of welfare state governmentality. Indeed, the identification of social policy as a kind of economic policy was at the heart of the European notion of welfare capitalism and its historic notions of *sozial ökonomie*, or social economy.[13] In the industrial era, social policy was framed within Keynesian discourses of humanpower and manual labor, while today they are concerned with the efficient utilization of social and human capital.[14]

The idea of social investment drew on a notion of efficiency that was directly linked to market efficiency and that contained a critique of the "old" Beveridgean welfare state as fundamentally inefficient and costly. New Labour's "new contract for welfare" contained a new approach to public spending in which public expenditure was redirected from areas considered "wasteful" to areas with strategic importance for the knowledge future. A key distinction was the careful separation between "good spending" and "bad spending"—between investments and costs. Good spending was spending designed to put people to work and extend education and learning; ". . . good, we like that." Bad spending was "spending on unemployment and people on benefit when they should be at work, bad, we want to decrease that."[15] A system of elaborate audits and standards was designed to monitor this move from costs to investments, "weed out waste," and make sure that investment paid off. In part, this applied to the management of public services and public sector reform, but weeding out waste also applied to the content of welfare and to the welfare subject.[16]

"Investment" and "cost" are not neutral economic concepts; they are powerful metaphors of progress and decay. The difference between what constitutes an investment and what constitutes a cost is at some level arbitrary; after all, both costs and investments demand resources from the present. Ultimately, the distinction between what constitutes spending as cost or spending as investment is the anticipation of rentability. A cost is a burden on resources because it leads to capital waste. An investment, on the other hand, represents resources used in the anticipation of future yield. Applied to welfare programs, these terms are not empirical descriptions of the anticipated economic role of a certain social program; rather, they contain deeply normative descriptions of who represents a cost and who represents an investment. The

British idea of social investment, which originated in the report of the British Commission on Social Justice and was taken up by the philosopher Anthony Giddens in his treatise on the Third Way, was strongly linked to New Labour's communitarian agenda on citizenship and its concern with breaking with a culture of dependency, thus cutting the costs for welfare bills. The social investment state was a new, active welfare state, a state that fostered achievement and aspiration. It did not "subvention failure." It "invested in success."[17]

This approach to welfare drew on distinctly liberal legacies around welfare and social policy as things that are latently on a par with market efficiency. New Labour is inspired by a very social democratic social interventionism. Meanwhile, it has broken with important legacies in the British progressive tradition around welfare, Richard Titmus's idea of universal entitlements, and T. H. Marshall's emphasis on the transformative role of social citizenship.[18] While leading in some areas to a more radical social policy agenda, social investment strategies also contain an approach to social policy that revokes Victorian legacies.[19] It is hard to avoid the conclusion that the flagship position given to the Sure Start program in New Labour policy is because children, in New Labour's moralistic approach to social citizenship, are seen as untainted blank sheets and not affected by the dichotomy of deserving and undeserving poor. Sure Start as a reform area was possible within the context of the values of Britishness and the liberal social contract, and investment in children was matched by strategies to "crack down" on welfare claimants and increase the conditionality of entitlements.

To that extent, the idea of the social investment state draws on a notion of efficiency that ultimately falls back on an outlook on social policy as a cost for idleness and dependency and as something that has to be circumscribed, controlled, and redesigned in order to bring out people's productive potential and not suffocate it.

This is a very different notion of efficiency from the one that historically informed Swedish welfare policies. A core notion in the discursive underpinning of the Swedish welfare state as it developed from the 1930s onward was the idea that the welfare state and its social policies were not costs for the mollification of markets but a productive investment in the efficient industrial economy. Historically, the Swedish notion of welfare, in contrast to its Anglo-Saxon connotations as assistance to people in need, signifies socioeconomic efficiency, an overall approach to the efficient functioning of economy and society, including aspects of social progress and individual well-being.[20]

Therefore, welfare is as much an economic as a social principle. It was this principle of welfare as efficiency that lay behind the productivism of the Swedish welfare state. To social democratic thinkers like Wigforss or the architect of universalism Gustav Möller, equality and social justice were not just moral but economic principles, to be placed at the core of a planned economy.[21]

Just like the social investment discourse of New Labour, this productivism was a multifaceted discourse, displaying the tensions between socializing and capitalizing that I discussed in earlier chapters. On the one hand, it put in place an economic defence around the emerging welfare state and principles of universalism, as principles not primarily of redistribution but of efficiency. As such, it called for the regulation of markets in the name of social citizenship.[22] On the other, the productivism of the Swedish model drew on legacies from an, at times, thoroughgoing social engineering rooted in economistic approaches to the social. Swedish universal social policies were born in the 1930s' discourses of the human material, *människomaterialet,* explicitly concerned with its quantity and quality.[23] It was the identification of children as a fundamental economic resource of the nation state that led to ideas of public responsibility for children's welfare and the development of family policy as a legitimate sphere of state intervention. The rational socioeconomic solution to problems of both falling birth rates and the poverty of the working class was sharing the burden for children, thereby also increasing the chances for children of good quality, equipped to contribute to society. This emphasis on sharing the costs for children became a central element in the rise of the modern welfare state. Indeed, it was framed within the language of investment.[24]

Thus, there are parallels across time between Swedish productivist approaches to welfare and New Labour's idea of social investment. Nevertheless, contemporary social investment strategies differ from these historical Swedish discourses in some substantial ways that cannot be explained simply in terms of the specific historic, economic, and social contexts in which they exist but that need to be discussed in terms of changing ideologies and changing definitions of the economic and the social in our present times. In the 1930s, the idea of social policy as a productive investment was framed within the logic of emerging Keynesianism and linked to ideas of the structural causes of social problems. It was part of a critique of the capitalist economy as notoriously unstable and prone to the destruction of social resources. Moreover, through its links to the emerging philosophy of universalism, this productivist social policy discourse in Sweden became linked to arguments for the structural transformation of society on the basis of social citizenship. As such, it was distinct from the conservative discourses on which it drew.[25]

This is not to reduce the deeply disciplining aspects of early Swedish social policies or the "dark side" of the People's Home, which have been elucidated in the last decade by Swedish historians. Discourses of efficiency gave rise, in Sweden as elsewhere in Europe, to thoroughly interventionist means of social engineering based on notions of human beings as productive or reproductive capital. In a sense, the universalism of Swedish social policy as it developed from the 1930s onward was dependent on the systematic exclusion of "asocial elements," through means such as the sterilization policies that, even though they were marginal in number, were a core feature of the Swedish welfare state.[26] Nevertheless, the crucial difference between the Swedish development and fascist eugenics was that efficiency discourses in Sweden were embedded in a historical tradition of individual rights, which acted as a bulwark against utilitarian social engineering and marked the decisive difference between fascism and social democracy. In Sweden, productivist discourses of social engineering merged with the principle of universalism.[27] Perhaps the virtual absence of the notion of social capital in Swedish discourse today is due to the association with a capitalization of human beings that it invokes in Swedish political memory.

New Labour's social investment discourse, in contrast, is tied to its pervasive notions of a common good created through discipline and obligation. It is the responsibility side of social citizenship that is associated with prosperity and efficiency, while the rights side of citizenship is fundamentally associated with dependency, idleness, and "waste." In addition, social investment discourses—through their link to social capital—occupy a central position on New Labour's communitarian agenda and its understanding of crime, asocial behavior, and delinquency as problems of social capital and as areas that should also be subject to strategic investment. In these areas, social investment refers to government activities aimed at preventing social costs; and as such it shares with Swedish productive social polices a prophylactic approach to social problems. But it differs fundamentally in its outlook on what causes them. The Swedish investment metaphor was aimed at "building away" problems of unemployment and poverty through structural means of economic and social planning and the universal welfare state. This side of investment is absent in the mentality of the social investment state. The famous slogan—"be tough on crime and tough on the causes of crime"—has resulted in some of the highest incarceration rates in Europe. What it shares with the productivism of Swedish social policies is the mercantilist emphasis on the role of the welfare state to increase the value in the future brainpower of the nation and the sanctions of those elements that do not fit in this ideology of efficiency. For instance, a policy paper of the Strategy Unit argued that governing individual behavior is more cost efficient than traditional welfare policies and accordingly labelled this approach "punitive universalism"—a kind of universalism in which the relative extension of social rights for some groups in society must be matched by increased conditionality and sanctions for others.[28]

The Safety Net and the Springboard:
Security and Opportunity

The economic argument around the welfare state as a productive investment was a central feature of SAP postwar ideology, and it provided the discursive underpinning of the welfare state, spanning the field from party rhetoric to the means of governance. The operative concept in economic and social planning throughout the postwar period was a notion of efficiency as social efficiency, *samhällsekonomisk effektivitet*, which took into account the effects of social programs not only on growth but on human welfare. The expansion of the public sector in the 1950s and 1960s was regarded in budgets as "productive spending" and not as consumption. In contrast, a central element of the SAP's Third Way experiment in the 1980s was its break with exactly this outlook on the welfare state as a productive investment. The 1970s economic crisis and the party's two lost elections led to a thoroughgoing debate in the party of the validity of the economic postulates around the welfare state, a process in which the modernizers on the party's right flank gained legitimacy for their critique of public spending as too wasteful and inefficient. The concept of socioeconomic efficiency was replaced by the concept of cost efficiency, followed by experiments with cost-benefit analysis and new public management models. The party toyed with notions of individual incentives and responsibility (see Chapter 3). These ideological principles lay behind the privatizations that took place in the Swedish welfare state beginning in the early 1990s. In the crisis management policies that began in 1982, individual security was set aside for fiscal stability, and the party silenced its notions of the productive role of social policy and the economic benefits of the welfare state.[29]

However, in line with the way that the party under Persson's leadership tried to reconnect with its classic heritage and break with its 1980s Third Way experiment, the party rediscovered these articulations and again put them at the heart of ideology.[30] Growth discourses of the 1990s defended the postulates of the Swedish model and the idea of the welfare state as a productive investment, essential to building the knowledge economy: "We should continue building the welfare state. Security in change stimulates innovation and provides the power to grow. Secure people dare. Security makes the economy more dynamic."[31] The economy does not need less security to function smoothly; it needs more.

This was based on an analysis of the process of modernization that is fundamentally different from that of New Labour. New Labour saw the process of modernization as driven by risk and opportunity and by individual willingness to assume these factors and turn them into success. Its approach to welfare state modernization has focused on fostering risk-taking individuals. Its reinvented idea of state responsibility in the modern era has followed from this conception of the primary individual responsibility to seize opportunity. The social investment state was also the "springboard"—a vision of the state as the trampoline that projected people into the air, not the safety net into which people fell and remained.[32] The springboard, like other New Labour metaphors such as the "ladder" or the "race," is a thoroughly meritocratic notion. It was more concerned with giving those willing to jump a bounce on their way up than with those who were afraid of heights or failed their jump. Its means of welfare were designed to push people to jump, through an intricate balance of encouragement and coercion.[33]

In contrast, the Swedish outlook on the process of change placed the main emphasis on the risks of modernization. Whereas the watchword of the process of modernization to New Labour was *opportunity*, in Sweden it was *security*. While Gordon Brown has repeatedly stated that there can be no security without change, the Swedish party leadership has insisted that there can be no change without security.[34] This is not a rejection of change itself or of the "inevitable" forces of globalization or technology; rather, the SAP argues that successful structural change depends on the capacity to uphold and defend the welfare state because the welfare state *is* the safety net that keeps people from falling into the abyss while doing pirouettes on a tightrope. This is a discourse that draws on the SAP's productivist discourse around the welfare state and its idea that a large public sector is a crucial element in a modern economy, creating the preconditions for smooth structural change. In the 1950s and 1960s, social democracy defended the expansion of the public sector with the argument that rapid structural change required a firm public commitment to security because insecurity would create intolerable rigidities. The idea was that structural change calls for collective responsibility to deal with the risks that individuals face in times of structural transition and that the increased risk of change has to be matched by a stronger commitment by the public and the welfare state to compensate for individual losses of well-being. The highly productivist orientation of the Rehn-Meidner model, with its insistence on labor mobility and individual adaptation, was also based on the recognition of the need for solidarity and the collective efforts of the welfare state. Security is, therefore, a productive force, closely associated with elements of growth and freedom, while insecurity, such as the insecurities brought on by globalization and a rapidly changing world, is a deeply destructive force that destroys potential and thwarts ambition:[35]

> If people fear the future, they will not realize or see its potentials. A woman who is afraid that unemployment might spoil her economy will not be ready to leave work in order to pursue higher education or start an enterprise to develop a skill or invention. A man who fears the economic consequences of getting fired will not speak up and criticize management decisions or risk finding new methods or markets. A couple that doesn't feel secure on the labor market or does not trust the future will be reluctant to have children and create a family.[36]

Insecurity creates inefficiencies and hampers growth, whereas security creates courageous individuals who dare to spend, to be creative, to criticize and express ideas in the workplace, to study, and to raise a family. Security creates growth.

This puts into place a notion of change and of individual motivation that is fundamentally different from the opportunity-driven discourse of New Labour. To Swedish social democracy, individuals are capable and curious, but they do not react positively to risk and fear. Rather they are spurred on by the instinct of solidarity. Modernization, in this Swedish interpretation, is a process driven by individual security and the boldness that security creates. Indeed, creativity stems from security. Secure people dare to be creative, to be entrepreneurs, and to take risks: "Secure people are creative people—people who are driven by the will to seek knowledge, not because they are driven with a whip, but because it makes them grow as individuals."[37]

This can be contrasted to how, in British discourse, creativity arises from competition, "the sharpest spur to improve productivity and the greatest guarantee of reward for talent and innovation."[38]

This is a very romantic Swedish discourse, regarding both individuals and the welfare state, and it has often been dismissed by party modernizers as well as by the Swedish Right as a kind of "security addiction" or "kindness disease" that stands in the way of proper change, an argument that was at the core of the 2006 election campaign. It is also a discourse that seems to silence the debate on the effects on insecurity that have arisen in the last decade due, arguably, to the twin challenge of economic transformation and organizational changes in the welfare state. A central point of the party's ideological change in the 1980s and the 1990s lies in the very notion of security. Security, today, is taken to include a higher individual acceptance of risk than was previously presumed, and the contemporary meaning of the notion contains a significant emphasis on incentives and increased individual responsibility.

The meaning of "security in change" is that change and a dynamic labor market need to be coupled with strong social institutions that guarantee individual security in periods of transition, particularly through high levels of compensation in the social insurance system.[39] The social insurance system is the "bridge of change," not the trampoline projecting people upward but the path on which people walk from one economy to the other. Unquestionably, this approach to flexibility is very different from the British one, first, in that it claims that security is not an obstacle change but a precondition for it and, second, in the way that it maintains that high levels of compensation for social risk are essentially a human capital investment.[40] Nevertheless, "security in change" draws on those contemporary labor market discourses that have effectively shifted the responsibility for unemployment from the public sphere to the individual. This conceptual slippage is clear in the new affinity between British and Swedish labor market policies in recent years. On one side of the North Sea, Gordon Brown has emphasized the importance of secure individuals, particularly in the context of the European social model. On the other side, Swedish policy makers have increasingly debated incentives, carrots and sticks. After Gordon Brown's speech to the Swedish Social Democrat's Economic Seminar in Almedalen in 2005, the Swedish Ministry of Finance and the British Treasury produced a joint report entitled *The Bridges of Change*. While the report spoke of the importance of security for creative individuals, it drew heavily on British language of flexibility and employability. Its main message was protecting people, not jobs, in a world where it is the responsibility of government to invest in people and opportunities and the responsibility of people to seize them.[41]

Between Welfare and Workfare:
Rights and Responsibilities

New Labour's New Deal for welfare was explicitly informed by the contractualism that has become fashionable in political philosophy and social science in recent decades. The New Deals were embedded in the language of "no rights without responsibilities," ultimately defined by "making work pay."[42] This relies heavily on a notion of individual responsibility, above all the duty of productive participation. In the knowledge age, the duty to work has been complemented by the duty to learn. It has sometimes been suggested that this "active" approach to citizenship draws on Scandinavian influences and Swedish-style active labor market policies and that New Labour's workfare strategies are not that different from the way that the strong social rights of the Swedish model were coupled with the emphasis on the duty to work.[43]

Despite occasional depictions by British and American observers to the contrary, the Swedish welfare state has never been a system of handouts for the idle and the weak. On the contrary, at its heart is a work ethic, which has, in history, led to the identification of various groups in social policy as crucial labor force reserves and to the creation of welfare means explicitly aimed at bringing out their productive potential. Historically, there has been a fine line between emancipatory discourses of the right to work and disciplining discourses of duty. The right to meaningful employment was a central claim of labor movements in the early twentieth century.[44] In Sweden, in contrast to the developments in the United Kingdom following the Beveridge report, this led to the development of active labor market policies, the creation of a large state bureaucracy around the organization and allocation of work, and the construction of a social insurance system based on principles of income relation.[45] In this manner, social rights in Sweden were directly tied to the principle of work. Swedish social democratic ideology is informed by a pervasive work ethic; and, throughout its history, the SAP has been deeply troubled by the existence of various groups and individuals who either seem not to share this ethic or are unable to be productive citizens in the social democratic meaning of the word. This is not just a matter of putting the notion of solidarity to the test; the existence of groups outside the labor market is a problem for the principle of universality that underpins the redistributive architecture of the Swedish welfare state because the core idea of this universalism is a principle of reciprocity close to Marx's principle of "from each according to his ability, to each according to his need," and thus stresses the productive participation of all.[46] Hence there is, if not the deserving–undeserving dichotomy of liberalism, the dichotomy of productive–unproductive and a concern with how to turn the latter into the former. This explains the underlying duality of the Swedish welfare state, between its strong—universal—entitlements in the social insurance system, based on labor market participation, and its much weaker, means-tested entitlements for groups outside the labor market.[47] In recent decades, these tensions between universalism and conditionality have become clearer, while the meanings of concepts such as welfare, security, and activation have become increasingly blurred.[48]

It needs to be pointed out, however, that the Swedish approach to the relationship between welfare and work differs fundamentally from the workfare strategies of the liberal model. Workfare strategies see rights as conditional on productive participation, as something earned through duties fulfilled, and they rely heavily on such means as contracts that define and regulate correct individual behavior.[49] In contrast, Swedish productivism drew on the idea that the extension of social entitlements and social security was the precondition for productive participation. The predominant emphasis was not on the duty to work but on the individual right to contribute productively to society. It is important to note that it saw this as dependent on the public responsibility for work to make it possible for everyone to participate according to capacity.[50]

This is distinct from workfare, and it reflects a social democratic tradition that New Labour has broken with. In its search for a new work ethic, it preferred American workfare contracts to expensive Scandinavian active labor market policies. Despite ambitions to put people to work, increasing conditionality has hardly been complemented by increased quality of services or higher spending on unemployment. U.K. spending on active labor market policy is still among the lowest in Europe; and, up to now, the predominant emphasis has been a quantitative focus on moving people off benefits and into work, substantially less so with the quality of that work (even if this is a shifting ground).[51] Again, it sees governing individual behavior as more cost efficient than intervening in structures. Meanwhile, a fundamental change in the Swedish welfare state has to do with the role of active labor market policies and the changing demarcations between work and welfare. In this process, social democracy's outlook on the unemployed as potentially productive citizens or idle has also been put to the test.[52]

Unemployment rose in Sweden from frictional unemployment around 4 percent to mass unemployment at 16 percent between 1991 and 1993. On its return to government in 1994, social democracy, faced with an exploding budget deficit, promised to reduce unemployment to 4 percent by the year 2000. It accomplished this task, even if numbers have since risen again. The social democratic government put a large group of unemployed in training and education through the knowledge lift so that they would be better prepared when the economy turned, and it restored unemployment insurance to 80 percent (which was still 10 percent lower than the original 90 percent) with the argument that high levels of unemployment benefit are a productive investment in human capital and prevent waste.[53] However, there have been significant changes in the design and content of active labor market policies concerning individuals who do not qualify for these 80 percent either because of long-term unemployment or because they have not previously been employed. In the aftermath of the 1990s recession, this group of people, who are more or less permanently outside the labor market, has grown substantially. Unemployment, together with other social effects of economic crisis, such as a dramatic increase in ill health and incapacity in the Swedish population, has resulted in falling rates of participation. This is a worrisome development because, in contrast to the situation in the United Kingdom or in other parts of Europe, long-term unemployment was virtually nonexistent in Sweden before the fall of the krona in 1992. This, then, is a new group in Swedish society, created, it seems, by the dramatic onset of the 1990s' crisis and further by the structural changes that occurred in the economy once the cycle changed and significant groups found themselves unemployable.[54] In addition, the rise of this group seems to stand in relationship to central changes in the bureaucracy of the welfare state itself. Since the 1990s, labor market policy has played an active role in the redefinition of long-term unemployment as a form of incapacity, by shuffling individuals between different parts of the system, activating them with activities whose meaningfulness is not easily deciphered, and, in fact, treating unemployed people as if they were disabled or deviant.[55] It is hard to avoid the conclusion that social democracy has played a role in this, partly in loss of control over the activities of the welfare bureaucracy and partly by accepting a relocation of responsibility from state to individual in its core ideological concepts. This Swedish development stands very much in contrast to the way in which the British emphasis on getting people off benefits has brought with it new framings of those not in employment as "able" and "capable."[56]

The active labor market policies of the Swedish model were put to a tremendous test after 1992 as the measures designed to deal with a small group of unemployed were suddenly to take care of a huge number of people, and resources were spread very thin. In the next decade, the nature of labor market policies in Sweden evolved into something that is much closer to workfare. Labor market policies were decoupled from the actual labor market and became increasingly concerned with the activation of the unemployed.[57] Indeed, activation was a new element in the employment strategy, dating from 1996, because inactivity was per se seen as a kind of human capital waste. Thus activation was defined as a human capital investment because it avoided the development of a dependency culture and the cost of passivity.[58] In Swedish conceptions of efficiency, it is now activation that is understood as being productive.

In the 1990s, unemployment policy as well as social assistance was decentralized, leaving more room for maneuvering by individual officials in the local employment offices and by local governments, which were given the right to demand that unemployed individuals take whatever work they were assigned under the threat of sanctions. Through what was known as the Activation Guarantee from 1999, which stated the government's responsibility to put individuals to work after 100 days of unemployment, entitlements were made conditional on individual activity.[59] Methodologies of employment offices became increasingly dependent on personalized interviews and contracts that aim to make the individuals aware of their shortcomings to develop into more employable characters. Such therapy-like interviews and contracts are a central feature of workfare.[60] In this process, the language of welfare and work changed toward ideas of a contract that regulates the relationship between the rights and responsibilities of government and citizen:

> Good labor market policies imply a mutual contract of obligation between society and citizen. Society takes on responsibilities toward the individual only to the extent that the individual fulfils his or her responsibilities. Individual responsibility resides in accepting the challenge of developing competence and actively seeking work.[61]

To the emphasis on the duty to work in the job strategy was added the individual duty to learn and develop competence. Indeed, a government committee charged with incentives problems in social insurance spoke of establishing a culture of work, of breaking with a culture of dependency, and of employment policy as self-help to independent, motivated, responsible individuals.[62]

Conclusion

It is striking that this language made it into Swedish social democratic discourse in the 1990s without the kind of ideological debate on the philosophical and moral foundations of welfare that was a central part of New Labour's attempt to create a new social contract. The treacherous nature of this silent process of discursive change is of course that modern activation discourse is deceivingly similar to productivist notions even when both its means and its underlying values differ substantially from the classical postulates of the

Swedish Model. Leading Social Democrats say that this new rights versus re-sponsibilities language does not differ significantly from the work ethic that has always informed party ideology and that the problem is not a new emphasis on responsibility. Rather, the party has lost touch with its old notions of duty and obligation; there has been too much talk of security, too much general nice-ness, and not enough activity. The crux, of course, is that the notion of "active" can cover anything from active labor market policies, "old-style"; to activation, from, as it were, an "old" Swedish notion of welfare; to notions of workfare. From this perspective, "security in change" is a congenial term with an opaque meaning, as is the party's emphasis in the last decade on welfare policy as an investment intended to bring out everyone's productive potential.[63]

While the relationship between the welfare state and processes of com-modification and decommodification is complex over time, nevertheless the Third Way marks a significant shift from social democratic traditions around the welfare state and social citizenship. As Sheri Berman points out, histori-cally, the welfare state was important to social democracy as the guardian of society against the effects of capitalism.[64] The objects of intervention were the economic and social structures that allow or deprive individuals from exer-cising their rights, the object of protection of the individual and core societal values. But to contemporary social democracy, the object of welfare state in-tervention is no longer the economy but the individual.

The language of responsibility is crucial for this shift. Governing the indi-vidual duty to work and learn is something fundamentally different from gov-erning the individual right to work and learn. The right to self-development and the duty to improve are not the same thing. "No rights without respon-sibilities" or "from each according to capacity, to each according to his need" are two very different strategies of reform. In fact, there is a social democratic world of difference between them.

8 Creating the Knowledge Individual

The Entrepreneur and Its Other

In previous chapters, I discussed the Third Way's idea of modernization as a process of improvement that takes place essentially within, through the upgrading of the human capital in our souls. I pointed to similarities between the Third Way's notions of improvement and social democracy's historic discourses. However, in its emphasis on change as something essentially taking place within us, the Third Way seems to differ substantially from social democracy historically. The historic emphasis on change as a process of collective improvement is replaced, in the Third Way, with a focus on the individual as the primary locus of change. At the heart of the process of modernization is the learning individual and the process of turning people into competent, dutiful, and knowledgeable citizens. This idea of the constantly learning and relearning individual is social democracy's utopia for the knowledge era. Social democracy has not rid itself of utopian reasoning; rather, it has relocated utopian projection from the collective sphere of mobilization to the individual sphere of self-improvement.

The idea of autonomous individuals has always, in some form, been at the heart of social democratic ideology. However, in the history of social democracy, the dream of free and emancipated people was part of its understanding of socialism's mission to break the chains of fettered individuals and of the idea that individual freedom rested on the shoulders of collective advancement: in short, that it is only through the solidarity of all that we are free. The Third Way, through its individualized discourses on flexibility, learning, and meritocratic ascendancy—discourses that shift the locus of social change, responsibility, and risk from the collective sphere to the individual—marks a break with this social democratic tradition regarding the role of the collective to free the potential of all. Despite its communitarian emphasis on the social embeddedness of individuals, the Third Way's idea of the learning individual reflects a concession to one of the utopias of neoliberalism, namely, that of the entrepreneurial and competitive person, one who is able to cast off the chains of circumstance and set his or her potential free.

In previous chapters, we have discussed the significant differences that exist between the parties in how they articulate the relationship between collective and individual advancement. The individual projected by the SAP is secure and solidaristic; in contrast, the New Labour person is a restless and calculating climber. These differences are not unimportant. On the contrary, they define the political subject, and, arguably, they are also constitutive of social relations, and perhaps even of politics themselves. These representations of the social democratic person are also representations of what social democracy considers to be the scope and limits of politics. Its narrative of modernization relies on the construction of its utopic knowledge individual. Its discourses of lifelong learning, autonomy, and responsibility are all intended to bring about this knowledgeable person.

Of course, it is arguable whether this really is a knowledgeable individual or, indeed, what kind of knowledge this utopic citizen is supposed to possess. Social democracy's vision of the knowledge citizen is dependent on its contemporary notion of knowledge as something having to do with particular dispositions and character—a kind of modernizing spirit that is defined first and foremost by the ability to constantly change and modernize, to learn and relearn. As we have seen, these dispositions are owned and embodied primarily by the entrepreneur: the individual who possesses useful knowledge and who knows how to make the most out of his or her potential. To that extent, the entrepreneur emerges as virtually the ideal social democratic citizen, the knowledgeable and virtuous individual who is able to see and grasp opportunity.

This representation of the entrepreneurial citizen comes with the projection of an Other, the individual who lacks potential. We can see this Other mirrored in the Third Way's discourses on social exclusion, in the concern with a digital divide and a class of "workless" or even "useless" people. Social exclusion is a deeply worrisome empirical phenomenon in contemporary societies, and there is no question that contemporary social democracy is very concerned about its human and social implications. Nevertheless, its discourses of exclusion seem to contain what is, at times, a disconcerting outlook on people as capital, people who are either carriers of useful knowledge or void of that knowledge. Social exclusion, like other forms of poverty and inequality in the knowledge era, has become understood in terms of its link to knowledge, talent, human and social capital—and defined as the absence of these things.[1] In a sense, the socially excluded represent the antithesis of modernization in Third Way discourse because they are the backward, laggard people who cannot keep up in the process of change, the ones who fail to improve. Just as the idea of the knowledge society (or economy) contains presumptions of a new global division of labor between those who create originals and those who produce copies, post-Fordist labor markets and education systems create new divides between "information haves" and "information have-nots," between critically minded and creative people and those who are not.[2] These are people who lack the modernizing spirit, who lack the virtues of citizenship. Therefore, the entrepreneur and the socially excluded can be seen as two central stereotypes of contemporary politics—quite as social democracy historically built its political project around the stereotypes of the good worker and the idle vagrant.

This is a highly normative vision of people, and it reflects the way that the idea of the knowledge economy and the knowledge society is an inherently powered discourse. It goes without saying that there are no people in the world who do not possess knowledge and potential. The crucial issue at hand is not that certain forms of knowledge are intrinsically worth more than others. There are many forms of work and social production in society that are essential to us even when their value is not quantified in economic terms.[3] Many other forms of creativity exist other than the entrepreneurial search for use and application, and many talents in society fall outside the growth policies of the Third Way. Rather, the key issue is how we ascribe value to individual potential. The knowledge economy and its language, institutions, and policies are active agents in the production of new subjects and new social hierarchies, just as new technologies actively create new forms of disabilities such as digital illiteracy or multiple stress disorders (through complicated social processes).[4] At the basis of our social hierarchies is the idea of use, value, and worth, to ourselves and to others. The definition of usefulness, that is, of who is a productive citizen, is per definition also a definition of who is not, of who is "useless." From this perspective, the idea of the knowledge society contains something deeply worrying for social democratic politics because of the way that it seems to draw on constant judgments of talent and potential. It is one thing to judge achievement but quite another to judge talent and innate potential. You are born with or born without. To that extent, potential is a notion of individual worth that, as Richard Sennett points out, is infinitely more devastating than notions of achievement because it comes down to a judgment of the self, a judgment of character:

> Judgements of potential ability are much more personal in character than judgements on personal achievement. An achievement compounds social and economic circumstance, fortune and chance, with self. Potential ability focuses only on the self. The statement "you lack potential" is much more devastating than "you messed up." It makes a more fundamental claim about who you are. It conveys uselessness in a more profound sense.[5]

The very idea of use, of useful knowledge and talent, stands in contrast to the social democratic idea of the equal worth of everyone and that all young people should be convinced of the worth of their own particular uniqueness and allowed to develop and explore their talents.

The Rise of the Useless

The problem of social exclusion is one that is deeply associated with late industrial modernity. In its modern form, the idea of social exclusion can be traced to the 1960s debates on the mechanisms of poverty and need in the affluent society, stemming from the postwar puzzlement that growth did not, as previously believed, trickle down to all groups of society. To use a modern phrase, the economic tide did not raise all boats. Rather, affluence seemed to have brought with it a whole new set of needs that had less to do with material want and more to do with intangible feelings of rootlessness and alienation. In late industrial capitalism, the old division between elites and the poor masses seemed to have been replaced by a growing middle-class mass and an increasingly marginalized group on the outside. This phenomenon was behind different political attempts to reshape agendas of poverty and find new means of social intervention in the 1960s. The American War on Poverty is the most well-known example.[6]

As multifaceted as they were, 1960s discourses on social exclusion contained a critique of the advanced industrial society and capitalism as something that systematically and structurally marginalized an important segment of society and deprived its members of a place in society and production. The postwar notion of progress was replaced by the fear of a deeply dichotomous social order, where some groups in society seemed to keep up with the accelerating pace of modernization while others fell mercilessly behind. The early works on a coming knowledge order, for instance the French sociologist Alain Touraine's work on the end of class, were concerned with the emergence of this two-tier society, a society in which the hierarchical class divisions of the factory were being replaced by social divisions around knowledge and creativity, inclusion and exclusion. This was part of a growing 1960s critique of growth and technology as something that actively shaped new social hierarchies, new forms of want, and new groups disabled by development. This critical perspective informed the rise of the New Left and its critique of social democracy in both Sweden and the United Kingdom.[7]

In the 1990s and 2000s, this idea of social exclusion was and continues to be discernable under another guise in the idea of the social web, in which inequalities are not conceptualized as hierarchies in status and power but in terms of spatial in-exclusion from the social web. This has similarities with postwar discourses on social exclusion, indeed, in contemporary ideas of a growing technological divide, where the crucial social line of demarcation runs between those who are included in the network and those who are excluded from it and who can therefore not take part in democratic processes or are rendered digitally illiterate.[8] In both the United Kingdom and Sweden, attempts to extend opportunities for upgrading skills, for distance learning, and for universal access to the Internet are reactions to this fear of the possibly exclusionary effects of ICT.[9] However, in line with the way that contemporary social democracy seems to have broken with its critical articulations of capitalism, these contemporary notions of social exclusion seem to be detached from any critique of knowledge capitalism. Contemporary discourses on social exclusion reflect fundamental changes in our understanding of social organization. Principles of citizenship, solidarity, and equality are replaced by an emphasis on work and individual compliance with the norms of the network as the main principle of inclusion. Through such conceptualizations, the problem that Touraine observed as a question of social hierarchies and, indeed, of class becomes a question of the individual's location inside or outside the social fabric. Equality has become social cohesion, a concern with social order, the social order that is also understood as a source of economic prosperity. This is social democracy's understanding of poverty in the era of the network.[10]

Social exclusion is a highly complex term, with very different definitions in different national institutional settings and political cultures.[11] The problem of social exclusion also takes very different empirical forms in the United

Kingdom and Sweden because of different prevailing inequalities in British and Swedish society. But national interpretations of social exclusion are also highly dependent on different ideological legacies around poverty. The meaning of the term in Swedish—*social utslagning*—is literally "knocked out," a metaphor that places a significant emphasis on the agents who strike.[12] In recent years, this language has changed because of the emphasis of the European Union on national action plans against social exclusion, which has meant that the European terminology of social cohesion and inclusion has also become central in Sweden, without much critical discussion of the normative assumptions that the concept brings with it.[13] In the United Kingdom, there has been an enormous production of policy concerning social exclusion, which was placed at the heart of the New Labour agenda with the creation of the Social Exclusion Unit under the aegis of the prime minister in 1997. The SEU was the flagship of New Labour's modern governance project, working in cross-sectoral partnership with other departments and in local communities and heavily reliant on modern technologies of government such as ICT and audits.[14] New Labour's language of social exclusion, however, echoes a liberal tradition of the deserving and undeserving poor and of the cultural theories of poverty and dependency that originated in the American War on Poverty and were brought to the United Kingdom by social theorists such as Charles Murray and Lawrence Mead.[15]

Wasted Potential

In both countries, social exclusion is framed in an economic language that has to do with the waste of human capital. This is the mirror image of the growth policies of the Third Way—if the key to growth in the new economy is people's potential, then social exclusion is that potential gone to waste because it represents people whose knowledge and talent are not put to use. Social exclusion is wasted human potential. As such, it cannot be accepted in a modern society where success hinges on the utilization of the potential of all.[16] This, like other articulations of the Third Way discussed in previous pages, is ambiguous, vacillating between a critique of capitalism and a discourse of efficiency and improvement. The idea of waste reflects social democracy's classic critique of inequalities as inefficient, of, as it were, capitalism's "inherent" tendency to destroy social resources and "use up" or "waste" people. But the notion of waste also stands in direct relationship to the Third Way's capitalization of people.

In the United Kingdom, social exclusion has been predominantly framed in the economic language that treats people as forms of capital. It is thus understood as a problem not only of human misery and plight—or even social injustice—but as a problem for a vibrant innovation economy.[17] There has been a crucial focus on the costs of social exclusion—not just in terms of wasted lives but in terms of the social costs of crime and welfare bills, the costs to business for reduced market demand and a reduced skilled labor force, and the costs for the knowledge economy in terms of lost entrepreneurs.[18] Just as New Labour has had an ambitious social agenda in other areas, it has certainly had a radical agenda on social exclusion, with means such as the Sure Start program, programs for extending educational opportunity, or the young apprentice program designed to provide room for all talents. However, it has also linked social exclusion to asociality, crime, and immoral behavior, adding up to a pervasive underclass discourse, which effectively centers in on the deviant behavior of the underclass.[19] This underclass discourse merged with New Labour's economistic understanding of social justice as a problem of prosperity and its approach to the social as the locus where crucial processes of wealth creation take place. Social exclusion is, thus, a problem for the creation of social capital—and as such a problem for the efficiency of knowledge capitalism.

New Labour's understanding of social exclusion reflects its cultural analysis of social problems, an analysis that stems not only from the underclass discourses of American theorists of poverty but also from its understanding of knowledge and learning as things that are culturally dependent and fostered. Social exclusion, within the communitarian agenda, is essentially seen as being caused by the breakdown of community values, indeed, the erosion of the sense of obligation and the individual lack of aspiration. Correspondingly, inclusion is a process that starts with the individual embracing these values and with the individual's coming to terms with problems of character.[20] There has been a dynamic emphasis in the concept of social exclusion—an emphasis, that is, on the mechanisms of exclusion. Investment into deprived communities and policies directed at urban renewal have been designed to create aspiration.[21] Ultimately, however, the drivers behind social exclusion are understood as cultural, as the cultural poverty of aspiration that is the result of decades of social decay. The dynamic emphasis, thus, is on the inclusion into the social fabric by learning the virtues of citizenship, embracing the work ethic, and accepting prevailing notions of duty.[22] In this manner, the individual willingness to improve, accept opportunity, become employable comes into the heart of politics, in the fusion between cultural analysis and economic argument that forms the basis of social democracy's understanding of the knowledge age.

There is a fundamental duality to this cultural analysis, between a progressive emphasis on helping people bring out their potential and a much more repressive emphasis on discipline and coercion to induce them to bring out their potential. On the one hand, in its fight against social exclusion, New Labour has struggled to extend educational opportunity and educational allowances also to those far from the general education system, specifically targeting 16- to 18-year-olds who leave school with small chances of making it in the labor market.[23] On the other, the conditionality in entitlements and the careful monitoring of progress through standards and audits apply to the socially excluded as well. The use of ICT as a new means of political governance reflects this duality. While ICT has been an important policy tool for creating services tailored to the special needs of those on the outside, through distance learning and web portals with information of entitlements, it has also been made into a tool of surveillance and coercion. For instance, to prevent truancy, schools have been enabled to send automatic text messages when children are not present at the beginning of the school day, and schools have also been allowed to publish pupils' academic performance on school websites.[24]

While fighting social exclusion has been at the heart of the New Labour agenda for over a decade, it is very striking that New Labour does not have much of a theory regarding the possibility that there is something in the new economy or in the process of capitalist transformation that creates social exclusion. It recognizes that rapidly changing demands for skills lead to an increased risk of social exclusion for those who fail to upgrade their skills, but its answer to this lies in its language of opportunity. If opportunity is provided through the expansion of education, then failure is truly an individual responsibility. It also seems oblivious to the argument that there might be something in its own policies—in the moralistic and authoritarian nature of its means of social intervention, its meritocratic language of excellence, and its economistic vision of a social order based on competitive strife—that might produce the kind of individual behavior it is trying to sanction. Competition, to New Labour, is a disciplining force, also when it comes to the socially excluded. Standards and audits apply also to them, monitoring their progress and inclusion.[25]

This is strikingly different from a sometimes highly romantic Swedish language of making room for everyone and making sure that "everyone gets on the train," which applies to social exclusion as well. The cement of society, to Swedish social democracy, is to be found in the individual allegiance to certain core social values: democracy, equality, and solidarity. Historically, in Sweden social exclusion has been understood as the incapacity to participate and exercise democratic rights, hence, of being outside of the *samhälle* and not being able to have a voice in the process of change. To the SAP, the problem of social exclusion fits into its overarching narrative of universalism and collective solidarity and responsibility—its emphasis on the "lift" and on "getting everybody on the train" or "bringing everybody along." These metaphors originated in the party's 1990s Program, which was concerned with an economic and technological development that might potentially leave a group behind while others were allowed to "board the train." It spoke of a worrying tendency in contemporary capitalism to divide opportunities and life chances between those who steadily gained in opportunity and those who found themselves "on the outside." It was clearly influenced by the idea of a two-tier society and the rise of a production order that might not have room for everyone. [26]

Nevertheless, the SAP's understanding of social exclusion also fits into a more classical social democratic understanding of inequalities and poverty as a form of waste that is caused by capitalism. Swedish social democracy has grappled with the problem of social exclusion since the 1960s, when a government Committee on Low Income concluded that significant groups in Swedish society had fallen behind despite the full employment and solidarity wage bargaining of the Swedish Model.[27] In the late 1960s, this was rapidly interpreted as an effect of the automation and rationalization of production, as something that led to the exhaustion of human production factors. Social exclusion was interpreted as a phenomenon related to industrialism and, as the 2001 Program put it, "capitalism's inherent tendency to destroy human and natural resources."[28] In a speech in 1978, Olof Palme spoke of social exclusion as the waste of the industrial society—"people on the garbage heap of the industrial society."[29] In the advanced industrial society, growth was no longer created by putting more people into work but seemed to be created by exhausting people's productive resources in intensified and rationalized production processes. The party's drive for economic democracy and workplace influence in the 1970s was a reaction against this development, an attempt to rethink the role of social democracy in capitalism and push the equality agenda even further, not only for the immediate working class but also for those "on the outside." Jonas Pontusson expressed this most astutely when he noted that its failure to implement economic democracy also proved to be the historic limit of Swedish social democracy.[30] One might say the same thing for the party's incapacity, or unwillingness, to incorporate social exclusion into its theory of progressive universalism.

To the SAP in the knowledge era, capitalism's waste of social resources appears to have been taken one step further, as growth no longer seems to need everyone to begin with. The phenomena of jobless growth and technological developments, which rapidly render new skills obsolete, seem to have created a group of undesired and unprofitable people in society—people who are effectively rendered useless. These are the "knowledge proletariat," or the underclass of knowledge-lacking people that the party sees as a feature of knowledge capitalism. The SAP's insistence, in the 1990s, on measures designed to increase the competence of all and extend access to higher education, particularly in regional colleges, for instance in the suburbs of Stockholm; the modernization of *folkbildning*; and the increased resources for early schooling; along with the knowledge lift for the long-term unemployed have all been aimed at thwarting such a development. Similarly, its employment policies have stressed that room must be made for all to participate based on their capacity and that working life needs to be adapted to the different needs and talents of the workforce, including matters of disabilities and differences in competitiveness.[31] The crucial difference to New Labour is that this contains a certain critique of what the party conceives as trends of knowledge capitalism, of a development in which competition and the quest for productivity gains drive up the process of change to the extent that there is no room left for those who do not meet required standards. This is a development that needs to be counteracted by the social democratic state, with protection for those who are, as it were, "weak."

This may seem to be a very ambiguous rhetoric, but it vacillates between emphases on the pressures of contemporary life, on the one hand, and the seeking of explanations to social exclusion in discourses on the weak, the less capable, and the less competitive, on the other. Arguably, this is an indication of the gap in the Swedish case between a kind of programmatic critique of capitalism in party discourse and the absence of a political analysis of economic and social change. However, it is also an indication of the fact that there is something about the idea of social exclusion that is fundamentally awkward to Swedish social democracy. Because of the historic role of the welfare state and the historically high levels of social equality and labor market participation in Sweden, social exclusion is, or at least has been, a much less prominent phenomenon in Sweden than in other European countries. Indeed, the comparison with the generationally entrenched poverty levels in British society is staggering. On the one hand, this makes social exclusion much less of a political problem; but, on the other, it also means that it is somehow more conspicuous. Social exclusion does not fit in with the SAP's worldview of Sweden as a good country in which to live—a society where no one should experience need or suffering, a society where indeed there are "no stepchildren and no favourites."[32] The mere phenomenon of social exclusion in Swedish society seems to hold a kind of accusation, namely, the suggestion that in the process of building the People's Home, the party might have missed some groups and effectively left someone behind. The cultural dependency or underclass discourse of New Labour is very far from its ideology; yet there is something so individual in the problem of social exclusion that it somehow seems difficult to explain in its normal social democratic language. Questions of truancy and welfare scrounging are a problem for principles of universalism and solidarity. In addition, the increased social inequalities and insecurities that have followed in the wake of the 1990s somehow seem to imply that the party did something wrong in its restructuring of Swedish public finances, in short, that it failed to protect the weakest. In integration policy and labor market policy, social democracy has been at pains to stress inclusion, but the means of inclusion are increasingly to be found in notions of individual responsibility, cultures of aspiration and hope, and individual activity. The Swedish action plans against social exclusion follow the conclusions of the Balance Sheet for Welfare, which stated that growing trends of social exclusion in Sweden have to do with groups that "fell off" the train in the 1990s and have not been able to get back on.[33] This is awkward to social democracy, which has been reluctant to talk about the social effects of crisis because this seems to address the issue of its own responsibility. In addition, while social exclusion is clearly acquiring an ethnic dimension in Sweden, Swedish social democracy is highly uneasy with the notion of structural discrimination, which critics of the Swedish welfare state have argued are an integral feature of "universalism."[34]

All of this means that the SAP tends to vacillate between explanations of structural factors—the stress of contemporary working life, the problems of integration and discrimination in Swedish society, segregation in suburban areas—and rather befuddled ideas regarding the causes of individual sadness and substance abuse in the midst of a resurrected People's Home. Sometimes party representatives clearly think that there is something ungrateful about people who may not *want* to belong in the first place. Thus, party policy falls back on what are ultimately highly individualized explanations of a social problem. In the 1960s, Social Democrats reacted to the discussion of social exclusion with an attitude that was captured in a famous radio debate with the Minister of Finance Gunnar Sträng—people who were earning low wages in the midst of Swedish society were quite simply not right in the head. In the 2000s, people are worried or a little sad.[35] It is indicative of the party's dearth of analyses of trends in Swedish society that the question of social exclusion or *"utanförskap"* was at the heart of the election campaign of 2006, as the Swedish Right made a powerful case for taking people off benefits and putting them into work by introducing tax credits and strengthening incentives for work. The "new Labour Party"—*nya Arbetarpartiet*—a reinvented the conservative party in the center field, campaigned to reform government bureaucracies that turn people into waste, or—as New Labour's critique of the "old" welfare state put it—"write people off" as if they were not capable of contributing to society.[36]

The Limits of Human Capital

In his 1973 book *The Coming of Post-Industrial Society*, the American sociologist Daniel Bell wrote of "exponential curves"—"the acceleration of doubling rates of all kinds." Bell was referring to the way that the growth of knowledge seemed to have passed a point where it was no longer humanly possible to keep up. Development seemed to defy saturation and to call for adaptation to constant acceleration. Exponential curves, Bell wrote, transform our lives.[37]

Notions of exponential curves inform the idea of the knowledge economy. We have seen them in ideas of the silicon revolution or Moore's Law, which presume the existence of a teleological logic of exponential expansion within the network. Similarly, the idea of human capital draws on a silent assumption that human capital, in contrast to the coal or steel or manual labor of the Industrial Revolution, will prove to be virtually limitless. Indeed, the idea of lifelong learning can be seen as a perpetual process of human capital expansion, a process that presumes that the expansion of the self and the expansion of the economy are virtually the same processes. In a sense, the knowledge economy seems to bring together the radical discourses of the late 1960s with social democracy's productivism and to claim that the dilemma between industrialism and individual emancipation was solved. Inherent in this is a hope that a life of work in the knowledge economy will be fundamentally different from a lifetime spent in the factory and that the knowledge economy avoids phenomena of exhaustion and exploitation because it works for self-fulfilment and will create happier and more creative individuals who quintessentially control their own lives. Hence, the 1960s debate on the limits to growth and the social and ecological costs of growth seems to have been replaced by assertions that the knowledge economy is clean; environmentally friendly and people friendly.[38]

These are very bold assumptions, and they seem oddly detached from serious analysis. Social democracy's virtual obsession with wealth creation and economic growth in last decade has meant that it has little theorization of the possible adverse effects of human capital expansion on human well-being. It might be argued that the limits of a productivity expansion driven by human capital must be the limits embedded—embodied—in that capital. These might be discussed in terms of the physical and cognitive scope and reach of human beings, the limits to our degree of adaptability, and our willingness and strength to learn and relearn, which do not, in contrast to presumptions of the constant expansion of productivity or the increasing efficiency of silicon, seem infinitely elastic. Studies show that work injuries are on a rise in contemporary societies and that physical work injuries are increasingly being replaced by disorders related to stress and insecurity. The French economist Daniel Cohen suggests that the phenomenon of burnout is endemic to modern capitalist societies and directly related to flexible production.[39]

There has been little debate about this in social democratic ideology. New Labour's idea of change as a competitive race to the top and its dismissal of individual needs for security in favor of an authoritarian call for opportunity leaves little room for questions of quality of life, happiness, and well-being, even if this is a discourse that has changed in the last years with a growing emphasis on the quality of jobs, work–life balance, and healthy workplaces. While this is, indisputably, a shifting ideological ground, these emerging discourses seem to remain firmly within New Labour's all-encompassing modernization narrative; healthy workplaces and happy people are arguments for efficiency and growth because they lead to more productive workplaces. Discourses of healthy workplaces are ultimately also about absence management and early intervention, which ensure that an employee will return to work at the earliest possible opportunity. [40]

In contrast, in Sweden, the idea of social exclusion has contained a certain, albeit hesitant, critique of the very process of modernization. The Persson years brought out a strand in social democratic ideology that is critical of modernization and growth, visible most clearly in the party's vision of a Green People's Home (*gröna folkhemmet*). Part of this strand has derailed into an unfortunate nostalgia for the People's Home, which has taken focus away from the work with a strategy for sustainable capitalism. Nevertheless, this has brought back a party discussion on the nature of progress and the relationship between growth and individual well-being. So the SAP states that progress cannot be considered progress if it leads to exclusion of people from working life because of increasing demands. The party's 2004 conference on growth concluded the following:

> Growth is not an end in itself. The objective of our policies is a better society. A society where people do not wear out early in life. A society where all can participate in production according to their ability . . . The objective of our growth policies is to make people grow. Our policies encourage entrepreneurship but also ensure that the sick can be rehabilitated and the disabled given a place in working life.[41]

Social democratic growth strategies of the 1990s contained an emphasis on the reform of working life by increasing the responsibility of employers for work environment and rehabilitation and by finding places, particularly in the public sector, for people who are not competitive.[42] The tripartite "Growth Conversations (*tillväxtsamtal*)" in 2003 and 2004 aimed toward the creation of a deal with employers, where government and trade unions agreed to tax reliefs for SMEs if business would accept increased responsibility for sick leaves, incapacity, and work injuries. This was a reaction to the soaring levels of long-term sick leaves and absenteeism in the first years of the 2000s, which were interpreted by the Swedish Right as "the Swedish disease," caused by allegedly perverted incentives in a far too generous social insurance system.[43] The growth conversations were not a success, mainly because of the SAP's failure to reach an agreement with the trade unions over taxes, which led to the subsequent withdrawal of business from the talks.[44] However, the social democratic emphasis on the roots stress related work injuries, and the party's attempt to strengthen employer responsibility is very different from the way that responsibility, in New Labour politics, has predominantly been a question of strengthening the individual work ethic. Ultimately, this is indicative of a more important difference, namely, that the SAP sees a potential limit to the process of modernization, a limit set by individuals and their life situations. Life, the party claims, is not a race.[45]

Conclusion

New Labour's idea of change as a competitive race and the Swedish rejection of change as exactly such a race are indicative of different notions of modernization and of the role of the individual in the process of change. While

New Labour seems to presume that individual adaptation is virtually limitless, Swedish social democracy stresses the possible tensions between change and well-being. Ultimately, this falls back on different conceptions of growth as economic or human growth and definitions of what constitutes progress.

Nevertheless, in both countries the individual has clearly emerged as the focal point of change. Social policies have gained a cultural emphasis, which stands in direct relationship to the way that modern economic policies see growth as stemming from certain individual attitudes and dispositions. Such a cultural approach permits a limited egalitarian agenda, where policies are aimed at breaking with the barriers that lock in potential, foster a culture of aspiration and achievement, and create a culture of learning, but where these barriers are ultimately seen as located within individuals themselves, in the incapacity or unwillingness to learn. It is this conception of economic change as beginning in individuals that leads to the highly specific understanding of social exclusion as a problem of character. A possible alternative explanation of rising social exclusion in the Western world today would arguably be, as Zygmunt Bauman has suggested, that exclusion is an integral characteristic of post-Fordist labor markets, creating an abundant population without value.[46]

9 The Future of Social Democracy: Epilogue

As I finish this book, climate change, the financial crisis, and the election of Barack Obama are changing the face of politics. Obama speaks to the idea that everything is possible, which is really precisely the opposite of what Third Wayers told us. The financial crisis challenges the rationale of the Third Way, the idea that the market economy is supreme and requires all our devotion. Crisis is indeed undoing the prosperous economy that was social democracy's pride, leaving us with the question of how much of the new economy was ever for real. The 1990s and early 2000s are rapidly becoming history.

Suddenly it is hard to think of a more outdated political slogan than the Third Way. European social democracy has spent the last years in a state of crisis—ranging from the fatigue of New Labour after Blair to the disintegration of French socialists who cannot agree on a road forward between anticapitalism, modernization, and old-style state socialism. Italian social democracy has once again lost the working class vote to Berlusconi. In Sweden, current opposition leader Mona Sahlin seems, more than anything, to have gone back to the 1980s and its themes of freedom, entrepreneurship, and meritocracy, struggling to face a new Right that seems, at times, more social democratic than social democracy itself.

The state of social democracy in the present leaves us with the question, Is the Third Way at an end, or is it merely at a critical juncture? As the historian David Marquand put it when Blair finally stepped down in the summer of 2007, the Third Way was a fudge, and one that seemed to degenerate over time into a Blairite project of what Marquand describes as "evangelical belligerence."[1] In the eyes of history, Blairism will no doubt be seen as a political project inseparable from the Iraq War, and as such it is decisively at an end. However, it would be premature and misconstrued to proclaim it dead. The Third Way was bigger than Blair. If we understand the Third Way to be a project of social democratic revisionism, similar to other projects of social democratic revisionism in history, then it is clear that its historical significance goes beyond the individuals who have carried it. Moreover, while the themes that have dominated social democratic thinking in the long decade from the mid-1990s to the present—choice, opportunity, entrepreneurship—may be less fresh and shiny policy responses to the issues facing social democracy today, it is also hard to discern an alternative vision to them in contemporary European social democracy. The financial crisis will, of course, force social democracy to think very hard about its choices, and it is also rapidly cracking open the fissures of the Third Way project. However, more than anything, crisis has shown us just how disoriented social democracy is in the present. It is hardly the political agent that has responded most vehemently to crisis—rather, with the possible exception for Gordon Brown, it seems to stand silently by as leaders of the Right bring Keynesianism back.

The ideological coherence of the Third Way should not be overstated, and many voices within contemporary social democracy have been left out in the previous pages. It is, and was always, a tension-ridden project, made up of discourses and counterdiscourses from various periods of revisionism and from the different factions of traditionalists and modernizers in the different constellations of social democracy that have defined the period from the 1970s onward. These tensions have become stronger with increasing electoral challenges and changes of leadership. Today, the Third Way is a problematic heritage for social democracy, and Social Democrats all over Europe are struggling to break out of its confined space. For a long time this struggle has looked like a strange waltz of two steps forward, one step back. Gordon Brown's willingness to break with the Blair years seemed highly debatable until financial crisis suddenly put him in the position to nationalize British banks. While financial crisis has meant a certain return to themes of "old" Labour, including even the dreaded notion of taxation, the newfound need to redistribute public money to banks and house owners has had hardly any visible effects on New Labour's morally conservative approach to those who were poor before the markets came tumbling down, even if two of Brown's first initiatives in government were the dismantling of Blair's flagships of the Social Exclusion Unit and the Respect agenda.

In Sweden, Göran Persson was forgotten the minute after he stepped down, and the Persson years are now openly seen as suffering from nostalgia and lack

of debate. The party's slogans in the election campaign in 2006 seemed to epit-
omize a political project that had turned its back on the future: "We are proud
but not satisfied"; "Sweden is a good country to live in." Persson's successor
Mona Sahlin has been a bold visionary in integration policy and an articulate
feminist. But Sahlin was also one of the young modernizers around Ingvar
Carlsson in the 1980s Third Way project. Her first speech as party leader announced a renewal that echoed of the themes of the 1980s and that spoke of
reclaiming the notion of freedom as the center of social democratic politics.[2]
In the following months, the party made hesitant statements on the need to
reform schools—without addressing a possible conflict between equality and
diversity in the voucher system—and on labor market policy, through promises to strengthen individual responsibility.[3] It has opened the door for an all-
party alliance around schools, based on principles of order and meritocracy,
also including the possibility of grades in early years—a principle that was
always a red flag to the SAP.

Taken together, the sheer magnitude of the issues facing us in the world
today should be ample material for a new social democratic vision of society.
Obama will surely have at least as big an influence on European social democracy as Clinton once did, as he has already begun to reshape the global
political landscape. But while Social Democrats today are calling for a new
future vision, for something that might define the soul of social democracy
for the future, it doesn't seem to be much closer to defining the content of that
vision.[4] In recent years, this future debate has suffered from a tangible instrumentalism. So the quest for a social democratic future has become more about
the need for a vision, the need for a "story" to persuade people with, than
about a progressive analysis of what is wrong with the world and how to define a better social order. To that extent, the social democratic future vision is
in a curious state, squeezed between calls for utopia and legacies of spin. This
is the result of the confined space that was and is the Third Way. Very strategically, Third Wayers, in Britain, Sweden, and elsewhere, constructed a political
space that would appeal to all and no one, and now they are stuck in it.

Meanwhile, it is possible (but by no means a given) that financial crisis
will challenge one of the central aspects of contemporary social democracy,
namely, its lack of a critique of capitalism. I have argued in the pages of this
book that what the Third Way did was to turn articulations that, in the history
of social democracy, were articulations in a critique of capitalism into arguments of efficiency and improvement; arguments, more than anything, for the

efficiency of markets. In this process, it took historic discourses of revisionism in the social democratic project one step further as it defined principles of equality and security as mere means to other more important ends and made culture, education, and equality into arguments for prosperity. It abdicated the sphere of utopia—what Roberto Mangabeira Ungar has called the "cause of the constructive imagination"—and it rejected the idea that there are forms of good and worth in society that stand in conflict to the economy.[5] This is important. While social democracy has rarely been an anticapitalist movement, nevertheless its utopian aspirations have had a critical function in the social democratic project because they have been the guiding stars of debates on the direction of change. In the history of social democracy, utopian discourses have given voice to the kind of critique that reminds a reformist movement of the fine but crucial line between adaptation and politics. The Third Way left these things behind when it argued that the role of politics was not shifting the goalposts of ideological debate but pragmatic management and the identification of what works, the appeal to mainstream values of the people and the creation of a common good reduced to prosperity. In the same process, ideology became a question of articulation, a question of shifting ideological elements after the presumed appeal of the electorate but not with shaping the values of people. The Third Way stands in an awkward relationship to postmodernism here, borrowing its postulates of articulated identities but stripping these of their emancipatory potential, believing in the power of political language and ideology production but not in the productive role of ideology.

From the confined space that this abdication of utopia created, it became very hard to talk of alternatives, indeed hard to imagine how something else could come about and what this something else could be. Rejecting utopia went beyond revisionism. It was a process much more serious than purging social democracy of outdated teleological blueprints or editing the books of old dogma that had long since lost their relevance. Leaving ideology behind did not free social democracy; rather, social democracy lost a worldview, an entire social democratic ontology without which it is very difficult to make sense of patterns and structures in society. So New Labour today finds itself in a space where it knows not how to speak of things because these things have become so detached from a critique of the structures of economy and society that what are left are vague concepts of fairness, inequalities (somehow less offensive in the plural form), and opportunity. In Sweden, social democracy has held on to its classical articulations of equality, security, and solidarity, but it has treated these notions as if they were stagnant, self-evident, and common sensical; and in doing so it has no less left the sphere of ideological reasoning. Indeed, the very striking feature of Swedish social democracy in the 1990s is the absence of debate and the party's silences around crucial issues. So when asked of the social democratic future vision, the then future Minister of Finance Pär Nuder replied, seemingly untroubled, that there was really no vision.[6] This lack of vision is an inherent feature of pragmatism, but arguably this pragmatic stance was taken one step further in the 1990s. Assertions of Sweden as the best society in the world can't help but reflect the nagging question, Is Sweden still the best society in the world? The SAP's use of history in the 1990s has in itself been a process of ideological rearticulation because, through careful constructions of continuity and through the careful reliance on the symbols and images of Nordic notions of modernity, the party has constructed a worldview in which nothing has changed. The road to the future goes through the past. The notion of the People's Home has become a tired trope, a past utopia of national unity, social harmony, and reformist rationality. This nostalgia is a very particular political strategy, and it is indicative of a political project that has little to say of the contemporary world.

There were consequences of the Third Way's reinterpretation of social democracy as a quintessentially pragmatic and even unpolitical project. It has left electorates deeply uncertain of what social democracy is and who, if anyone, can protect them in a runaway world. It opened up a new political space for a new and modernizing Right that in both countries is now struggling to present itself as a better centrist than is social democracy. In Sweden, the right-wing Alliance for Sweden campaigned in 2006 as the new Labour party (*det nya arbetarpartiet*). In the United Kingdom, David Cameron has very strategically tried to profile himself as a new Blair, firmly in the center ground on previously polarized issues of education and crime. Possibly this political competition in the middle will force social democracy to think seriously about ideology. But what is perhaps more dangerous than the rise of a new and self-professed moderate Right or a disenchanted electorate is that the Third Way also left Social Democrats themselves deeply uncertain about their role in the world. The search for future vision is also a search for identity and purpose, for those many people who joined politics and social democracy because they believe in it.

So far, the call for vision has seemed detached from analysis of the times we live in, and, indeed, from attempts to provide a progressive analysis of contemporary capitalism. Meanwhile, there are many issues in our surrounding world, less spectacular than financial breakdown and rising temperatures but that nevertheless also go well beyond the scope of the individual and call for new political responsibilities. The process of welfare state retrenchment has created new risks, many of them arising precisely from the praised principles of choice.[7] Inequalities are growing, in the domestic arena and on the global level. Galloping private consumption and the transformation of many crucial public goods into private ones in the last decades has opened up new divides in the access to housing, education, pensions, and care, not least in Sweden. There is thus nothing historically predetermined about the demise of social democracy, nothing, to my mind, that would render it obsolete. Rather, social democracy seems to have a relevance that is maybe greater than ever.

From this perspective, the enduring historic paradox of the Third Way is perhaps that it came into existence in a moment, in the 1990s, that seemed to call out for a new social democratic project but that it somehow failed to provide a social democratic analysis of our times. In retrospect, the decade from the mid-1990s was a time in which the great right-wing tide started to roll back. It saw the emergence of new social movements calling for utopian visions of another world. Historically, such utopian critique has invigorated social democracy, and maybe it will in the coming decade, but in the 1990s social democracy's response to this critique was its message of adaptation to globalization and capital as forces beyond political control. The 1990s also saw—through the hard work of social democratic politicians like Blair and Persson—the end of the neoliberal critique of the welfare state. The welfare state is today more or less universally acknowledged as a necessary part of capitalism. Social democracy seems to have won the historic battle over its claim that what is fair is also efficient. New Labour has succeeded in establishing a progressive social policy agenda in many areas, and the historic feat of Swedish social democracy in the 1990s is arguably that it has successfully established that the Swedish model is not deficient but valid for another era. But the tough verdict on the last decade is that social democracy did not use its momentum in the 1990s to push forward an egalitarian agenda or defend the uniqueness of the social democratic project.

This forces us to consider very carefully what social democracy *is*. On some level, of course, social democracy is what social democracy *does*, as was suggested in the early literature on the Third Way. From this perspective, the Third Way was just social democracy recast for a new era, and there was nothing in it that set it apart from the social democratic project in principled terms. But social democracy is arguably a historic project construed around certain values that are not instrumental or exchangeable but that define its soul. The objective of equality is such a goal, such a utopian aspiration to a better social order, without which it is very hard to be and think social democrat. As Sheri Berman has recently argued, social democracy is historically defined not by its anticapitalist stances but by the way that it historically set certain values—equality, democracy, solidarity—as values that were superior to the economic. The importance of these values is that they established what Berman calls "the primacy of politics," the idea that there is a political sphere defined by values that override the market. This is where the Third Way marks a decisive break with the historic project of social democracy. Indeed, Sheri Berman writes that the proponents of the Third Way "appear not to understand that one of the core principles of social democracy has always been a belief in the primacy of politics."[8]

Berman reasserts an argument that has been made by many other students of social democracy and by critics of New Labour since its very naissance. But Berman argues that the twentieth century marked the historic victory of social democracy, through the long historic struggle to put values of equality and democracy and principles of social citizenship at the basis of our societies and gradually transform them.[9] Similarly, it has been argued that the rise of a new center Right would reflect a hegemonic victory of social democratic values over neoliberalism, that the Third Way has succeeded in establishing the values of social democracy as consensus values in the population, and that the Right is now left with stealing social democracy's clothes.[10] There is clearly some truth in this. There are, as Berman points out, few political projects today that question the social embeddedness and democratic regulation of capitalism. However, historically, social democracy did something more than "just" embed the market—it debated its alternatives, its limits, its notions of value and good, and its effects on people's lives. It may be true that there are few proponents of the free market in contemporary politics, but there also few critics of capitalism. Arguably, the specificity of the values of equality and democracy in the social democratic project was that they were linked to a critique of capitalism and to the structures of economy and production that infringe on human fulfilment. This critique of capitalism was a central aspect of social democracy's struggle for the primacy of politics: through welfare state intervention and social policy, through economic planning, through education and cultural debate, and through the conscientious protection of certain spheres in society. In the 1990s, Third Wayers mistakenly assumed that such a critique of capitalism necessarily called for the nationalization of the means of the production and that speaking of capitalism presumes understanding it as a stage-driven development of static and recognizable patterns.

It is true that social democracy has made that mistake in history, but historically it has also criticized exactly these assumptions of Marxism and socialism with its appeal to human will and potential, to democracy, and to the transformative role of social citizenship. In history, social democracy's understanding of capitalism was tied to a utopian aspiration and critique, the notion that a different and better society was possible and that this society had to be built on a critique of the economic and social structures that caused inequality and waste in the present. So the Swedish "modernizer" Ernst Wigforss spoke of "provisory utopias" (*provisoriska utopier*): the dreams that were within the realm of political possibility but had to be radical enough as to function as guiding stars for the process of pragmatic reform if social democracy were to keep track of its defining values.[11] In the absence of such utopian vision and in the absence of a critique of capitalism that link the lives of people with the way we organize society and economy, the Third Way is, as Roberto Ungar puts it, merely the first way with sugar, "the sweetener of compensatory social policy and social insurance to make up for a failure to achieve any fundamental broadening of opportunity."[12] This is not the historic victory of social democracy, but the historic retreat of social democracy from exactly those things that historically defined its soul.

This would suggest that the move to the center is possible only because social democratic articulations are today so innocuous that they can easily also be embraced by the Right. The vision of equality, in contemporary social democratic discourse, is void of its utopian elements, reduced, in the case of New Labour, to an instrumentalism that has to speak of equality as a means for other things and first and foremost as a route to prosperity, or, in the Swedish case, detached from analysis of current trends in inequality.[13] This is not to say that there are no important differences between the contemporary social democratic project and the new Right, whatever the latter will turn out to be.[14] But it is not entirely easy today to distinguish what sets social democratic articulations apart from modernized versions of social conservatism or social liberalism, both of which have become integrated elements in social democratic ideology. Arguably the contemporary acclaim of welfare statism in the political middle is that today it is a project of social order and not of social change, a project of prosperity and growth and not of equality, a project that sees social citizenship and the common good as a question of the adherence to market values and not as a radical principle for social transformation. Social democracy's contemporary articulations of meritocracy, opportunity, and potential do not challenge the social order. Its notions of efficiency and prosperity have become so narrow that these are today but notions of market efficiency, decoupled from arguments of what a good society should be like or the importance of public good for equality and solidarity. The middle class that is the target of the new Labour parties on the political Right is in significant parts social democracy's own creation. In the 1930s, social democracy appealed to the common good in the form of solidarity and to the "people" as historical actors who could be convinced to carry a political project of social transformation. In the 1990s, it appealed to a people whom it saw as naturally conservative, made up of self-interested consumers and imbued with a national identity inseparable from market values.

So freedom of choice and diversity became more important than democracy, opportunity more important than equality, responsibility more important than rights. The shift in notions of citizenship from rights to responsibility and obligation is a sea change because it reorients the entire political project around the subject individual. Many changes in the organization of the welfare state seem to have serious adverse effects on the status of citizenship and on the very ties of reciprocity and mutuality in society. To that extent, the Third Way seems to have missed its historic opportunity and failed to provide a progressive account of our times. In the same logic, it also seems to have failed to create a progressive account out of the knowledge economy.

The central argument of the Third Way is the revocation of the old socialist claim that the role of politics is to bring out the potential of all, to allow all individuals to grow and pursue their talents and become what they have it in themselves to become, now in an age that allegedly gives people new opportunities to pursue that potential. But it seems in fact to have no real answer to the question of what opportunity and human potential are, or what defines the common good in an era where individuals may be increasingly concerned with the cultivation of their selves but also seem to ask for new forms of belonging, where on the one hand mills are disappearing but on the other they are also replaced by call centers and outsourcing, and where opportunity does not seem to automatically spread but to concentrate. Education and culture that have a fundamental role for the creation and liberation of human potential have been turned into market goods in a global running for competitiveness. There seem to be virtually no values, to contemporary social democracy, that are not also economic values.

This reflects what I have described as a process of capitalization: The Third Way turns notions of good that historically were noneconomic goods, such as creativity or curiosity, into new commodities and indeed new forms of capital. This could be put more bluntly: In the Third Way, social democracy's critique of capitalism has been replaced by a theory of capital, by a theory of how to create value in the knowledge economy. In so doing it elevates principles of prosperity and efficiency into hegemonic notions of value and worth and makes alternative definitions of value seem frivolous. In this process—in the process of constantly defining everything in terms of its potential use value in the new economy—social democracy is an active agent in the constitution of an economy that might make us prosperous in some ways and infinitely poorer in others.

In itself, this capitalizing logic is not new to social democracy, and it would be a mistake therefore to think that the Third Way is somehow an unhappy accident or anomaly in the social democratic tradition. The Third Way draws on fundamental elements in the social democratic tradition. However, it does so through a very selective process of rereading social democracy's past ideologies, a rereading in which it strategically picks certain elements while silencing others. So it speaks of community and social cohesion but leaves out the long-standing critique of the market as a threat to social order that is an important feature of social democracy's historic notion of community. It speaks of culture as a way of creating fulfilled and whole-knowledge citizens but leaves out William's critique of industrialism or Morris's and Sandler's utopias of education and beauty. It speaks of the human capital waste of inequality and social exclusion—but shies away from critiquing structures in favor of an argument where, essentially, people waste themselves. Human capital discourse, to the Third Way, is about putting people to use, tapping the potential of us all. It blames people, not capitalism; it corrects people, not structures. So New Labour reenacts a kind of productivist social interventionism or social engineering that is deep in the heart of social democracy, a logic that historically is prone to see people as capital; but it forgets that the aspiration to equality, democracy, and solidarity was the bulwark that once steered that productivism into a progressive argument of social transformation instead of a conservative or even fascist narrative of social order. It leans on Scandinavian influences of work ethic but is oblivious of the transformative role of social citizenship. In the process, it leaves out a whole sphere of utopian thought in the history of social democracy, without which social democratic politics are reduced to creating prosperity and people reduced to productive capital. Without a critique of the structures of knowledge capitalism, the Third Way's slogan of "tapping potential" leads to a dangerous capitalization of the human self.

The notion of capitalism has not been prized in the politics of the Left lately, despite the rise of movements such as Attack or Italian *Ya basta!*. Maybe the failure of these movements lies exactly in the fact that they also did not manage to produce a theory of our times but remained radical protesters. While this book is about two particular versions of social democracy, it is hard to find other and more viable debates about capitalism in other social democratic parties. In France, PS has occasionally—pushed by a small but vocal French communist Left—debated the theme of knowledge capitalism and post-Fordism. But French politics of the Left are also incapable of mounting an alternative worldview to that of the Right.

It is possible, finally, that the knowledge economy was nothing but fluff, a strategic invention of a coalition of business and political interests to define desired political changes as contingently necessary. If so, it says something about social democracy's inability to invent its own strategy to change the world. Social democracy needs to go back to an understanding of capitalism as something that not only creates riches but also impoverishes our world.

Notes

Notes

Introduction

1. Influential studies of this first wave were Alex Callinicos, *Against the Third Way* (Cambridge, U.K., and Malden, MA: Polity Press; Blackwell, 2001); Steven Driver and Luke Martell, *New Labour: Politics after Thatcherism* (Cambridge, U.K.: Polity Press, 1998); Stuart Hall, "The Great Moving Nowhere Show," *Marxism Today* (1998); Colin Hay, *The Political Economy of New Labour* (Manchester, U.K.: Manchester University Press, 1998); Richard Heffernan, *New Labour and Thatcherism: Political Change in Britain* (Basingstoke, U.K., and New York: Macmillan; St. Martin's Press, 2000). For Sweden, see J. Magnus Ryner, *Capitalist Restructuring, Globalisation and the Third Way: Lessons from the Swedish Model, Routledge/RIPE Studies in Global Political Economy; 5* (London: Routledge, 2002).

2. See Tony Blair, *New Britain. My Vision of a Young Country* (London: Fourth Estate Limited, 1996); Tony Blair, *The Third Way: New Politics for the New Century* (London: Fabian Society, 1998); Department for Trade and Industry, "Our Competitive Future. Building the Knowledge Economy" (London: DfTI, 1998).

3. Gordon Brown, "The Politics of Potential. A New Agenda for Labour," in *Reinventing the Left*, ed. David Miliband (Cambridge, U.K.: Polity Press, 1994).

4. Brown, "The Politics of Potential. A New Agenda for Labour," p. 116.

5. Göran Persson, speech to Örebro Universitets invigning, in Göran Persson, *Tankar och tal 1996–2000* (Stockholm: Hjalmarson och Högerberg, 2000), p. 163; Sveriges socialdemokratiska arbetarparti, *Ett decennium av satsningar på utbildning och*

forskning ledde till framgång. Socialdemokratisk utbildningspolitik 1994–2004 (Stockholm: Socialdemokraterna, 2004).

6. See Joel Mokyr, *The Gifts of Athena. Historical Origins of the Knowledge Economy* (Princeton, NJ, and Oxford, U.K.: Princeton University Press, 2002); Deirdre McCloskey, *The Bourgeois Virtues* (Chicago: University of Chicago Press, 2005).

7. Steve Bastow and James Martin, *Third Way Discourse: European Ideologies in the Twentieth Century* (Edinburgh: Edinburgh University Press, 2003), pp. 59–66; Giuliano Bonoli and Martin Powell, "Third Ways in Europe?" *Social Policy and Society*, 1, 1 (2002); Anthony Giddens, *The Global Third Way Debate* (Cambridge, U.K.: Polity Press, 2001).

Chapter 1

1. Donald Sassoon, *One Hundred Years of Socialism: The West European Left in the Twentieth Century* (London: Tauris, 1996); Francis Castles, *The Social Democratic Image of Society* (London: Routledge, Keegan Paul, 1978).

2. Bob Jessop, *The Future of the Capitalist State* (Cambridge, U.K.: Polity Press, 2002); Bob Jessop, "Critical Semiotic Analysis and Cultural Political Economy," in *Critical Discourse Studies*, 1, 2 (October 2004), pp. 159–174. Compare Fred Block, *Postindustrial Possibilities: A Critique of Economic Discourse* (Berkeley: University of California Press, 1990).

3. I make no attempt in this book to define the very nebulous concept of the knowledge, or knowledge-based, economy, or any of the other equally problematic terms that surround it, such as *post-Fordism, the information age,* or *the knowledge society.* The meaning of these terms is anything but clear, as is their correspondence to empirical reality. But from the perspective that the concept "the knowledge economy" has a critical function in setting the direction and content of reform, thus defining the role of modern politics, it is worthy of our attention. Under its conveniently wide umbrella, social democracy does some things that it already did before but that acquire new meaning because they are set in the context of the new economy, and other things whose relevance to social democratic politics is motivated by the idea of the knowledge economy.

4. Ruth Levitas, *The Concept of Utopia* (Syracuse, NY: Syracuse University Press, 1990); Peter Beilharz, *Labour's Utopias: Bolshevism, Fabianism, Social Democracy* (London: Routledge, 1992).

5. John Callaghan and Ilaria Favretto, *Transitions in Social Democracy* (Manchester, U.K.: Manchester University Press, 2007).

6. See particularly Colin Hay, *The Political Economy of New Labour* (Manchester, U.K.: Manchester University Press, 1998); J. Magnus Ryner, *Capitalist Restructuring, Globalisation and the Third Way: Lessons from the Swedish Model* (London: Routledge, 2002).

7. Ilaria Favretto, *The Long Search for a Third Way: The British Labour Party and the Italian Left since 1945* (Basingstoke, U.K.: Palgrave Macmillan, 2003), p. 3.

8. Sheri Berman, *The Primacy of Politics. Social Democracy and the Making of Europe's 20th Century* (Cambridge, U.K.: Cambridge University Press, 2006).

9. Jonas Hinnfors, *Reinterpreting Social Democracy. A History of Stability in the British Labour Party and Swedish Social Democratic Party* (Manchester, U.K.: Manchester University Press, 2006).

10. Sassoon, *One Hundred Years of Socialism*.

11. See Gordon Brown, "Equality—Then and Now," in *Crosland and New Labour*, ed. D Leonard (London: Macmillan, 1999); Raymond Plant, "Crosland, Equality and New Labour," in *Crosland and New Labour*, ed. D Leonard (London: Macmillan, 1999); Stephen Fielding, *The Labour Party: Continuity and Change in the Making of New Labour* (Basingstoke, U.K.: Palgrave Macmillan, 2003).

12. Jenny Andersson, *Between Growth and Security. Swedish Social Democracy from a Strong Society to a Third Way* (Manchester, U.K.: Manchester University Press, 2006).

13. Åsa Linderborg, *Socialdemokraterna skriver historia: historieskrivning som ideologisk maktresurs 1892–2000* (Stockholm: Atlas, 2001); Patrick Diamond, ed., *New Labour's Old Roots. Revisionist Thinkers in Labour's History 1931–1997* (Exeter, U.K.: Imprint Academic, 2004).

14. Brown, "Equality—Then and Now": SAP, *Framtid för Sverige. Handlingslinjer för att föra Sverige ur krisen* (Stockholm, 1981).

15. Gerassimos Moschonas, *In the Name of Social Democracy. The Great Transformation: 1945 to the Present* (London: Verso, 2002), p. 293.

16. See Ruth Levitas, *The Inclusive Society: Social Exclusion and New Labour* (New York: Routledge, 2005).

17. David Miliband, *Reinventing the Left* (Cambridge, U.K.: Polity Press, 1994).

18. Geoff Eley, *Forging Democracy. The History of the Left in Europe 1850–2000.* (Oxford, U.K.: Oxford University Press, 2002), p. 7.

19. Gøsta Esping-Andersen, *The Three Worlds of Welfare Capitalism* (Cambridge, U.K.: Polity Press, 1990); Claus Offe, *Contradictions of the Welfare State* (Cambridge, MA: MIT Press, 1984).

20. Steve Bastow and James Martin, *Third Way Discourse: European Ideologies in the Twentieth Century* (Edinburgh: Edinburgh University Press, 2003).

21. Sheri Berman, *The Social Democratic Moment* (Cambridge, MA: Harvard University Press, 1998).

22. See Kevin Manton, *Socialism and Education in Britain 1883–1902* (London: Woburn Press, 2001).

23. See Will Leggett, Luke Martell, and Sarah Hale, ed., *The Third Way and Beyond: Criticisms, Futures, Alternatives* (Manchester, U.K.: Manchester University Press, 2004).

24. Eley, *Forging Democracy.* p. 7.

25. John D. Stephens, *The Transition from Capitalism to Socialism* (London: Macmillan, 1979); Gösta Esping-Andersen, *Politics against Markets* (Princeton, NJ: Princeton University Press, 1985).

26. Vivienne A. Schmidt, "Values and Discourse in the Politics of Adjustment," in Vivienne Schmidt and Fritz Scharpf, eds., *Work and Welfare in the Open Economy* (Oxford, U.K.: Oxford University Press, 2000), pp. 228–309.

27. Mark Blyth, *Great Transformations: Economic Ideas and Institutional Change in the Twentieth Century* (New York: Cambridge University Press, 2002); Ryner, *Capitalist Restructuring, Globalisation and the Third Way*; Andersson, *Between Growth and Security*; Urban Lundberg, *Social Democracy Lost—The Pension Reform in Sweden*, Working Paper (Stockholm: Institute for Futures Studies, 2005); Jonas Pontusson, "At the End of the Third Road: Swedish Social Democracy in Crisis," *Politics and Society*, 20, 3 (1992), pp. 305–332.

28. Hugh Heclo and Henrik Madsen, *Policy and Politics in Sweden: Principled Pragmatism* (Philadelphia: Temple University Press, 1987); Tim Tilton, *The Political Theory of Swedish Social Democracy. Through the Welfare State to Revolution* (New York: Clarendon Press, 1990).

29. Interview, Ed Miliband, House of Commons, October 18, 2005.

30. Several of my British and Swedish interviewees have suggested this.

31. Bobo Hombach, *The New Centre, Die Neue Mitte* (Cambridge, U.K.: Polity, 1998).

32. There was disagreement, for instance in the Third Way meeting in Florence in November 1999 or in the meeting of European socialists in Malmö in 1997. See *Progressive Governance for the XXI Century,* Centro Studi di Politica Internazionale (Florence, 1999); Simon Lightfoot, *Europeanizing Social Democracy? The Rise of the Party of European Socialists* (London/New York: Routledge, 2005).

33. Anthony Giddens, ed., *The Global Third Way Debate* (Cambridge, U.K.: Polity, 2001); Anthon Hemericjk, Maurizio Ferrera, and Martin Rhodes, eds., *The Future of Social Europe, Recasting Work and Welfare in the New Economy* (Oeiras: Celta Editoria, 2004), pp.17, 54.

34. John Gray, *After Social Democracy: Politics, Capitalism and the Common Life* (London: Demos, 1996); Francis Fukuyama, *The End of History and the Last Man* (New York/Toronto: Free Press; Maxwell Macmillan Canada, 1992); Andrew Gamble, *The New Social Democracy* (Oxford, U.K.: Blackwell, 1999).

35. David Marquand, *The Progressive Dilemma: From Lloyd George to Blair* (London: Phoenix Giant, 1999).

36. Tony Blair, *The Third Way: New Politics for the New Century* (London: Fabian Society, 1998); Geoff Mulgan, *Life after Politics* (1997).

37. Anthony Giddens, *The Third Way: The Renewal of Social Democracy* (Cambridge, U.K.: Polity Press, 1998).

38. See Alan Finlayson, *Making Sense of New Labour* (London: Lawrence and Wishart, 2003); Alex Callinicos, *Against the Third Way* (Cambridge, U.K.: Polity Press, 2001).

39. Finlayson, *Making Sense of New Labour.*

40. Raymond Williams, "May Day Manifesto, 1968," quoted in Andrew Scott, *Running on Empty. 'Modernising' the British and Australian Labour Parties.* (Sydney/London: Pluto Press, Comerford and Miller, 2000), p. 72.

41. Nikolas Rose, *Powers of Freedom: Reframing Political Thought* (Cambridge, U.K.: Cambridge University Press, 1999), p. 8.

42. Chantal Mouffe, *On the Political* (New York/London: Routledge, 2005).

43. Lars Trägårdh, "Crisis and the Politics of National Community. Germany and Sweden 1933/1994," in Nina Witoszek and Lars Trägårdh, eds., *Crisis and the Construction of Identity* (Oxford, U.K.: Berghahn Books, 2002), pp. 75–110.

44. Ulrich Beck, *Risk Society: Towards a New Modernity* (London: Sage, 1992). See Nico Stehr, *Knowledge Societies* (London: Sage, 1994), p. 41.

45. Tage Erlander, *Människor i samverkan* (Stockholm: Tiden, 1954); Tage Erlander, *Framstegens politik* (Stockholm: Tiden, 1956); Tage Erlander, *Valfrihetens samhälle* (Stockholm: Tiden, 1962).

46. Zygmunt Bauman, *Liquid Modernity* (Cambridge, U.K.: Polity Press, 2000).

47. Fredric Jameson, "The Politics of Utopia," *New Left Review*, 25 (2004), pp. 35–54.

48. Charles Taylor, *Modern Social Imaginaries* (Durham, NC: Duke University Press, 2004), p. 7.

49. See Bob Jessop, "Narrating the Future of the National Economy and the Nation State: Remarks on Remapping Regulation and Reinventing Governance," in George Steinmetz, ed., *State/Culture: State Formation After the Cultural Turn* (Ithaca, NY: Cornell University Press, 1999), pp. 378–406.

50. Steven Driver and Luke Martell, *New Labour: Politics after Thatcherism* (Cambridge, U.K.: Polity Press, 1998), p. 46f.

51. Progressive Governance Summit, Budapest 2004.

52. Stephen Driver, "Third Ways," ed. Schmidtke (2002), p. 95. See Robert Cox, "The Path-Dependency of an Idea: Why Scandinavian Welfare States Remain Distinct," *Social Policy and Administration*, 38, 2 (April 2004), pp. 204–219.

53. Peter A. Hall and David Soskice, *Varieties of Capitalism: The Institutional Foundations of Comparative Advantage* (Oxford and New York: Oxford University Press, 2001); Evelyne Huber and John D. Stephens, *Development and Crisis of the Welfare State: Parties and Policies in Global Markets* (Chicago: University of Chicago Press, 2001).

54. Taylor, *Modern Social Imaginaries*, pp. 23, 25, 27.

55. See Jonas Pontusson, *Inequality and prosperity. Social Europe vs. Liberal America* (Ithaca, NY: Cornell University Press, 2005).

56. Birgit Pfau Effinger, "Culture and Welfare State Policies: Reflections on a Complex Interrelation," *Journal of Social Policy*, 34, 1 (2005), pp. 3–20; Colin Hay, "Globalization, European Integration and the Discursive Construction of Economic Imperatives," *Journal of European Public Policy* 9, 2 (April 2002), pp. 147–167. The historian of ideas Mark Bevir has made a similar argument for an interpretative approach to politics; see Mark Bevir, *New Labour: A Critique* (London: Routledge, 2005).

57. Schmidt, "Values and Discourse in the Politics of Adjustment," p. 263.

58. Interview, Bo Ringholm, Stockholm, September 15, 2005.

59. Urban Lundberg, *Juvelen i kronan: Socialdemokraterna och den allmänna pensionen* (Stockholm: Hjalmarson & Högberg, 2003).

60. See Johannes Lindvall, *The Politics of Purpose: Swedish Macroeconomic Policy after the Golden Age*, Göteborg Studies in Politics, 84 (Göteborg, Sweden: Department of Political Science, Gothenburg University, 2004).

61. Christina Garsten and Kerstin Jacobsson, *Learning to Be Employable: New Agendas on Work, Responsibility, and Learning in a Globalizing World* (Basingstoke, U.K.: Palgrave Macmillan, 2004); Bo Stråth and Peter Wagner, eds., *After Full Employment. European Discourses on Work and Flexibility* (Brussels: P.I.E. Peter Lang, 2000).

62. Paula Blomqvist and Bo Rothstein, *Välfärdsstatens nya ansikte: Demokrati och marknadsreformer inom den offentliga sektorn* (Stockholm: Agora, 2000); Arbetarrörelsens tankesmedja, *Kunskap som klassfråga* (Stockholm: Arbetarrörelsens tankesmedja, 2002).

63. For an evaluation of New Labour policies, see Polly Toynbee and David Walker, *Better or Worse? Has New Labour Delivered?* (London: Bloomsbury, 2005).

64. Nick Pearce and Will Paxton, *Social Justice, Building a Fairer Britain* (London: IPPR, 2005).

65. Interview, Ed Balls, House of Commons, London, October 19, 2005.

66. Anne Daguerre and Peter Taylor-Gooby, "Neglecting Europe: Explaining the Predominance of American Ideas in New Labour's Welfare Policies since 1997," *Journal of European Social Policy*, 14, 1 (2004), pp. 25–39; Desmond King and Mark Wickham-Jones, "Bridging the Atlantic: Democratic (Party) Origins of Welfare-to-Work," in Martin Powell, ed., *New Labour, New Welfare State: The Third Way in British Social Policy* (Bristol, U.K.: Policy Press, 1998) pp. 257–270.

67. Gwendolyn Mink, *Welfare's End* (Ithaca, NY: Cornell University Press, 1998).

68. Ed Miliband, "Northern Lights," *Progress Magazine*, June 30, 2006. Available online at www.progressonline.org.uk/magazine/article.asp?a=1249 (last accessed June 15, 2009).

69. See Scott, *Running on Empty*, p. 75.

70. C. A. R. Crosland, *The Future of Socialism* (London/Southampton: Camelot Press, 1956), p. 143; Robert Taylor, *Sweden: Proof That a Better World Is Possible* (London: Compass, 2005).

71. Göran Persson, speech to SAP Conference 1997.

Chapter 2

1. Peter F. Drucker, *Post-Capitalist Society* (New York: HarperBusiness, 1993).

2. Alan Finlayson, *Making Sense of New Labour* (London: Lawrence and Wishart, 2003), p. 185.

3. Ibid., p. 196.

4. Colin Hay and Matthew Watson, "The Discourse of Globalisation and the Logic of No Alternative: Rendering the Contingent Necessary in the Political Economy of New Labour," *Policy and Politics* 31, 3 (2003), pp. 289–305.

5. Stephen Driver and Luke Martell, *New Labour: Politics after Thatcherism* (Cambridge, U.K.: Polity Press, 1998); Andrew Glyn, *Social Democracy in Neoliberal Times: The Left and Economic Policy since 1980* (Oxford, U.K.: Oxford University Press, 2001); Chris Howell, *Trade Unions and the State. The Construction of Industrial Relations Institutions in Britain, 1890–2000* (Princeton, NJ: Princeton University Press, 2005).

6. Colin Hay, *The Political Economy of New Labour* (Manchester, U.K.: Manchester University Press, 1998), p. 145.

7. J. Magnus Ryner, *Capitalist Restructuring, Globalisation and the Third Way: Lessons from the Swedish Model* (London: Routledge, 2002).

8. Andrew Gamble, *The Free Economy and the Strong State: The Politics of Thatcherism*, (Basingstoke, U.K.: Macmillan, 1988).

9. Gordon Brown, "The Politics of Potential. A New Agenda for Labour," in David Miliband, ed., *Reinventing the Left, a New Agenda for Labour* (Cambridge, U.K.: Polity Press, 1994), pp. 113–122.

10. Finlayson, *Making Sense of New Labour*, p. 198; see also Mark Bevir, *New Labour, a Critique* (London: Routledge, 2005), p. 121.

11. Charles Leadbeater, *Living on Thin Air. The New Economy.* (London: Penguin, 2000).

12. Björn Elmbrant, *Dansen kring guldkalven* (Stockholm: Atlas, 2004).

13. *The Wellbeing of Nations. The Role of Human and Social Capital* (Paris: OECD, 2001); *Employment and Growth in the Knowledge Based Economy* (Paris: OECD, 1996).

14. George Liagouras, "The Political Economy of Post-Industrial Capitalism," *Thesis Eleven*, 81 (May 2005), pp. 20–35.

15. Paul Pierson, *The New Politics of the Welfare State* (Oxford, U.K.: Oxford University Press, 2001).

16. David Coates, *Prolonged Labour. The Slow Birth of New Labour Britain* (New York: PalgraveMacmillan, 2005); HM Treasury, *Supporting Young People to Achieve: Towards a New Deal for Skills* (London: HMSO, 2004).

17. See William Keegan, *The Prudence of Mr Gordon Brown* (London: John Wiley and Sons, 2003); Göran Persson, *Den som är satt i skuld är icke fri. Min berättelse om hur Sverige återfick sunda statsfinanser* (Stockholm: Atlas, 1997).

18. Ed Balls, *Open Macro-Economics in an Open Economy* (London: Centre for Economic Performance, 1997); Gordon Brown, "Prudence Will Be Our Watchword," Mansion House speech, 1998.

19. Mark Blyth, *Great Transformations. Economic Ideas and Institutional Change in the 20th Century* (New York: Cambridge University Press, 2002); Johannes Lindvall, *The Politics of Purpose: Swedish Macro-Economic Policy after the Golden Age* (Göteborg, Sweden: Department of Political Science, 2004); Peter H. Lindert, *Growing Public: Social*

Spending and Economic Growth since the Eighteenth Century (Cambridge, U.K.: Cambridge University Press, 2004).

20. Michael Power, *The Audit Society. Rituals of Verification* (Oxford, U.K.: Oxford University Press, 1997).

21. Ed Balls and Gus O'Donnell, eds., *Reforming Britain's Economic and Financial Policy* (London: Palgrave/Treasury, 2002); HM Treasury, *Modern Public Services for Britain, Investing in Reform* (London: HMSO, 1998); Finansdepartementet, *Budgetprocessen*, (Stockholm: SOU 2000:61).

22. HM Treasury, *Modern Public Services for Britain*, Comprehensive spending review 1999, Performance and Innovation Unit, *Innovation in the Public Sector* (London: HMSO, 2003).

23. David Marquand, *Decline of the Public: The Hollowing-Out of Citizenship* (Cambridge, U.K.: Polity Press, 2004).

24. HM Treasury, *Prudent for a Purpose: Working for a Stronger and Fairer Britain* (London: HMSO, 2000).

25. Paul Romer, "The Origins of Endogenous Growth," *Journal of Economic Perspectives* 8, 1 (1994); Gregory Mankiw and David Romer, *New Keynesian Economics* (Cambridge, MA: MIT Press, 1991).

26. Robert B. Reich, *The Work of Nations: Capitalism in the 21st Century* (New York: Knopf, 1991).

27. Department for Education and Skills, *Towards Full Employment in a Modern Society* (London: HMSO, 2001); Regeringen och Sveriges socialdemokratiska arbetareparti, *En nation i arbete: ett handlingsprogram mot arbetslöshet*, Politisk redovisning, 1995:2 (Stockholm: Socialdemokraterna, 1995); Government bill, *Sysselsättningspropositionen. Åtgärder för att minska arbetslösheten. Regeringens proposition 1995/96:222* (1995).

28. Mitchell Dean, "Governing the Unemployed Self in an Active Society," *Economy and Society* 24 (1995), pp. 559–583; Bo Stråth, "After Full Employment. The Breakdown of Conventions of Social Responsibility," in Bo Stråth, ed., *After Full Employment. European Discourses on Work and Flexibility* (Brussels: P. I. E. Peter Lang, 2000); Noel Whiteside, "From Full employment to Flexibility: Britain and France in Comparison," in Stråth, *After Full Employment*, pp. 107–124.

29. Balls-O'Donnell, *Reforming Britain's Economic and Financial Policy*; HM Treasury, *The Modernisation of Britain's Tax and Benefits System*, 6, "Tackling Poverty and Making Work Pay, Tax Credits for the 21st Century" (March 2000).

30. Janet Newman, *Modernising Governance* (London: Sage, 2001), p. 155; Finlayson, *Making Sense of New Labour*, pp. 144f.

31. Bob Jessop, *The Future of the Capitalist State* (Cambridge, U.K.: Polity Press, 2002), p. 155.

32. Coates, *Prolonged Labour*.

33. Sveriges socialdemokratiska arbetareparti, *En ny ekonomisk politik: Socialdemokraternas ekonomiska politik för arbete, tillväxt och sunda statsfinanser*, Politisk

redovisning, 1993:3 (Stockholm: Socialdemokraterna, 1993); *Blågul tillväxt*, Program-debatt/Socialdemokraterna, 7 (Stockholm, 1993); Sveriges socialdemokratiska ar-betareparti, *Näringspolitik för tillväxt, Vårt alternativ,* 5 (Stockholm: Socialdemokra-terna, 1994); Sveriges socialdemokratiska arbetarparti, *Näringspolitik för arbete och tillväxt* (Stockholm: Socialdemokraterna, 2006).

34. Mats Benner, *The Politics of Growth: Economic Regulation in Sweden 1930–1994* (Lund, Sweden: Arkiv, 1997), p. 161; IT-kommissionen, *Informationsteknologin. Vin-gar åt människornas förmåga. Betänkande av IT-kommissionen* (Stockholm: Fritzes, 1994); *Produktivitetsdelegationen* (Stockholm: SOU 1991:82); *Lindbeckskommissionen* (Stockholm: SOU 1993:10).

35. HM Treasury, *Productivity in the UK* (London: HMSO, 2000); HM Treasury, *Microeconomic Reform in Britain: Delivering Opportunities for All* (London: Treasury/ Palgrave McMillan, 2004); Sveriges socialdemokratiska arbetareparti, *Näringspolitik för tillväxt.*

36. Institute for Public Policy Research, *Promoting Prosperity* (London: IPPR, 1997); Department for Trade and Industry, *Our Competitive Future. Building the Knowledge Economy* (London: HMSO, 1998); *Innovativa Sverige. En strategi för till-växt genom förnyelse.* (Stockholm: Näringsdepartmentet, Utbildningsdepartementet, Ds 2004:36); Government bill 1997/98:62, *Regional tillväxt för arbete och välfärd.*

37. Lars Ilshammar, *Offentlighetens nya rum. Teknik och politik i Sverige 1969–1999.* (Örebro, Sweden: Örebro Universitet, 2002); Government bill 1995/1996: 125, *Åtgärder för att öka användandet av IT*; Government bill, *Ett informationssamhälle åt alla* (1999).

38. The national grid for learning was scrapped in 2006. See also Cabinet Office, *Electronic Networks, Challenges for the Next Decade* (London: Strategy Unit, 2002).

39. *Innovativa Sverige.*

40. Benner, *The Politics of Growth.*

41. Mark Wickham-Jones, "Recasting Social Democracy," *Political Studies* 43, 4 (1995): pp. 698–702.

42. Finlayson, *Making Sense of New Labour,* p. 179.

43. HM Government Policy Review, *Building on Progress: Public Services* (Lon-don: HMSO, 2007).

44. Sue Tomlinson, *Education in a Post-Welfare Society* (London: Open Univer-sity Press, 2005).

45. Skolverket, *Fristående grundskolor* (Stockholm: Skolverket, 2001:3925).

46. After the policy failed there were attempts in the United Kingdom to create a replacement scheme with increased influence of participants (Department for Educa-tion and Skills, *Individual learning accounts, a consultation exercise on a new ILA style programme* [London: DfES research report 339, 2002]).

47. *Individuellt kompetenssparande* (Stockholm: SOU, 2000:119). Government bill 2001/02:175, *Ett system för individuell kompetensutveckling.*

48. Department for Education and Skills, *Higher Standards, Better Schools for All. More Choice for Parents and Pupils* (London: HMSO, 2005).

49. Claus Belfrage, unpublished PhD manuscript, University of Birmingham, U.K., "Neoliberal Reform in Sweden."

50. Compare Walter Korpi, *The Democratic Class Struggle* (London: Routledge & Kegan Paul, 1983).

51. Geoffrey M Hodgson, *Economics and Utopia. Why the Learning Economy Is Not the End of History* (London/New York: Routledge, 1999).

52. Charles F. Sabel and Jonathan Zeitlin, *World of Possibilities: Flexibility and Mass Production in Western Industrialization* (Cambridge, U.K.: Cambridge University Press, 1997).

53. The notion of partnership should not be confused with Will Hutton's idea of stakeholding, which New Labour toyed with for a while in the mid-1990s and then replaced with the notion of partnership. See Coates, *Prolonged Labour*, p. 21; and Will Hutton, *The State We're In. Why Britain Is in Crisis and How to Overcome It* (Cambridge, U.K.: Polity Press, 1996).

54. Cabinet Office, *Modernising Government*, Department of Trade and Industry, *Fairness at work* (London: HMSO, 1998). Compare Francis Fukuyama, *Trust: The Social Virtues and the Creation of Prosperity* (New York: Free Press, 1995).

55. Gösta Esping-Andersen, *Politics against Markets* (Princeton, NJ: Princeton University Press, 1985).

56. Howell, *Trade Unions and the State*, p. 174.

57. Institute for Public Policy Research, *Promoting Prosperity* (London: IPPR, 1997).

58. Olle Svenning, *Göran Persson och hans värld* (Stockholm: Norstedt, 2005).

59. *Industriavtalet*, Agreement on Industrial Development and Wage Formation; Nils Elvander, *Industriavtalet i tillämpning. The Industrial Agreement, an Analysis of Its Ideas and Performance* (Sandviken, Sweden: Almega, 1999).

60. Bo Stråth, *The Organisation of Labour Markets: Modernity, Culture and Governance in Germany, Sweden, Britain and Japan* (London: Routledge, 1996).

61. Ryner, *Lessons from the Swedish Model*, p. 52; Åke Sandberg, ed., *Technological Change and Co-Determination in Sweden* (Philadelphia: Temple University Press, 1992).

62. Finlayson, *Making Sense of New Labour.*

63. Daniel Cohen, *Nos temps modernes* (Paris: Flammarion, 1999).

64. John Kenneth Galbraith, *The Affluent Society* (London: Hamish Hamilton, 1958).

65. See Coates, *Prolonged Labour*, pp. 61, 68, 69.

66. See Jenny Andersson, *Between Growth and Security. Swedish Social Democracy from a Strong Society to a Third Way* (Manchester, U.K.: Manchester University Press, 2006).

67. Mark Bevir, *New Labour, a Critique* (London and New York: Routledge, 2004).

68. Vivienne Schmidt, "Values and Discourse in the Politics of Adjustment," in Fritz Scharpf and Vivienne Schmidt, ed., *Welfare and Work in the Open Economy* (Oxford, U.K.: Oxford University Press, 1999), p. 243.

69. *The Wellbeing of Nations. The Role of Human and Social Capital*, p. 17.

70. Gary Becker, *Human Capital: A Theoretical and Empirical Analysis, with Special Reference to Education* (New York: Columbia University Press, 1964).

71. Pete Woolcock, "Social Capital," in *Theory and Society* 27, 2 (1998); Ismail Serageldin and Partha Dasgupta, *Social Capital: A Multifaceted Perspective* (Washington, DC: World Bank, 2000).

72. J. Coleman, *Foundations of Social Theory* (Cambridge, MA: Harvard University Press, 1990); John Rae, "Foreword," in Scott L. McLean, David A. Schultz, and Manfred B. Steger, eds., *Social Capital. Critical Perspectives on Community and Bowling Alone* (New York: New York University Press, 2002).

73. Michael Freeden, "The Political Ideology of New Labour," *Political Quarterly* 70, 1 (1999), pp. 42–51.

74. Desmond King, *In the Name of Liberalism: Iliberal Social Policies in the United States and Britain* (Oxford, U.K.: Oxford University Press, 1999).

Chapter 3

1. Norman Fairclough, *New Labour, New Language* (London: Routledge, 2000), p. 18; Stuart Hall, "The Great Moving Nowhere Show," *Marxism Today* (1998), pp. 9–15.

2. Labour Party, *New Labour: Because Britain Deserves Better* (London: Labour Party, 1997).

3. The concept of renewal was temporarily used in the mid-1980s, as *förnya folkhemmet*. See Jenny Andersson, *Between Growth and Security. Swedish Social Democracy from a Strong Society to a Third Way* (Manchester, U.K.: Manchester University Press, 2006), p. 118.

4. Tony Blair, *New Britain. My Vision of a Young Country*. (London: Fourth Estate Limited, 1996), p. 98.

5. See Pär Nuder, *Stolt men inte nöjd: en kärleksförklaring till politiken* (Stockholm: Norstedts, 2008).

6. Kjell Östberg, "Swedish Social Democracy and Intellectuals," paper to the conference "Rethinking Social Democracy," London, April 15–17, 2004.

7. Mats Benner, *The Politics of Growth: Economic Regulation in Sweden 1930–1994*, Scandinavian Studies in Social Science and History, 2 (Lund, Sweden: Arkiv, 1997); Johannes Lindvall, *The Politics of Purpose: Swedish Macroeconomic Policy after the Golden Age* (Göteborg, Sweden: Department of Political Science, 2004).

8. Sveriges socialdemokratiska arbetarparti, *Framtid för Sverige—program för att ta Sverige ur krisen* (Stockholm: Tiden, 1981).

9. Olle Svenning, *Göran Persson och hans värld* (Stockholm: Norstedt, 2005); Jesper Bengtsson, *Det måttfulla upproret. Lindh, Sahlin, Wallström och 20 år av politisk förnyelse* (Stockholm: Norstedts, 2004).

10. Labour Party, *The New Hope for Britain* (London: Labour Party, 1983); Eric Shaw, *The Labour Party since 1945* (London: Blackwell, 1996); Steven Driver and Luke Martell, *New Labour: Politics after Thatcherism* (Cambridge, U.K.: Polity Press, 1998), pp. 10–20.

11. Kjell-Olof Feldt, *Den tredje vägen: en politik för Sverige* (Stockholm: Tiden, 1985).

12. Andersson, *Between Growth and Security*.

13. Jonas Pontusson, *The Limits of Social Democracy: Investment Politics in Sweden*, Cornell Studies in Political Economy (Ithaca, NY: Cornell University Press, 1992).

14. Lars Ekdahl, *Mot en tredje väg: En biografi över Rudolf Meidner. 2, Facklig expert och demokratisk socialist* (Lund, Sweden: Arkiv, 2005).

15. Stuart Hall and Martin Jacques, eds., *New Times* (London: Verso, 1989), pp. 29, 116.

16. Daniel Bell, *The Coming of Postindustrial Society* (London: Heineman, 1973); Alain Touraine, *La Société Post-Industrielle* (Paris: Bibliotheque Médiation, 1969); André Gorz, *Farewell to the Working Class: An Essay on Postindustrial Socialism* (London: Pluto Press, 1982).

17. Hall and Jacques, *New Times*, p. 16.

18. Stuart Hall developed these notions in *Thatcherism and the Crisis of the Left* (London: Verso, 1988).

19. *Marxism Today*, "Special Issue: Wrong" (1998).

20. Geoff Mulgan, *Connexity. How to Live in a Connected World* (London: Chatto and Windus, 1997), p. 35.

21. Interview with Geoff Mulgan, Institute for Community Studies, April 4, 2005.

22. Sveriges socialdemokratiska arbetarparti, *Framtiden i hela folkets händer* (Stockholm: Tiden, 1984).

23. Olof Palme, speech to party conference, 1984.

24. *Det genuint mänskliga behovet av idealitet, av något som bär bortom vars och ens timliga existens*. Sveriges socialdemokratiska arbetarparti, *90-talsprogrammet* (Stockholm: Tiden, 1989), p. 39.

25. Ibid., p. 32.

26. Ibid., p. 33.

27. Ibid., p. 49.

28. The *folkrörelse*—voluntary organizations and social movements such as the Christian *broderskapsrörelsen* or the ABF, the workers' movement for self-education (*Arbetarnas bildningsförbund*), are a traditional recruiting ground for Swedish social democracy, and many leading Social Democrats have their roots there.

29. *90-talsprogrammet*, p. 49.

30. Alan Finlayson, *Making Sense of New Labour* (London: Lawrence and Wishart, 2003).

31. Labour Party, *Meet the Challenge, Make the Change. A New Agenda for Britain: Final Report of Labour's Policy Review for the 1990s* (London: Labour Party,1989).

32. Labour Party, *New Labour: Because Britain Deserves Better*; Tony Blair, *New Britain. My Vision of a Young Country,* p. 98.

33. Gordon Brown, speech "Prosperity and Justice for All," September 27, 2004.

34. Disraeli, Benjamin, Lord Beaconsfield, 1804–1881: "The continent will [not] suffer Britain to be the workshop of the world . . ." House of Commons, March 15, 1838.

35. Tristram Hunt, *Building Jerusalem. The Rise and Fall of the Victorian City* (London: Penguin, 2005), p. 4.

36. British Commission for Social Justice, *Social Justice in a Changing World* (London: IPPR, 1993); David Miliband, *Reinventing the Left* (Cambridge, U.K.: Polity Press, 1994); David Miliband and Andrew Glyn, *Paying for Inequality: The Economic Cost of Social Injustice* (London: IPPR/Rivers Oram Press, 1994).

37. Blair, *New Britain,* p. x.

38. Labour Party, *New Labour: Because Britain Deserves Better*; Labour Party, *Ambitions for Britain. Labour's 2001 Manifesto* (London: Labour Party, 2001).

39. Gordon Brown, "Prudence Will Be Our Watchword," Mansion House speech, 1998, published in Andrew Chadwick and Richard Heffernan, *The New Labour Reader* (Cambridge, U.K.:Polity Press, 2003), pp. 101–104.

40. Ibid.

41. Gordon Brown, "The Future of Britishness," speech to the Fabian Society's New Year's Conference, January 14, 2006.

42. Gordon Brown, "Exploiting the British Genius—The Key to Long Term Economic Success," speech to the Confederation of British Industry, May 20, 1997.

43. George Orwell, *The Lion and the Unicorn. Socialism and the English Genius* (London: Searchlight Books, Secker and Warburg, 1941).

44. Gordon Brown, "Britishness and the Future of the British Economy," speech to the London Business School, April 27, 2005.

45. Gordon Brown, "The Spectator Lecture. The British Genius," November 4, 1997; Linda Colley, "Downing Street Millennium Lecture: Britishness in the 21st Century," February 20, 2003.

46. Brown, "Exploiting the British Genius—The Key to Long Term Economic Success."

47. Jonas Johansson, *Du sköna nya tid? Debatten om informationssamhället i riksdag och storting under 1990–talet*, Linköping Studies in Arts and Science No 349 (Linköping, Sweden: Tema kommunikation, Linköpings universitet, 2006).

48. Kazimierz Musial, *Roots of the Scandinavian Model. Images of Progress in the Era of Modernisation* (Baden Baden: NomosVerlagsgesellschaft, 2000), p. 10; Bo Stråth and Øystein Sørensen, *The Cultural Construction of Norden* (Oslo: Scandinavian University

Press, 1997); Bo Stråth, "Nordic Modernity: Origins, Trajectories and Prospects," in *Thesis Eleven* 77, 1 (2004), pp. 5–23.

49. Marquis William Childs, *Sweden: The Middle Way* (London: Faber, 1936).

50. See Peter H. Lindert, *Growing Public: Social Spending and Economic Growth since the Eighteenth Century* (Cambridge, U.K.: Cambridge University Press, 2004).

51. Göran Persson, *Den som är satt i skuld är icke fri. Min berättelse om hur Sverige återfick sunda statsfinanser* (Stockholm: Atlas, 1997), p. 98.

52. Persson opening address to conference, March 10, 2000, in Göran Persson, *Tankar och tal 1996–2000* (Stockholm: Hjalmarson och Högberg, 2000).

53. Sveriges socialdemokratiska arbetarparti, *Samtal om framtiden* (Stockholm: Socialdemokraterna, 1996); Sveriges socialdemokratiska arbetarparti, *Steget in i 2000-talet: riktlinjer antagna av framtidskongressen i Sundsvall* (Stockholm: Socialdemokraterna, 1997).

54. Sveriges socialdemokratiska arbetarparti, *Riktlinjer* (Stockholm: Socialdemokraterna,1997), p. 2.

55. The speaker is Hans Erik Svensson from Gotland, Conference protocol 1997 vol. 2, p. 7.

56. Göran Persson speech, "Tal vid folkbildningskonferensen perspektiv på folkbildningen" (September 27, 2005); Per Sundgren, *Kulturen och arbetarrörelsen. Kulturpolitiska strävanden från August Palm till Tage Erlander* (Stockholm: Carlssons, 2007).

57. Göran Persson speech to the inauguration of Örebro University, February 6, 1999, in Persson, *Tankar och tal 1996–2000*, p. 159.

58. Pär Nuder, speech "Tal vid Strängseminariet," March 5, 2005; Göran Persson, speech to the Swedish Federation of Industry (SIF), November 15, 2004.

Chapter 4

1. Gordon Brown, "The Politics of Potential. A New Agenda for Labour," in David Miliband, ed., *Reinventing the Left* (Cambridge, U.K.: Polity Press, 1994), pp. 114–122.

2. Charles Leadbeater, *Living on Thin Air. The New Economy* (London: Penguin, 2000).

3. Daniel Cohen, *Nos temps modernes* (Paris: Flammarion, 1999).

4. Gordon Brown, *Fair Is Efficient* (London: Fabian Society, 1994), p. 3.

5. See Bob Jessop, *The Future of the Capitalist State* (Cambridge, U.K.: Polity Press, 2002); Ellen Meiksins Wood, "Modernity, Postmodernity, or Capitalism?" in Robert W. McChesney, Ellen M. Wood, and John B. Foster, eds., *Capitalism and the Information Age. The Political Economy of the Global Communications Era* (New York: Monthly Review Press, 1998), pp. 27–49.

6. Cohen, *Nos Temps Modernes*; Luc Boltanski and Eve Chiapello, *Le nouvel esprit du capitalisme* (Paris: NRF Gallimard, 2002).

7. D. Barney, *Prometheus Wired, the Hope for Democracy in the Age of Network Technology* (Chicago: University of Chicago Press, 2000), p. 153.

8. Richard Sennett, *The Corrosion of Character: The Personal Consequences of Work in the New Capitalism* (New York: W. W. Norton, 1998).

9. Richard Sennett, *The Culture of the New Capitalism* (New Haven and London: Yale University Press, 2006), p. 84.

10. Brown, "The Politics of Potential."

11. C. A. R. Crosland, *The Future of Socialism* (London/Southampton: Camelot Press, 1956).

12. Brown, *Fair Is Efficient*, p. 3.

13. Brown, "The Politics of Potential," p. 114.

14. Brown, *Fair Is Efficient*, p. 3

15. Brown, "The Politics of Potential," p. 116.

16. Tony Blair, *Socialism* (London: Fabian Society, 1994).

17. Tony Blair, foreword to National Advisory Committee on Creative and Cultural Education, *All Our Futures* (London: Department of Culture, Media and Sports, 1998).

18. Labour Party Constitution, 1995.

19. Blair, *The Third Way: New Politics for the New Century* (London: Fabian Society, 1994).

20. Alan Finlayson, "Nexus Downing Street Seminar Report," available online at www.netnexus.org/mail_archive/uk-policy.cur/0100.html.

21. Blair, *Socialism*.

22. Lars Trägårdh, "Crisis and the Politics of National Community. Germany and Sweden 1933/1994," in Nina Witoszek and Lars Trägårdh, eds., *Crisis and the Construction of Identity* (Oxford, U.K.: Berghahn Books, 2002), pp. 75–110.

23. Labour Party, *Because Britain Deserves Better* (1997); Institute for Public Policy Research, *Promoting Prosperity* (London: IPPR, 1997).

24. Sheri Berman, *The Primacy of Politics. Social Democracy and the Making of Europe's 20th Century* (New York: Cambridge University Press, 2006), pp. 172f.

25. Bo Stråth, *Mellan två fonder. LO och den svenska modellen* (Stockholm: Atlas, 1998).

26. Sveriges socialdemokratiska arbetareparti, *Partiprogram för socialdemokraterna: antaget vid den 34e ordinarie partikongressen Västeråskongressen 5–11 November 2001*, p. 5.

27. Ibid.

28. Ibid.

29. Ibid., p. 6.

30. See *Socialdemokratins partiprogram 1897–1990* (Labour Movement's Archives: Stockholm, 2001).

31. Göran Persson, speech to Party Conference, 2001.

32. *Partiprogram för socialdemokraterna, 2001*, pp. 1–2.

33. Ibid., p. 20.

34. Ibid., p. 1. *Frihet och jämlikhet handlar både om individuella rättigheter och kollektiva lösningar för att skapa det gemensamma bästa, som utgör grunden till den enskildes liv och möjligheter. Människan är en social varelse som utvecklas och växer i samspel med andra, och mycket av det som är viktigt för den enskildes välfärd kan bara skapas i gemenskap med andra. Detta gemensamma bästa förutsätter solidaritet. Solidaritet är den sammanhållning som kommer ur insikten att vi alla är ömsesidigt beroende av varandra, och att det samhälle är bäst, som byggs i samverkan i ömsesidig hänsyn och respekt. Alla måste ha samma rätt och möjlighet att påverka lösningarna, alla måste ha samma skyldighet att ta ansvar för dem. Solidaritet utesluter inte strävan till individuell utveckling och framgång, men väl den egoism som gör det tillåtet att utnyttja andra för egna fördelar.*

35. Ibid., p. 19. *Socialdemokratin avvisar en samhällsutveckling där kapital och marknad dominerar och kommersialiserar sociala, kulturella, och mänskliga relationer. Marknadens normer får aldrig avgöra människors värde eller bilda norm för det sociala och kulturella livet.*

36. Ibid.

37. Crosland, *The Future of Socialism*, p. 211.

38. Ernst Wigforss, *Skrifter i urval* (Stockholm: Tiden, 1980), vol. 4, p. 212.

39. Gordon Brown, "Equality—Then and Now," in D. Leonard, ed., *Crosland and New Labour* (London: MacMillan, 1999), p. 37.

40. Stuart White, "Welfare Philosophy and the Third Way," in Jane Lewis and Rebecca Surrender, eds., *Welfare State Change. Towards a Third Way?* (Oxford, U.K.: Oxford University Press, 2004), pp. 25–47.

41. Blair, "The Opportunity Society," speech to Conference, 2004.

42. Crosland, *The Future of Socialism*, p. 221.

43. Ibid., p. 217.

44. *Fria och jämlika människor är socialismens mål.*

45. Sveriges socialdemokratiska arbetareparti, *Partiprogram för socialdemokraterna 2001*, p. 8.

46. Persson, speech to party conference, 2001.

47. Interview with Anne Marie Lindgren, December 2006, Stockholm.

48. Tage Erlander, *Valfrihetens Samhälle* (Stockholm: Tiden, 1962).

49. Gerassimos Moschonas, *In the Name of Social Democracy* (London: Verso, 2002), p. 158.

50. Brown, "Equality—Then and Now," p. 42.

51. See Richard Brooks, "Time to Rewrite Clause IV Again?" (London: Fabian Society, 2004); Anthony Giddens and Patrick Diamond, eds, *The New Egalitarianism* (London: Policy Network, 2005).

Chapter 5

1. Tony Blair, "The Labour Party—The Party of Wealth Creation," speech at Canary Wharf, April 14, 2005.

2. H. W. Arndt, *Economic Development. The History of an Idea* (Chicago: University of Chicago Press, 1987).

3. Raymond Williams, *Culture and Society* (New York: Columbia University Press, 1983 [1958]).

4. It was the architect of universalism Gustav Möller who introduced the concept of economic growth to Swedish social democracy because he saw it as the necessary foundation for the welfare state. See Eva Friman, *No Limits: The 20th Century Discourse of Economic Growth* (Umeå. Sweden: Institutionen för historiska studier, Umeå University, 2002).

5. Gail Stedward, "Education as Industrial Policy: New Labour's Marriage of the Social and the Economic," in *Policy and Politics* 31: 2 (2003); Lindsey Paterson, "The Three Educational Ideologies of the British Labour Party, 1997–2001," *Oxford Review of Education* 29: 2 (2003); Jean Bocock and Taylor Richard, "The Labour Party and Higher Education: The Nature of the Relationship," *Higher Education Quarterly* 57: 3 (July 2003); Lennart Svensson, "Life Long Learning, a Clash between a Production Logic and a Learning Logic," in Christina Garsten and Kerstin Jacobsson, eds., *Learning to Be Employable: New Agendas on Work, Responsibility, and Learning in a Globalizing World* (Basingstoke, U.K.: Palgrave Macmillan, 2004), pp. 83–107.

6. Bob Jessop, "Cultural Political Economy, the Knowledge-Based Economy, and the State," in Don Slater and Andrew Barry, eds., *The Technological Economy* (London: Routledge, 2005), pp. 144-166

7. Sveriges socialdemokratiska arbetareparti, *Blågul tillväxt* (Stockholm: 1993); Declaration of Government, October 6, 1998.

8. Department for Trade and Industry, *Our Competitive Future. Building the Knowledge Economy* (London: HMSO, 1998).

9. *Innovativa Sverige, En strategi för tillväxt genom förnyelse,* Ds 2004:36.

10. Ibid., National Curriculum in Action, "What Is Creativity?"

11. Gordon Brown, "Britishness and the Future of the British Economy," speech to the London Business School, April 27, 2005.

12. Government bill, 2004/05:11, *Kvalitet i förskolan,* Sveriges socialdemokratiska arbetareparti, *Nationell utvecklingsplan för förskola, skola och vuxenutbildning*, Politisk redovisning, 1997:8 (Stockholm: Socialdemokraterna, 1997); Sveriges socialdemokratiska arbetarparti, *Framtidens förskola* (Stockholm: Socialdemokraterna, 2005).

13. NUTEK, "Nationellt entreprenörskapsprogram."

14. Lena Hallengren, Leif Pagrotsky, and Ibrahim Baylan, "Kultur och lärande går hand i hand," in *Folket* (2005); Riksdagens skrivelse 2005/06:206, *Ett Sverige för barn: redogörelse för regeringens barnpolitik;* Government bill, *Kulturpolitik. Regeringens*

proposition 1996/97:3; Lena Hallengren speech, "Kultur för lust och lärande" October 18, 2004.

15. Institute for Public Policy Research, *Promoting Prosperity* (London: IPPR, 1997); Department for Education and Employment, *Excellence in Schools* (London: HMSO, 1997); Department for Education and Employment, *The Learning Age: A Renaissance for Britain* (London: HMSO, 1998).

16. Helga Nowotny, Peter Scott, and Michael Gibbons, *Rethinking Science. Knowledge and the Public in an Age of Uncertainty* (Cambridge, U.K.: Polity Press, 2001).

17. *Innovativa Sverige*; HM Treasury, *Building a Stronger Economic Future for Britain* (London, HMSO, 1999); *Our Competitive Future*, pp. 7, 14, 28.

18. National Advisory Committee on Education, *All Our Futures* (London: DCMS, 1998).

19. DfEE, *The Learning Age: A Renaissance for Britain.*

20. See Denis Lawton, *Education and Labour Party Ideologies, 1900–2001 and Beyond* (London and New York: RoutledgeFalmer, 2004), pp. viii, 12; Kevin Manton, *Socialism and Education in Britain 1883–1902* (London: Woburn Press, 2001).

21. Ronny Ambjörnsson, *Den skötsamme arbetaren. Ideer och ideal i ett norrländskt sågverkssamhälle 1880–1930* (Stockholm: Carlssons, 1988); Inge Johansson, *Bildning och klasskamp. Om arbetarbildningens historia, ideer och utveckling* (Stockholm: ABF, 2002); Bernt Gustavsson, *Bildningens väg. Tre bildningsideal i svensk arbetarrörelse 1880–1930* (Stockholm: Wahlström och Widstrand, 1991). There were important links between Swedish and British debates around self-education, mutuality, and cooperation at the end of the nineteenth and the beginning of the twentieth century. *Folkbildning* has had a central role in Swedish political culture. Many leading social democratic politicians have come out of the ABF, *Arbetarnas bildningsförbund.*

22. Lawton, *Education and Labour Party Ideologies.*

23. Francis Sejersted, *Socialdemokratins tidsålder: Sverige och Norge under 1900-talet.* (Nora, Sweden: Nya Doxa, 2005).

24. Ilaria Favretto, *The Long Search for a Third Way: The British Labour Party and the Italian Left since 1945* (Basingstoke, U.K.: Palgrave McMillan, 2003), p. 57.

25. DfEE, *The Learning Age: A Renaissance for Britain.*

26. Ibid.

27. Government bill 1997/1998:62, *Regional tillväxt för arbete och välfärd.*

28. Lena Hallengren speech, "Perspektiv på folkbildningen," September 27, 2005; Government bill, *Lära, växa, förändra. Regeringens folkbildningsproposition* 2005/06:192; *Folkbildning i brytningstid* (Stockholm: SOU, 2004:30).

29. The Kennedy Report, *Widening Participation in Further Education* (London: Design Council, 1998).

30. *Innovativa Sverige;* Chris Smith, *Creative Britain* (London: Faber and Faber, 1998).

31. Joel Mokyr, *The Lever of Riches: Technological Creativity and Economic Progress* (New York: Oxford University Press, 1990).

32. In 2006 Sweden opened a virtual embassy in Lindenland to promote Swedish culture abroad. Accessed May 30, 2007, at www.sweden.se/templates/cs/Article _16345.aspx.

33. Chris Smith, *Creative Futures: Culture, Identity and National Renewal* (London: Fabian Society, 1997); *Creative Britain*.

34. Jo Littler, "Creative Accounting: Consumer Culture, the 'Creative Economy,' and the Cultural Policies of New Labour," in Timothy Bewes and Jeremy Gilbert, eds., *Cultural Capitalism* (London: Lawrence and Wishart, 2000), pp. 203–223; E. McLaughlin, *Rebranding Britain: The Life and Times of Cool Britannia* (London: Open University/BBC); Panel 2000, "Towards a Cool Britannia." Retrieved on February 18, 2006, from: wwp.greenwhich2000.com/millennium/info/panel2000/htm.

35. Mark Leonard, *Britain TM—Renewing Our Identity* (London: Demos, 1997).

36. It leaned on the work of the postmodern historian Benedict Anderson, *Imagined Communities*, and the British historian Linda Colley's work on the forging of British identity in the eighteenth century, *Britons: Forging the Nation, 1707–1837* (London: Vintage, 1996).

37. Fabian Society, *Creative Futures: Culture, Identity and National Renewal*.

38. The Parekh report, *The Future of Multiethnic Britain* (London: Profile Books, 2000).

39. "The Britishness Issue," special Fabian review (London: Fabian Society, 2006).

40. Government bill, *Framtidsformer: Förslag till handlingsprogram för arkitektur, formgivning och design,* 1997/1998:117; Leif Pagrotsky speech, "Design som ett verktyg i näringspolitiken," October 15, 2003.

41. *Innovativa Sverige*, p. 24; Sveriges socialdemokratiska arbetarparti, *Näringspolitik för arbete och tillväxt. Rapport från socialdemokraternas näringspolitiska grupp* (Stockholm: Socialdemokraterna, 2006), p. 5.

42. Leif Pagrotsky speech, "Branding Sweden," June 8, 2005.

43. Ibid.

44. Ibid.

45. Raymond Williams, *Culture* (Glasgow: Fontana, 1981); Raymond Williams, *Culture and Society, 1780–1950* (London: Chatto and Windus, 1958).

46. Fredric Jameson, *Postmodernism or the Cultural Logic of Late Capitalism* (Durham, NC: Duke University Press, 1991); David Lloyd and Paul Thomas, *Culture and the State* (London and New York: Routledge, 1998).

47. *Kulturpolitikens inriktning* (Stockholm: SOU, 1995:84); Government bill, *Kulturpolitik*, 1996/97:3.

48. Per Sundgren, *Kulturen och arbetarrörelsen. Kulturpolitiska strävanden från August Palm till Tage Erlander* (Stockholm: Carlssons, 2007), p. 285.

49. Sveriges socialdemokratiska arbetarparti, *Människan i nutiden* (Stockholm: Tiden, 1952); *Ny kulturpolitik* (Stockholm: SOU, 1972:67, 1972:66): Government bill, *Den statliga kulturpolitiken*, 1974:28.

50. Sveriges socialdemokratiska arbetareparti, *Partiprogram för socialdemokraterna: antaget vid partikongressen 2001*, p. 19; *Socialdemokratin avvisar en samhällsutveckling där kapital och marknad dominerar och kommersialiserar sociala, kulturella och mänskliga relationer.*

51. Ibid. p. 30: *Kunskap och kultur är verktyg för människors personliga frihet och växande likaväl som för samhällets utveckling och för ekonomisk tillväxt och välfärd. Kunskap och kultur ger människor möjlighet att växa och att vidga sina perspektiv, frigör människors tankar och människors skapande förmåga. Denna frigörande förmåga är en avgörande motvikt mot ekonomiska och sociala eliters strävan efter att ta makten över tanken.*

52. Government bill, *Kulturpolitik*, 1996/97:3.

53. Timothy Bewes, "Cultural Politics/Political Culture," in *Cultural Capitalism*, pp. 20–40; Littler, "Creative Accounting."

54. Thomas Östros speech, "Tal vid konferensen design och arbetsliv," January 2005; Swedish Government, "Designår 2005," retrieved on February 19, 2006, from: www.regeringen.se/sb/d/5231/a37952, and "Design för alla," retrieved on June 15, 2009, from: www.regeringen.se/sb/d/1928/a/19728; Kultur- och utbildningsdepartementet, *Framtidsformer: Förslag till handlingsprogram för arkitektur och formgivning* (Stockholm: Ds, 1997:86).

55. Tessa Jowell speech, "Britain's Cultural Identity," 2001; Department for Culture, Media and Sport, *Government and the Value of Culture* (London: DCMS, 2002),; Department for Culture, Media and Sport, *Better Places to Live. Government, Identity and the Value of the Historic and Built Environment* (London: DCMS, 2005).

56. Department for Culture, Media and Sport, *The Historic Environment: A Force for Our Future* (London: DCMS, 2001).

57. See David Miliband and Tristram Hunt, "Learn from Victorians," *Guardian*, September 10, 2004.

58. James Purnell speech, "Making Britain the World's Creative Hub," June 16, 2005.

59. Jo Littler, "Introduction. British Heritage and the Legacies of Race," in Jo Littler and Roshi Naidoo, eds., *The Politics of Heritage* (London and New York: Routledge, 2005), pp. 1–21.

60. Ibid., p. 10.

61. Ruth Levitas, *The Concept of Utopia*, Utopianism and Communitarianism (Syracuse, NY: Syracuse University Press, 1990).

62. Williams, *Culture and Society*, p. 34.

63. Yasmin Alibhai Brown, *Who Do We Think We Are? Imagining the New Britain* (London: Allen Lane, the Penguin Press, 2000).

64. Tim Edensor, *National Identity, Popular Culture, and Everyday Life* (Oxford, U.K.: Berg, 2002), p. 171 ff.; Jeremy Gilbert, "Beyond the Hegemony of New Labour," in *Cultural Capitalism,* pp. 231–232; BBC, "Virtual Tour of the Millennium Dome," available online at http://news.bbc.co.uk/hi/english/static/in_depth/uk/2000/dome_tour/default.stm.

65. Yvonne Hirdman, *Att lägga livet till rätta: studier i svensk folkhemspolitik* (Stockholm: Carlsson, 1989).

66. Gilbert, "Beyond the Hegemony of New Labour."

67. Bewes, "Cultural Politics/Political Culture," p. 31.

Chapter 6

1. Manuel Castells, *The Network Society: A Cross-Cultural Perspective* (Northampton, MA: Edward Elgar Publishing, 2004).

2. HM Treasury, *Opportunity and Security for All. Investing in an Enterprising, Fairer Britain* (London: HMSO, 2002).

3. Bob Jessop, *The Future of the Capitalist State* (Cambridge, U.K.: Polity Press, 2002); Nikolas Rose, *Powers of Freedom: Reframing Political Thought* (Cambridge, U.K.: Cambridge University Press, 1999).

4. Mark Bevir, *New Labour, a Critique* (New York: Routledge, 2004), p. 127.

5. George Steinmetz, *Regulating the Social. The Welfare State and Local Politics in Imperial Germany* (Princeton, NJ: Princeton University Press, 1993), pp. 2, 52; Jacques Donzelot, *L'invention du social. Essai sur le déclin des passions politiques* (Paris: Fayard, 1984).

6. David Marquand, *The Progressive Dilemma: From Lloyd George to Blair* (London: Phoenix Giant, 1999); Michael Freeden, *Liberal Languages. Ideological Imaginaries and 20th Century Progressive Thought* (Princeton, NJ, and Oxford, U.K.: Princeton University Press, 2005).

7. Janet Newman, *Modernising Governance. New Labour, Policy and Society* (Bristol, U.K.: Policy Press, 2001).

8. Steven Driver and Luke Martell, "New Labour's Communitarianism," *Critical Social Policy* 17, 3 (1997); Michael Freeden, "The Ideology of New Labour," *Political Quarterly* 70, 1 (1999); Sarah Hale, "The Communitarian 'Philosophy' of New Labour," in Will Leggett, Luke Martell, and Sarah Hale, eds., *The Third Way and Beyond: Criticisms, Futures and Alternatives* (Manchester, U.K.: Manchester University Press, 2004), pp. 87–95.

9. Sarah Hale, "The Communitarian 'Philosophy' of New Labour," pp. 90–91.

10. Ruth Levitas, *The Inclusive Society. Social Exclusion and New Labour* (New York: Routledge, 2005).

11. See the Commission for Social Justice, *Social Justice. Strategies for National Renewal* (London: Vintage, 1994); Tony Blair, *New Britain. My Vision of a Young Country* (London: Fourth Estate Limited, 1996).

12. David Blunkett speech, "Civil Renewal—A New Agenda," June 11, 2003.

13. Bevir, *New Labour, a Critique*, p. 71.

14. Department of Communities and Local Government, *Our Towns and Cities: The Future* (London: HMSO, 2005); *Strong and Prosperous Communities* (London: HMSO, 2006).

15. Rob Imrie and Mike Raco, *Urban Renaissance? New Labour, Community, and Urban Policy* (Bristol, U.K.: Policy Press, 2003), pp. 33–37.

16. Amitai Etzioni, *The Third Way to a Good Society* (London: Demos, 2000).

17. Geoff Mulgan, *Connexity. How to Live in a Connected World* (London: Chatto and Windus, 1997), p. 35.

18. Cabinet Office, *Modernising Government*(London: HMSO, 1999).

19. David Blunkett, speech to the Performance and Innovation Unit, "How Government Can Help Build Social Capital," March 26, 2002.

20. Robert D. Putnam, *Bowling Alone. The Collapse and Revival of American Community* (New York: Simon and Schuster, 2000).

21. John Rae, "Foreword," in S. L. McLean, D. A. Schultz, and M. B. Steger, eds., *Social Capital. Critical Perspectives on Community and Bowling Alone* (New York: NYU Press, 2002).

22. David Halpern, *Social Capital* (Cambridge, U.K.: Polity Press, 2005), p. 44.

23. This celebration of the two-parent family has come with policies to help single parents and also to recognize work–life balance. See Stephen Driver and Luke Martell, "New Labour, Work, and the Family," in *Social Policy and Administration* 36, 1 (2002); and Mary Daley, "Changing Conceptions of Family and Gender Relations in European Welfare States and the Third Way," in Jane Lewis and Rebecca Surender, eds., *Welfare State Change, Towards a Third Way?* (Oxford, U.K.: Oxford University Press, 2004), pp. 135–156.

24. Halpern, *Social Capital*, p. 53.

25. Simon Szreter, "A New Political Economy: The Importance of Social Capital," in Anthony Giddens, ed., *The Global Third Way Debate* (2001); Halpern, *Social Capital*, p. 22.

26. Debates on social capital have systematically avoided references to the French sociologist Pierre Bourdieu, who saw social capital as a symbolic individual resource in a powered field of social hierarchies; see Bourdieu, "The Forms of Capital," in J. G. Richardson, ed., *Handbook of Theory and Research for the Sociology of Education* (New York: Greenwood Press, 1986), pp. 241–258.

27. David Blunkett, speech to the IPPR, "The Asset State— the Future of Welfare," July 5, 2005. The baby bonds were designed to counter the determining effects on individual life chances of asset-owning by giving each newborn child a small trust. It might be pointed out here that encouraging a culture of property is an old means of disciplining for social democracy, beginning with nineteenth-century credit institutions and friendly societies.

28. Ben Fine, *Social Capital vs. Social Theory. Political Economy and Social Science at the End of the Millennium* (New York: Routledge, 2001); Ben Fine and F. Green,

"Economics, Social Capital, and the Colonisation of the Social Sciences," in Tom Schuller, Steven Davon, and John Field, eds., *Social Capital. Critical Perspectives* (Oxford, U.K.: Oxford University Press, 2000), p. 87.

29. Interview with Amitai Etizioni, Budapest, July 2005.

30. Henrik Berggren and Lars Trägårdh, *Är svensken människa?* (Stockholm: Norstedts, 2006).

31. Fredrika Lagergren, *På andra sidan välfärdsstaten: en studie i politiska idéers betydelse* (Eslöv, Sweden: B. Östlings bokförl. Symposion, 1999); Henrik Björck, "Till frågan om folkhemmets rötter," in *Lychnos* (Göteborg, Sweden: Annual of the Swedish History of Science Society, Swedish Science Press, 2000), pp. 139–170.

32. See Göran Persson, *Den som är satt i skuld är icke fri. Min berättelse om hur Sverige återfick sunda statsfinanser* (Stockholm: Atlas 1997); Göran Persson, *Se dig själv i andra* (Stockholm: Hjalmarson och Högberg, 2006).

33. In recent years there has been a vital debate in Sweden on the possible conflict between the values of universalism and diversity. See *Integrationens svarta bok: Agenda för jämlikhet och social sammanhållning* (Stockholm: SOU, 2006:79).

34. See Sten O. Karlsson, *Det intelligenta samhället: en omtolkning av socialdemokratins idéhistoria* (Stockholm: Carlsson, 2001); Jenny Andersson, "A Productive Social Citizenship? Reflections on the Notion of Productive Social Policies in the European Tradition," in Bo Stråth and Lars Magnusson, eds, *A European Social Citizenship* (Brussels: PIE Peter Lang, 2004); Magnus Ryner, *Capitalist Restructuring, Globalisation and the Third Way: Lessons from the Swedish Model* (London and New York: Routledge, 2002), p. 72.

35. Francis Sejersted, *Socialdemokratins tidsålder: Sverige och Norge under 1900–talet.* (Nora: Nya Doxa, 2005).

36. Bo Rothstein, *Just Institutions Matter. The Moral and Political Logic of the Universal Welfare State* (Cambrige, U.K.: Cambridge University Press, 1998).

37. Sveriges socialdemokratiska arbetareparti, *Partiprogram för socialdemokraterna: antaget vid partikongressen 2001*, p. 30; *Att ge alla möjlighet och förutsättningar till kunskap är centralt för att bryta klassmönstren. Kunskap och kompetens blir allt mer de arbetsredskap som bestämmer den enskildes möjligheter i arbetslivet. Stora skillnader i tillgång till dessa redskap ökar klyftorna i samhället och därmed i samhället. En hög kunskaps-och kompetensnivå hos alla i arbetslivet innebär däremot att de klassmönster som skapas av produktionslivet förändras. Hög kompetens hos alla i arbetslivet ökar samtidigt styrkan och slagkraften i produktionslivet, och det innebär ökade resurser för välfärden. Den nya produktionsordning som växer fram bygger i mycket på hanteringen av information. Informationsflödena har aldrig varit så omfattande som idag, och den moderna informationstekniken betyder en verklig demokratisering av tillgången till kunskap. Men den makt som kunskapen ger handlar inte bara om tillgång till information utan lika mycket om förmågan att kunna tolka informationen. All kunskapsförmedling måste bygga på respekt för fakta, men den måste också ge alla*

redskapen att självständigt tolka och värdera information, se sociala sammanhang och skilja mellan fakta och värderingar. Först då kan man tala om en verklig demokratisering av kunskapen. Socialdemokratins uppgift är nu att skapa ett verkligt kunskapssamhälle, byggt både på bildning och utbildning, öppet och tillgängligt för alla på likvärdiga villkor.

38. Government bill, *Lära, växa, förändra. Regeringens folkbildningsproposition.* 2005/06:192 (Stockholm, 2005).

39. Jonas Johansson, *Du sköna nya tid? Debatten om informationssamhället i riksdag och storting under 1990-talet* (Linköping, Sweden: Linköping Studies in Arts and Science, 2006).

40. *Individuellt kompetenssparande* (Stockholm: SOU, 2000:119); *Livslångt lärande i arbetslivet—steg på vägen mot ett kunskapssamhälle* (Stockholm: SOU, 1996:164).

41. See Paulina De los Reyes, *Mångfald och differentiering. Diskurs, olikhet och normbildning inom svensk forskning och samhällsdebatt* (Stockholm: SALTSA, Swedish National Institute for Working Life, 2001), p. 82; Wuocko Knocke and Fredrik Herzberg, *Mångfaldens barn söker sin plats* (Stockholm: Swedish National Institute for Working Life), p. 26.

42. Blunkett, "Civil Renewal—a New Agenda."

43. Lindsey Paterson, "The Three Educational Ideologies of the British Labour Party, 1997–2001," *Oxford Review of Education* 29, 2 (2003), p. 176; Elisabeth Fraser, "Citizenship Education: Antipolitical Culture and Political Education in Britain," *Political Studies,* 48 (2000). The National curriculum is available online at www.direct.gov.uk/en/RightsAndResponsibilities/index.htm.

44. Alva Myrdal, *Förskolan, 1980-talets viktigaste skola* (Stockholm: Tiden, 1982).

45. Sveriges socialdemokratiska arbetareparti, *Nationell utvecklingsplan för förskola, skola och vuxenutbildning*, Politisk redovisning, 1997:8 (Stockholm: Socialdemokraterna, 1997); Sveriges socialdemokratiska arbetareparti, *Förskola för alla barn* (Stockholm: Socialdemokraterna, 1985); Sveriges socialdemokratiska arbetareparti, *Framtidens förskola* (Stockholm: Socialdemokraterna, 2005); *Partiprogram för socialdemokraterna*, pp. 30–34.

46. *Läroplan för det obligatoriska skolväsendet, förskoleklassen och fritidshemmet,* 1994, p. 3.

47. Ronald Dearing, *Higher Education in the Learning Society* (London: HMSO, 1997); Helena Kennedy, *Learning Works. Widening Participation in Further Education* (Coventry, U.K.: Further Education Funding Council, 1998); Department for Education and Employment, *Learning Works. Further Education for the New Millennium* (London: DfEE, 1998).

48. Denis Lawton, *Education and Labour Party Ideologies, 1900–2001 and Beyond* (London and New York: RoutledgeFalmer, 2004).

49. Blair, conference speech, 1996; Sue Tomlinson, *Education in a Post-Welfare Society* (London: Open University Press, 2005), pp. 86f.

50. See Department for Education and Skills, *Higher Standards, Better Schools for All. More Choice for Parents and Pupils. Education White Paper* (London: HMO, 2005); Compass paper, *Shaping the Education Bill. Reaching for Consensus. Alternative White Paper* (London: Compass, 2005); Fiona Millar and Melissa Benn, *A Comprehensive Future. Quality and Equality for All Our Children* (London: Compass, 2005).

51. Francis Sejersted, *Socialdemokratins tidsålder: Sverige och Norge under 1900–talet* (Nora, Sweden: Nya Doxa, 2005).

52. Sveriges socialdemokratiska arbetarparti, *En kunskapsskola för alla* (Stockholm: Socialdemokraterna, 2006).

53. Kunskapslyftskommittén, *Kunskapsbygget 2000. Det livslånga lärandet* (Stockholm, SOU, 2000:28); Kommittén om ett nationellt kunskapslyft för vuxna, *En strategi för kunskapslyft och livslångt lärande* (Stockholm: SOU, 1996:27); Government bill, *Sysselsättningspropositionen. Åtgärder för att minska arbetslösheten. 1995/96:222.*

54. See Thomas Englund, ed., *Utbildningspolitiskt systemskifte?* (Stockholm: HLS förlag, 1995). Anyone with sufficient capital can start a "free" school. Schools are not allowed to choose students by ability unless this is because of specific abilities such as musical talent or sports. (In the United Kingdom, specialization schools can choose up to 10 percent of their students.) Voucher schools are subject to inspection, but control has so far been lax. Until 2007, public schooling had to be provided in each community, so public schools in each area were to some extent protected against voucher schools, but this has now changed. After the change of government, applications for voucher schools have increased dramatically, and there are now places where the last remaining comprehensive school is under threat of takeover, to the objections of many parents and teachers.

55. After the lost election, the SAP admits that uneven standards are a problem, but it does not mention the voucher schools and their effect in creating inequalities.

56. Skolverket, *Resultat av inspektion av fristående skolor 2003–2006* (Stockholm: Skolverket, 2006).

57. Interview with Bosse Ringholm, October 3, 2005, Stockholm.

58. Socialdemokraterna, *En kunskapsskola för alla.*

59. *Skolans uppgift är att låta varje elev finna sin unika egenart och därigenom kunna delta i samhällslivet genom att ge sitt bästa i ansvarig frihet.*

60. Michael Power, *The Audit Society. Rituals of Verification* (Oxford, U.K.: Oxford University Press, 1997). See Bengt Jacobsson and Kerstin Sahlin Andersson, *Skolan och det nya verket* (Stockholm: Nerenius Santerus, 1995).

61. Denis Lawton, *Education and Labour Party Ideologies, 1900–2001 and Beyond* (London and New York: RoutledgeFalmer, 2004).

62. Michael Young, *The Rise of the Meritocracy 1870–2033: An Essay on Education and Equality* (London: Thames and Hudson, 1961).

63. Lawton, *Education and Labour Party Ideologies*; Bernt Gustavsson, *Bildningens väg. Tre bildningsideal i svensk arbetarrörelse 1880–1930* (Stockholm: Wahlström och Widstrand, 1991).

64. Francis Sejersted, *Socialdemokratins tidsålder,* p. 297.

65. *Learning for Success, The Learning Age*; Department for Education and Skills, *Higher Standards, Better Schools for All. More Choice for Parents and Pupils. Education White Paper* (London: HMSO, 2005), p. 17.

66. *Excellence in Schools,* 1997.

67. Interview with Michael Barber, October 20, 2005.

68. *Higher Standards, Better Schools for All.*

69. Ibid.

70. Compare Stuart White, "Welfare Philosophy and the Third Way," in Jane Lewis and Rebecca Surender, eds., *Welfare State Change. Towards a Third Way?* (Oxford, U.K.: Oxford University Press, 2004), pp. 25–47.

71. Richard Sennett, *The Culture of the New Capitalism,* The Castles Lectures in Ethics, Politics and Economics (New Haven and London: Yale University Press, 2006).

72. Francis Sejersted, *Socialdemokratins tidsålder.*

Chapter 7

1. Steve Bastow and James Martin, *Third Way Discourse: European Ideologies in the Twentieth Century* (Edinburgh: Edinburgh University Press, 2003).

2. Gøsta Esping-Andersen, *Politics against Markets* (Princeton, NJ: Princeton University Press, 1985); Claus Offe, *Contradictions of the Welfare State* (Cambridge, MA: MIT Press, 1984); Bob Jessop, *The Future of the Welfare State* (Oxford, U.K.: Polity Press, 2001).

3. Department of Social Security and Department for Employment and Education, *New Ambitions for Our Country: A New Contract for Welfare* (London: HMSO, 1998).

4. John D. Stephens, *The Transition from Capitalism to Socialism* (London: Macmillan, 1979).

5. Jenny Andersson, *Between Growth and Security. Swedish Social Democracy from a Strong Society to a Third Way* (Manchester, U.K.: Manchester University Press, 2006).

6. The concept of social investment gained a significant emphasis on the European level following the summits of Lisbon and Nice.

7. HM Treasury, *Modern Public Services for Britain, Investing in Reform* (London: HMSO, 1998).

8. Gordon Brown, budget speech, April 16, 2002.

9. Ruth Lister, "Investing in the Citizen Workers of the Future, Transformations in Citizenship and the State under New Labour," in *Social Policy and Administration* 37, 5 (October 2003), pp. 427–443, p. 431.

10. Jane Jenson and Denis Saint-Martin, "New Routes to Social Cohesion. Citizenship and the Social Investment State," *Canadian Journal of Sociology* 28, 1 (2003), pp. 77–99.

11. Ibid.

12. Lister, "Investing in the Citizen Workers of the Future."

13. Daniel Rodgers, *Atlantic Crossings. Social Politics in a Progressive Age* (Cambridge, MA: Harvard University Press, 1998).

14. Jenny Andersson, "A Productive Social Citizenship? Reflections on the Notion of Productive Social Policies in the European Tradition," in *A European Social Citizenship* (Brussels: PIE Peter Lang, 2004).

15. Tony Blair, quoted in Martin A. Powell, ed., *New Labour, New Welfare State? The "Third Way" in British Social Policy* (Bristol, U.K.: Policy Press, 1999), p. 21.

16. See Pre-budget Reports, 1997–2006, and Comprehensive Spending Reviews, 2002, 2004.

17. British Commission on Social Justice, *Social Justice, Strategies for National Renewal* (London: Vintage, 1994), pp. 96–106, 110–113; Social Exclusion Unit, *Bringing Britain Together* (London: SEU, 1998), p. 7.

18. Marshall's argument does not need to be recounted here, but it should be pointed out that while Marshall certainly saw responsibilities as a part of citizenship, his argument on social transformation was linked to the rights side of citizenship. See T. H. Marshall, *Citizenship and Social Class* (London: Pluto Press, 1992); Ruth Lister, *Citizenship. Feminist Perspectives* (Basingstoke, U.K.: Macmillan, 1997), p. 14; and Stuart White, "Social Rights and the Social Contract—Political Theory and the New Welfare Politics," in *British Journal of Political Science* 30 (2000), pp. 507–532, p. 511.

19. Desmond King, *In the Name of Liberalism. Illiberal Social Policy in the U.S. and Britain* (Oxford, U.K.: Oxford University Press, 1999); William Walters, *Unemployment and Government. Genealogies of the Social* (Cambridge, U.K.: Cambridge University Press, 2000).

20. Andersson, *Between Growth and Security*; Tim Tilton, *The Political Theory of Swedish Social Democracy. Through the Welfare State to Revolution* (New York: Clarendon Press, 1990).

21. Andersson, *Between Growth and Security*.

22. Esping-Andersen, *Politics against Markets*.

23. See Teresa Kulawik, "A Productivist Welfare State, the Swedish Model Revisited," in Tadeusz Borkowski, ed., *Social Policies in a Time of Transformation* (Krakow: Goethe Institute and Jagellonian University, 1991).

24. Lena Sommestad, "Human Reproduction and the Rise of Welfare States: An Economic-Demographic Approach to Welfare State Formation in the United States and Sweden," *Scandinavian Economic History Review* 46, 2 (1998), pp. 97–116; Allan Constantine Carlson, *The Swedish Experiment in Family Politics: The Myrdals and the Interwar Population Crisis* (New Brunswick, NJ: Transaction, 1990).

25. Andersson, "A Productive Social Citizenship?"

26. Maija Runcis, *Steriliseringar i folkhemmet* (Stockholm: Ordfront, 1998); Gunnar Broberg and Mattias Tydén, "Eugenics in Sweden: Efficient Care," in Gunnar Broberg and Nils Roll-Hansen, eds., *Eugenics in the Welfare State* (Ann Arbor: University of

Michigan Press, 1996); A. Spektorowski and E. Mizrachi, "Eugenics and the Welfare State in Sweden. The Politics of Social Margins and the Idea of a Productive Society," in *Journal of Contemporary History* 39, 3 (2004), pp. 333–352.

27. See Rothstein, *Just Institutions Matter. The Moral and Political Logic of the Universal Welfare State* (Cambridge, U.K.: Cambridge University Press, 1998); Sheri Berman, *The Social Democratic Moment* (Cambridge, MA: Harvard University Press, 1998).

28. Discussion paper, "Personal Responsibility and Changing Behaviour: The State of Knowledge and the Implications for Public Policy" (London: Strategy Unit, 2004), pp. 10, 64; Levitas, *The Inclusive Society* (New York: Routledge, 2005), p. 227.

29. Andersson, *Between Growth and Security.*

30. Sveriges socialdemokratiska arbetareparti, *Steget in i 2000-talet: Riktlinjer antagna av framtidskongressen i Sundsvall* (Stockholm: Socialdemokraterna, 1997).

31. Government budget bill, 2002/2003:1, p. 25. *Välfärden ska fortsätta att byggas ut. Trygghet i förändring stimulerar nytänkande och ger växtkraft. Trygga människor vågar. Trygghet gör ekonomin mera dynamisk.* This has been a standing theme since Ingvar Carlsson's 1994 government, but the slogan "security in change" was coined in 1997.

32. David Blunkett speech, "The Asset State—the Future of Welfare," July 5, 2005; Gordon Brown, *Fair Is Efficient* (London: Fabian Society, 1994).

33. HM Treasury, *The Modernisation of Britain's Tax and Benefits System*, nr. 4 and 6.

34. Gordon Brown speech, "Prosperity and Justice for All," September 27, 2004; Göran Persson speech, "Economic and Social Policy, the Swedish way," Wellington, New Zealand, February 14, 2005.

35. The Swedish term for security, *trygghet*, is a much more immaterial term than the English notions of security and alludes also to psychological and cognitive security and the political capacity to accommodate for individual need in processes of structural transformation.

36. Göran Persson speech to the Progressive Governance Summit, Budapest, 2004.

37. Göran Persson to the Congress of Swedish Industry (SIF), November 15, 2002. *Människor i trygghet är skapande människor. Människor som drivs av en äkta vilja att söka kunskap inte därför att man drivs av en piska, utan för att man växer själv som individ.*

38. DfTI, *Our Competitive Future.*

39. Sofia Murhem, "Flexicurity in Sweden," unpublished research paper (Uppsala: Department of Economic History, Uppsala University, 2007).

40. See, for instance, the Pär Nuder speech, "Tal vid Strängseminariet," March 5, 2005, and Nuder's speech to the Harvard Center for European Studies, November 15, 2006.

41. HM Treasury and the Swedish Ministry of Finance, "Social Bridges. Meeting the Challenges of Globalisation" (HM Treasury, Regeringskansliet, 2006); Conversation with Jens Henriksson, special advisor to Pär Nuder.

42. *New Ambitions for Our Country: A New Contract for Welfare*.

43. See Stuart White, "Welfare Philosophy and the Third Way," in Jane Lewis and Rebecca Surender, eds., *Welfare State Change. Towards a Third Way?* (Oxford, U.K.: Oxford University Press, 2004), p. 40; also Claire Annesley and Andrew Gamble, "Economic and Welfare Policy," in Steve Ludlam, ed., *Governing as New Labour* (Basingstoke, U.K.: Palgrave Macmillan, 2003), pp. 144–159.

44. Michael Freeden, *The New Liberalism: An Ideology of Social Reform* (Oxford, U.K.: Clarendon Press, 1978).

45. Bo Rothstein, *The Social Democratic State: The Swedish Model and the Bureaucratic Problem of Social Reforms*, Pitt Series in Policy and Institutional Studies (Pittsburgh, PA: University of Pittsburgh Press, 1996).

46. See Steffen Mau, *The Moral Economy of Welfare States* (New York and London: Routledge, 2004).

47. See Lena Eriksson, *Arbete till varje pris, arbetslinjen i 1920–talets arbetslöshetspolitik* (Stockholm: Stockholm Studies in History, 2004); Åke Bergmark, "Activated to Work? Activation Policies in Sweden in the 1990s," in *Revue Francaise des Affaires Sociales*, 4, (2003), pp. 291–306.

48. The epicentre of this debate is the term *arbetslinjen*, meaning the work strategy. *Arbetslinjen* is a term that is used today by all political actors in Swedish society, and correspondingly it can signify everything from the right to work to the duty to work and anything from active labor market policy to activation policies. See Socialförsäkringsutredningen, *Vad är arbetslinjen? Samtal om socialförsäkring nr 4* (Stockholm: Riksförsäkringsverket, 2005).

49. Mark Canadine, *Enterprising States. The Public Management of Welfare to Work* (Cambridge, U.K.: Cambridge University Press, 2001).

50. As such, it is also codified in the Swedish constitution: the right of all to security and work.

51. Anne Daguerre and Peter Taylor-Gooby, "Neglecting Europe: Explaining the Predominance of American Ideas in New Labour's Welfare Policies since 1997," *Journal of European Social Policy* 14, 1 (2004), pp. 24-39; Jochen Clasen and Daniel Clegg, "Does the Third Way Work? The Left and Labour Market Reform in Britain, France and Germany," in Lewis and Surender, eds., *Welfare State Change*, pp. 89–111.

52. John Stephens, "The Scandinavian Welfare States. Achievements, Crisis and Prospects," in Gösta Esping Andersen. ed., *Welfare States in Transition. National Adaptations in Global Economies* (New York: Sage, 1996), pp. 32–66.

53. Government bill 1995/96:207. *En politik för att halvera den öppna arbetslösheten till år 2000*.

54. Håkan Johansson, *Svensk aktiveringspolitik i nordisk belysning* (Stockholm: ESO, 2006); Joakim Palme et al., "Welfare Trends in Sweden: Balancing the Books for the 1990s," *Journal of European Social Policy* 12, 4 (2002); Johannes Lindvall, *Ett land som alla andra. Från full sysselsättning till massarbetslöshet* (Stockholm: Atlas, 2006).

55. Julia Peralta, *Den sjuka arbetslösheten* (Uppsala, Sweden: Uppsala Studies in Economic History, 2006); Christina Garsten and Kerstin Jacobsson, *Learning to Be Employable: New Agendas on Work, Responsibility, and Learning in a Globalizing World* (Basingstoke, U.K.: Palgrave Macmillan, 2004); Jessica Lindvert, *Ihålig arbetsmarknadspolitik? Organisering och legitimitet igår och idag* (Umeå, Sweden: Borea, 2006).

56. DfWP, *A New Deal for Welfare*, 2006.

57. Sven E. Hort, "Sweden, Still a Civilised Version of Welfare?" in Noel Gilbert and Rebecca vaan Vorhis, eds., *Activating the Unemployed* (New Brunswick, NJ: Transaction Publishers), pp. 243–267.

58. Government bill 1995/96:207. *En politik för att halvera den öppna arbetslösheten till år 2000.*

59. Johansson, *Svensk aktiveringspolitik i nordisk belysning.* Government bill 1999/2000:98, *Förnyad arbetsmarknadspolitik för delaktighet och tillväxt, Kontrakt för arbete. Rättvisa och tydliga regler i arbetslöshetsförsäkringen* (Stockholm: Ds, 1999:58).

60. Renita Thedvall, "Do It Yourself. Making Up the Selfemployed Individual in the Swedish Public Employment Service," in Garsten and Jacobsson, *Learning to Be Employable*, pp. 131–152.

61. *En god arbetsmarknadspolitik innebär ett ömsesidigt åtagande mellan samhället och medborgaren. Samhället ikläder sig skyldigheter gentemot individen enbart i den mån individen uppfyller sitt ansvar. Det egna ansvaret ligger i att anta utmaningen om att utveckla kompetens och aktivt söka arbete.* Government bill 1995/96:207, *En politik för att halvera den öppna arbetslösheten till år 2000.*

62. What is traditionally referred to in Swedish as *arbetslinjen* has thus become *arbets-och kompetenslinjen* in the 1990s; see 1998, *The Budget Statement and Summary*, p. 19.

63. I am particularly grateful for discussions with Joakim Palme, Bosse Ringholm, and Anna Hedborg here.

64. Sheri Berman, *The Primacy of Politics. Social Democracy and the Making of Europe's 20th Century* (New York: Cambridge University Press, 2006), p. 178.

Chapter 8

1. Gilles Raveaud and Robert Salais, "Fighting against Social Exclusion in a Knowledge Based Society," in David Mayes, Jos Berghamn, and Robert Salais, eds. *Social Exclusion and European Policy* (Cheltenham, U.K.: Edward Elgar, 2001).

2. Perry 6 and Ben Jupp, *Divided by Information. The Digital Divide and the Implications of the New Meritocracy* (London: Demos, 2001).

3. Jean Gardiner, *Gender, Care and Economics,* (Basingstoke, U.K.: Macmillan, 1997).

4. Daniel Cohen, *Nos Temps Modernes* (Paris: Flammarion, 1999).

5. Richard Sennett, *The Culture of the New Capitalism*, The Castles Lectures in Ethics, Politics and Economics (New Haven and London: Yale University Press, 2006), p. 123.

6. Michael Katz, *The Undeserving Poor. From President Johnson's War on Poverty to Reagan's War on Welfare* (New York: Pantheon Books, 1989).

7. Alain Touraine, *The Post-Industrial Society, Tomorrow's Social History* (New York: Random House, 1971).

8. Manuel Castells, *The Information Age: Economy, Society and Culture* (Malden, MA: Blackwell, 1996); Manuel Castells, *The Network Society: A Cross-Cultural Perspective* (Northampton, MA: Edward Elgar Publishing, 2004).

9. Government bill, *Ett informationssamhälle åt alla* (Stockholm, 1999); Social Exclusion Unit, *Inclusion through Innovation: Tackling Social Exclusion through New Technologies* (London: SEU, 2005).

10. Compare Ruth Levitas, *The Inclusive Society. Social Exclusion and New Labour* (New York: Routledge, 2005).

11. Hilary Silver, "Social Exclusion and Social Solidarity: Three Paradigms," in *International Labour Review* nr. 5/6, 133, 1994.

12. I have discussed the origins of the term *social exclusion* in Sweden in Jenny Andersson, *Between Growth and Security. Swedish Social Democracy from a Strong Society to a Third Way* (Manchester, U.K.: Manchester University Press, 2006).

13. In the Swedish action plans against social exclusion, *utslagning* has become *utestängning,* which is much milder, meaning not the "knocked out" but the "closed out," and in the election campaign 2006 it became milder again, *utanförskap*—those "outside." See *Sveriges handlingsplan mot fattigdom och social utslagning 2001–2003, Bilaga till protokoll vid regeringssammanträde 2001-05-23 nr 11, Sveriges handlingsplan mot fattigdom och social utestängning 2003–2005, bilaga till protokoll vid regeringssammanträde 2003-07-03.*

14. Janet Newman, *Modernising Governance. New Labour, Policy and Society* (London: Sage, 2001).

15. Levitas, *The Inclusive Society?*; Charles Murray, *The Emerging British Underclass* (London: Institute for Economic Affairs, 1990).

16. Social Exclusion Unit, *Bringing Britain Together* (London: SEU, 1998); *Bridging the Gap: New Opportunities for 16–18 Year-Olds Not in Education, Employment or Training* (London: SEU, 1999).

17. Social Exclusion Unit, *Preventing Social Exclusion* (London: SEU, 2001).

18. Ibid.

19. Levitas, *The Inclusive Society.*

20. This became a near-dominant discourse of poverty in the late 1990s, not least because of the policy production of the European Union. See Mary Daley, "Social Exclusion as Concept and Policy Template in the European Union," Working paper, Center for European Studies, Harvard, 2005, nr. 135.

21. Department for Communities and Local Government, *Strong and Prosperous Communities* (London: TSO, 2006).

22. Levitas, *The Inclusive Society.*

23. Department for Education and Employment, *Raising Expectations: Staying in Education and Training Post-16* (London: DfEE, 2007); Social Exclusion Unit, *Bridging the Gap.*

24. Social Exclusion Unit, *Inclusion through Innovation.*

25. Newman, *Modernising Governance.*

26. Sveriges socialdemokratiska arbetarparti, *90-talsprogrammet* (Stockholm: Tiden, 1989).

27. See *Låginkomstutredningen.*

28. See LO 1966, *Fackföreningsrörelsen och den tekniska utvecklingen,* Sveriges socialdemokratiska arbetareparti, *Partiprogram för socialdemokraterna: antaget vid partikongressen 2001.*

29. Olof Palme speech to party conference, 1978.

30. Jonas Pontusson, *The Limits of Social Democracy: Investment Politics in Sweden,* Cornell Studies in Political Economy (Ithaca, NY: Cornell University Press, 1992).

31. Government bill, *Sysselsättningspropositionen* (1995): Government bill, *Vuxnas lärande och utvecklingen av vuxenutbildningen* (2000).

32. This was the original metaphor of the People's Home, from Per Albin Hansson's famous speech in 1928.

33. A Welfare Balance Sheet for the 1990s: Final Report of the Swedish Welfare Commission, *Scandinavian Journal of Public Health,* Supplement, 60 (Stockholm: Umeå, 2003).

34. *Integrationens svarta bok: agenda för jämlikhet och social sammanhållning. Slutbetänkande av utredningen om makt, integration och strukturell diskriminering* (Stockholm: SOU 2006:79).

35. Anna Hedborg to seminar on the future of welfare, Stockholm, Ministry of Social Affairs, October 2005.

36. Department of Work and Pensions, *A New Deal for Welfare: Empowering People to Work* (London: DWP, 2006).

37. Daniel Bell, *The Coming of Post-Industrial Society. A Venture in Social Forecasting* (New York: Basic Books, 1973), p. 170.

38. Fred Hirsch, *Social Limits to Growth* (Cambridge, MA: Harvard University Press, 1977).

39. Cohen, *Nos Temps Modernes.*

40. Department of Trade and Industry, *A New Deal for Welfare: Empowering People to Work, Success at Work, Protecting Vulnerable Workers, Supporting Good Employers* (London: D T I, 2006); Department of Work and Pensions, *Workplace Health, Work and Wellbeing* (London: DWP, 2005).

41. Sveriges socialdemokratiska arbetarparti, *Politiska riktlinjer beslutade av mellankongressen* (Stockholm: Socialdemokraterna, 2004), p. 2.

42. Declaration of Government, 2004; and *Finansplanen* 2004/05:1; Government bill 2004; *Tillväxt i hela landet. En hållbar tillväxt* (Stockholm: Socialdemokraterna, 2004); and *Ett mänskligare arbetsliv* (Stockholm: Socialdemokraterna, 2004).

43. Kjell Nyman et al., *Den svenska sjukan: Sjukfrånvaron i åtta läder* (Stockholm: ESO, 2002:49).

44. In the recently published interviews with the political journalist Erik Fichtelius, Göran Persson says that social democracy was ready to abolish wealth, inheritance, and property tax in 2004. Inheritance tax was dropped in 2004. The right-wing government abolished wealth and property tax in April 2007. Erik Fichtelius and Göran Persson, *Aldrig ensam, alltid ensam: samtalen med Göran Persson 1996–2006* (Stockholm: Norstedt, 2007).

45. Sveriges socialdemokratiska arbetareparti, *Steget in i 2000–talet: riktlinjer antagna av framtidskongressen i Sundsvall* (Stockholm: Socialdemokraterna, 1997); *En svensk strategi för hållbar utveckling* (Stockholm: Miljödepartementet, Regeringskansliet, 2004).

46. Zygmunt Bauman, *Work, Consumerism and the New Poor* (Philadelphia: Open University Press, 1998).

Chapter 9

1. David Marquand, "A Man without History," in *New Statesman*, May 7, 2007.

2. Mona Sahlin speech to party conference, March 18, 2007, available online at at www.sap.se.

3. Mona Sahlin, "Självkritik är nödvändig på viktiga politikområden," in *Dagens nyheter*, June 13, 2007.

4. See SAP, *With a View to the Future. Thoughts to Inspire*, paper to congress March 16–18, 2007; Nick Pearce and Julia Margo, eds., *Politics for a New Generation* (London: IPPR, Palgrave, 2007).

5. Roberto Mangabeira Ungar, *What Should the Left Propose?* (London: Verso, 2005), p. 22.

6. Per Nuder to panel debate, SAP Party Headquarters, January 2004.

7. Peter Taylor Gooby, ed., *Risk, Trust and Welfare* (Basingstoke, U.K.: Palgrave Macmillan, 2000).

8. Sheri Berman, *The Primacy of Politics. Social Democracy and the Making of Europe's 20th Century* (Cambridge, U.K.: Cambridge University Press, 2006), p. 211.

9. Berman, *The Primacy of Politics.*

10. Bo Rothstein, "Valet en triumph för socialdemokraterna," in *Dagens nyheter,* September 20, 2006.

11. Ernst Wigforss, *Minnen* (1–3, 1950–1954), pp. 86–119.

12. Roberto Ungar, *What Should the Left Propose?*, p. 2.

13. The party has announced a new committee on equality, which will report before the next election.

14. Tony Fitzpatrick, *New Theories of Welfare* (Basingstoke, U.K.: Palgrave Macmillan, 2005).

Index